Computer Aptitude for Competitive Examinations

Reema Thareja
Assistant Professor
Shyama Prasad Mukherji College
University of Delhi

Universities Press

All rights reserved. No part of this book may be modified, reproduced or utilised in any form, or by any means, electronic or mechanical, including photocopying, recording or by any information storage and retrieval system, in any form of binding or cover other than in which it is published, without permission in writing from the publisher.

COMPUTER APTITUDE FOR COMPETITIVE EXAMINATIONS

UNIVERSITIES PRESS (INDIA) PRIVATE LIMITED

Registered office
3-6-747/1/A & 3-6-754/1, Himayatnagar, Hyderabad 500 029, Telangana, India
info@universitiespress.com; www.universitiespress.com

Distributed by
Orient Blackswan Private Limited

Registered office
3-6-752 Himayatnagar, Hyderabad 500 029, Telangana, India

Other offices
Bengaluru, Chennai, Guwahati, Hyderabad, Kolkata,
Mumbai, New Delhi, Noida, Patna, Visakhapatnam

© Universities Press (India) Private Ltd 2024

ISBN: 978-93-89211-94-8

Cover and book design
© Universities Press (India) Private Ltd 2024

Typeset in Times New Roman PS Std 10 by
SRS Publishing Services, Puducherry

Printed in India by
Rajiv Book Binding House, Delhi

Published by
Universities Press (India) Private Limited
3-6-747/1/A & 3-6-754/1, Himayatnagar, Hyderabad 500 029, Telangana, India

Disclaimer
Care has been taken to confirm the accuracy of information printed in this book. The author and the publisher, however, cannot accept any responsibility for errors or omissions or for consequences from application of the information in this book and make no warranty, express or implied, with respect to its contents. This textbook does not constitute a standard, specification or regulation. The trademarks or manufacturer's names appear/are used in this book only because they are considered essential to the object of subject discussion and do not necessarily constitute endorsement of product/standard by the author or publisher. All products and company names are trademarks[TM] or registered[®] trademarks of their respective holders. Use of them do not imply any affiliation with or endorsement by them.

I dedicate this book to my mother Smt Usha Thareja and my father Sh Janak Raj Thareja. Without their love, guidance, blessings and support, I would have never been able to become an author.

Contents

Preface .... *vi*
About the Author .... *viii*

Chapter 1: Introduction to Computer 1

Chapter 2: GUI-based Operating Systems 9

Chapter 3: Data Organization and Database Management System 15

Chapter 4: Internet, WWW and Web Browsers 35

Chapter 5: Communication and Collaboration 49

Chapter 6: Application of Digital Financial Services 59

Chapter 7: IT and Its Applications in Business 65

Chapter 8: Data Security and Encryption 72

Chapter 9: Elements of Word Processing 88

Chapter 10: Spreadsheet 93

Chapter 11: Microsoft PowerPoint 97

Chapter 12: Microsoft Access 100

Solved Paper – 1 108

Solved Paper – 2 115

Solved Paper – 3 122

Solved Paper – 4   129

Solved Paper – 5   135

Solved Paper – 6   142

Solved Paper – 7   148

Solved Paper – 8   154

Solved Paper – 9   160

MCQ Sets from Various Papers   166

Preface

Computer awareness is an important section for various staff selection exams such as those conducted by IBPS, SBI (Bank PO and Clerk), SSC, Railway, Police, Insurance companies, RBI, NABARD, NIACL, and also for many other competitive exams held at the state and national levels. Therefore, it is vital to have a sound knowledge of computers to qualify in these exams.

Computer Aptitude for Competitive Examinations helps readers to learn and revise the concepts that help to enhance their computer awareness, and practice answering the test questions in minimal time. The book has been written after considering the syllabi and patterns of various entrance examinations. Thus, it provides the best learning material to guide students and professionals to gain a comprehensive understanding of the world of computers.

A wide range of topics, from computer fundamentals to the latest advancements in technology (such as IoT, Big Data, Artificial Intelligence, Knowledge Management, Data Warehousing) has been discussed in the book. It has more than 1700 MCQs and 800 True-or-False type questions that can be used for all competitive exams.

The book comprises of 12 chapters and has 9 solved papers. In addition, there are four MCQ sets for practice. There are plenty of illustrative diagrams, keywords and topic highlights. Some defining features of the book that make it a must-buy product are:

Pictorial Approach: Numerous well-labelled diagrams are provided throughout the text for clear understanding of the concepts.

Practical Orientation: Loads of solved examples that enables the students to check their understanding of the concepts.

Comprehensive Coverage: The book provides comprehensive coverage of important topics.

Glossary: A list of key terms included is provided in each chapter to facilitate revision of important topics learned.

Easy to Understand: The book uses a very simple language to explain the concepts.

Complementary App: Students can download the free mobile app Jruma from Google Play Store or Apple Store for additional learning resources. The app would help them to recapitulate and test their understanding of the concepts. From time-to-time the author would take interactive online sessions on weekends to help readers resolve their doubts and queries.

ACKNOWLEDGMENTS

The writing of this text book was a mammoth task for which a lot of help was required from many people. Fortunately, I have had the fine support of my family, friends and fellow members of the teaching staff at the Shyama Prasad Mukherji College.

My special thanks would always go to my father Late Sh Janak Raj Thareja, my mother Smt Usha Thareja, my brother Pallav and sisters Kimi and Rashi who were a source of abiding inspiration and divine blessings for me. I am especially thankful to my son Goransh who has been very patient and cooperative in letting me realize my dreams. My sincere thanks go to my uncle Mr B L Theraja for his inspiration and guidance in writing this book.

Last but not the least, my acknowledgements will always be incomplete if I do not thank the editorial team at Universities Press (India) Private Limited that gave me this brilliant opportunity to utilize my writing skills.

Reema Thareja
reema_thareja@yahoo.com

About the Author

Dr Reema Thareja is Assistant Professor, Department of Computer Science, at Shyama Prasad Mukherji College, University of Delhi. In her 18 years of teaching experience, she has taught several courses including BA, BSc, MSc, BBA, MBA, BCA, MCA. She has authored several books in Computer Science and her books have been well-accepted across the globe. She has also published more than 22 researcher papers in international journals of repute and file four patents. A recipient of 64 Google Scholar Citations, she has launched a mobile learning and quizzing app, Jruma, for both Android and iOS devices to promote incentive-based learning through quizzing.

Besides being an author, Dr Thareja is also an eminent speaker. She has conducted several Faculty Development Programs, Seminars, Webinars and Student's Workshop in India, UAE and the USA. She was also invited as a speaker for the Global Virtual Summit in New York. She is a member of Board of Subject Experts for multiple colleges in India and a member of Technical Advisory Board of the Refactor Academy.

A member of Computer Society of India, Editorial Board and Elite Speakers group of the IMRF Conference Board, Dr Thareja is a skilled motivator who helps students utilize their untapped skills and reinvent themselves. For her immense contributions in the field of education, she has received multiple awards and recognitions.

CHAPTER 1
Introduction to Computer

KEY POINTS

- With each new generation of computers, there has been advancement in computer technology.
- Besides being very fast and accurate, computers are automatic devices that execute programs without any user intervention.
- The computer storage space stores not only the data and programs but also the intermediate results and the final results of processing.
- Application software is designed to solve a particular problem for users. Examples of application software include MS Word, PowerPoint, Excel, games, web browser, etc.
- System Software provides a general programming environment in which programmers can create specific applications to suit their needs.
- The primary goal of an operating system is to make the computer system (or any other device in which it is installed, like the cell phone) *convenient and efficient to use*.
- Compilers and interpreters are special types of programs that convert source code written in a programming language (the *source language*) into machine language comprising of just two digits – 1s and 0s (the *target language*).
- Multimedia includes a combination of text, audio, still images, animation, video, and interactivity content forms.
- A programming language is a language specifically designed to express computations that can be performed by the computer.
- Data processing is the process by which facts and figures are collected, assigned meaning, displayed to users and stored for future use.

KEYWORDS

Data: A collection of raw facts or figures.

Information: Processed data that provide answers to the *"who", "what", "where"* and *"when"* type of questions.

Knowledge: Application of data and information to answer the *"how"* part of the question.

Instructions: Commands given to the computer that tells what it has to do.

Computer: A machine that takes instructions and performs computations based on the provided instructions.

Software: A set of programs.

Input: The process of entering data and instructions into the computer system.

Storage: The process of saving data and instructions permanently in the computer so that it can be used for processing.

Processing: The process of performing operations on the data as per the instructions specified by the user.

Output: The process of giving the result of data processing to the outside world.

Clicking: Pressing either the left or the right button of the mouse.

Dragging: Moving an object to the desired position by pressing the left button of the mouse.

OMR: Stands for Optical Mark Recognition. It is the process of electronically extracting data from marked fields.

Soft copy output devices: Output devices which produce an electronic version of output.

Hard copy output devices: Output devices which produce a physical form of output.

Memory: An internal storage area in the computer used to store data and programs either temporarily or permanently.

Program: A set of instructions arranged in a sequence to guide a computer to find a solution for the given problem.

OMR is an input device for reading marks on a sheet of paper

Programming: The process of writing a program.

Assembler: System software that converts the code written in assembly language into machine language.

Loader: A special type of program that copies programs from a storage device to the main memory, where they can be executed.

Bit: Bit is the short form of binary digit. It is the smallest possible unit of data. In computerized data a bit can either be 0 or 1.

Nibble: Nibble is a group of four binary digits.

Byte: Byte is a group of eight bits.

Word: A group of two bytes is called a word.

E-governance: Governing a country or a state by using Information and Communication Technologies (ICT).

MODEL QUESTION PAPER

Multiple Choice Questions

1. A computer works on _____ given to it.
   (a) computations   (b) instructions   (c) data   (d) b and c

2. Computers are used in which of the following machine(s)?
   (a) GPS   (b) ATM   (c) Gas Pumps   (d) All of these

3. Computer is a/an _____ machine.
   (a) electrical   (b) mechanical   (c) electronic   (d) physical

4. _____ is a collection of raw facts or figures.
   (a) Data   (b) Information   (c) Knowledge   (d) Instructions

5. _____ comprises of processed data.
   (a) Data (b) Information (c) Knowledge (d) Instructions

6. Commands given to the computer that tells what it has to do.
   (a) Data (b) Information (c) Knowledge (d) Instructions

7. A set of programs is called _____.
   (a) hardware (b) software (c) instructions (d) manuals

8. Which generation of computers was used in the period 1955–1964?
   (a) First (b) Second (c) Third (d) Fourth

9. First generation computers were manufactured using which of the following?
   (a) Vacuum tubes (b) Transistors (c) Integrated chips (d) ULSI

10. Select the computer(s) in the first generation of computers.
    (a) ENIAC (b) EDVAC (c) EDSAC (d) All of these.

11. Second generation computers were manufactured using which of the following?
    (a) Vacuum tubes (b) Transistors (c) Integrated chips (d) ULSI

12. Select the computer(s) in the second generation of computers.
    (a) UNIVAC LARC (b) EDVAC (c) EDSAC (d) All of these.

13. Which generation computers were manufactured using ICs with LSI and later with VLSI technology?
    (a) First (b) Second (c) Third (d) Fourth

14. Microcomputers came into existence in which computer generation?
    (a) First (b) Second (c) Third (d) Fourth

15. Currently on which generation of computers are we working?
    (a) First (b) Fifth (c) Third (d) Fourth

16. Which type of software enables you to create page layouts for entire books?
    (a) Chatting (b) Word Processing (c) Desktop publishing (d) Spreadsheet

17. Name an Indian supercomputer:
    (a) UNIVAC LARC (b) EDVAC (c) EDSAC (d) CRAY XMP

18. CRAY XMP is used for _____.
    (a) education (b) multimedia and entertainment
    (c) weather forecasting (d) banking

19. Which type of computer system is used by managers to analyze their business?
    (a) Robots (b) DSS (c) Expert system (d) Supercomputer

20. Which type of computer system is best for analyzing the credit histories for loan approval?
    (a) Robots (b) DSS (c) Expert system (d) Supercomputer

21. The process of entering data and instructions in to the computer system is called _____.
    (a) Input (b) Output (c) Processing (d) Result

22. Computer understands only _____ language.
    (a) Assembly (b) Binary (c) High-level (d) SQL

23. All computations are performed in which part of the CPU?
    (a) CU (b) MU (c) ALU (d) Registers

24. Which of the following is called the brain of the computer system?
    (a) CU (b) MU (c) ALU (d) CPU

25. _____ is the main input device.
    (a) Mouse (b) Joystick (c) Keyboard (d) Touchscreen

26. Which keys are used by applications and operating systems to perform specific commands?
    (a) Function (b) Numeric (c) Arrow (d) Typing

27. Which key cancels the selected option and also pauses a command in progress?
    (a) Home (b) End (c) Page Up (d) Esc

28. Which key captures everything on the screen as an image?
    (a) Control (b) Function (c) Print screen (d) Insert

29. GUI stands for _____.
    (a) Graphical User Interface
    (b) Graphical User Input
    (c) Graphically Used Interface
    (d) Geometrical User Input

30. Name a cursor control device widely used in computer games and CAD/CAM applications.
    (a) Keyboard (b) Joystick
    (c) Mouse (d) Stylus

Joystick: Input device for pointing and clicking on computer screen

31. _____ is a pen-shaped input device used to enter information or write on the touch screen of a phone.
    (a) Keyboard (b) Joystick
    (c) Mouse (d) Stylus

32. Which input device will be used to convert a printout into its digital image?
    (a) Bar code Reader (b) MICR Reader
    (c) Scanner (d) OMR

33. Which of the following converts audio data into digital data?
    (a) Sound card (b) Video card
    (c) Headphone (d) Microphone

Bar Code Reader: Input device using OCR to read characters

34. Digital camera and web camera are popular examples of a _____ input device.
    (a) audio (b) video (c) graphics (d) pointing

35. Which output device is used in home theater systems?
    (a) Printer (b) Plotter (c) Projector (d) Speakers

36. Which device allows users to talk and listen at the same time?
    (a) Speaker (b) Headphone (c) Microphone (d) Headset

37. A printer can print carbon copies of a document. Which printer are we talking about?
    (a) Laser (b) Inkjet (c) Dot matrix (d) Thermal

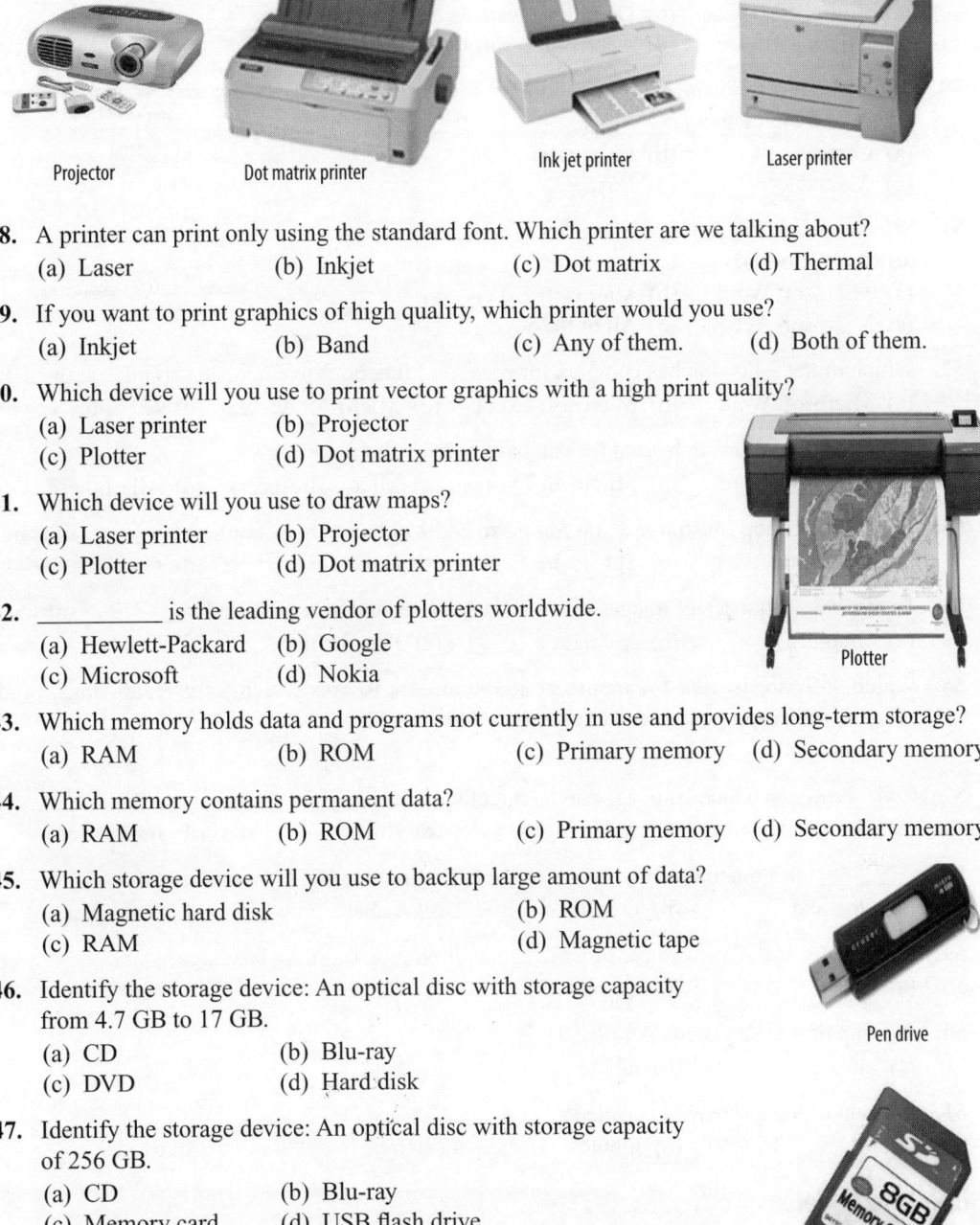

Projector   Dot matrix printer   Ink jet printer   Laser printer

38. A printer can print only using the standard font. Which printer are we talking about?
    (a) Laser (b) Inkjet (c) Dot matrix (d) Thermal

39. If you want to print graphics of high quality, which printer would you use?
    (a) Inkjet (b) Band (c) Any of them. (d) Both of them.

40. Which device will you use to print vector graphics with a high print quality?
    (a) Laser printer (b) Projector
    (c) Plotter (d) Dot matrix printer

41. Which device will you use to draw maps?
    (a) Laser printer (b) Projector
    (c) Plotter (d) Dot matrix printer

42. _____ is the leading vendor of plotters worldwide.
    (a) Hewlett-Packard (b) Google
    (c) Microsoft (d) Nokia

Plotter

43. Which memory holds data and programs not currently in use and provides long-term storage?
    (a) RAM (b) ROM (c) Primary memory (d) Secondary memory

44. Which memory contains permanent data?
    (a) RAM (b) ROM (c) Primary memory (d) Secondary memory

45. Which storage device will you use to backup large amount of data?
    (a) Magnetic hard disk (b) ROM
    (c) RAM (d) Magnetic tape

46. Identify the storage device: An optical disc with storage capacity from 4.7 GB to 17 GB.
    (a) CD (b) Blu-ray
    (c) DVD (d) Hard disk

Pen drive

47. Identify the storage device: An optical disc with storage capacity of 256 GB.
    (a) CD (b) Blu-ray
    (c) Memory card (d) USB flash drive

48. Which of the following enables the users to interact with hardware components efficiently?
    (a) Application software (b) Communication software
    (c) Presentation software (d) System software

Memory card

49. Which of the following ensures that the system resources are utilized efficiently?
    (a) Compiler   (b) Operating system
    (c) Utility software (d) Application software

50. Which of the following copies programs from a storage device to main memory?
    (a) Compiler   (b) Interpreter
    (c) Assembler   (d) Loader

51. Which application software is used to write letters, memos, resumes or forms?
    (a) Microsoft Word (b) Microsoft Excel
    (c) Microsoft Access (d) All of these.

52. Which of the following has complex formulas and functions to calculate variables in the data?
    (a) Microsoft Word (b) Microsoft Excel (c) Microsoft Access (d) All of these

53. Which of the following is used for database queries and reporting?
    (a) Microsoft Word (b) Microsoft Excel (c) Microsoft Access (d) All of these.

54. Adobe Photoshop Illustrator, Paint Shop Pro and MS Paint are examples of _____ software.
    (a) Word processing (b) Spreadsheet (c) Database (d) Graphics

55. To display a sequence of images in a fraction of a second, you will need a _____ software.
    (a) Graphics (b) Animation (c) Presentation (d) Utility

56. Which software is used by architects and engineers to create architectural drawings, product designs, landscaping plans and engineering drawings?
    (a) Graphics (b) CAD (c) Presentation (d) CAM

57. Code written in which language can be directly executed by the computer?
    (a) Compiled (b) Assembly (c) Binary (d) Interpreter

58. _____ is a mnemonic that specifies the operation that has to be performed.
    (a) Operand (b) Opcode (c) Label (d) Comment

59. Query language is an example of which generation programming language?
    (a) First (b) Second (c) Third (d) Fourth

60. A group of 4 binary digits is called a _____.
    (a) bit (b) nibble (c) byte (d) word

61. A group of 8 binary digits is called a _____.
    (a) bit (b) nibble (c) byte (d) word

State True or False

1. A computer can perform thousands of instructions in one second.
2. First generation computers required an entire room for installation.
3. First generation computers were used for commercial applications.
4. Knowledge is the application of data and information.

5. Computer and all its physical parts are known as software.
6. 1942–1955 marks the second generation of computers.
7. Machine/assembly language was used in the first generation of computers.
8. Vacuum tubes and transistors emit large amount of heat.
9. The first generation of computers were more expensive than the third generation of computers.
10. The third generation of computers were more difficult to install and maintain than the computers of first generation.
11. In the second generation of computers, high-level programming languages were used.
12. Computers of the fourth generation are faster, smaller, cheaper, reliable and more powerful than the computers of first generation.
13. SSI and MSI technology was used in the fourth generation of computers.
14. Pascal, COBOL, FORTRAN and BASIC are all low-level programming languages.
15. High-speed computer networks in the form of LANs, WANs and MANs were used in the third generation of computers.
16. Computer is a reliable machine.
17. If input data is wrong then the output will also be erroneous.
18. When data and programs have to be used, they are copied from the primary memory into the secondary memory.
19. Computers cannot make decisions on their own.
20. Robots are computer-controlled machines.
21. Robots cannot work in high temperature, high pressure conditions or in processes which demand very high level of accuracy.
22. Managers use DSS to plan effective strategies for penetrating their markets.
23. Secondary memory is faster than primary memory.
24. Your computer has more primary memory than secondary memory.
25. CPU can directly access primary memory.
26. Primary memory can be used for storing data permanently.
27. ALU manages and controls all the components of the computer system.
28. VDU is an input device.
29. Mouse can be used to create graphics such as lines, curves and freehand shape on the screen.
30. Scanner is an input device.
31. OMR is used to verify the legitimacy or originality of paper documents.
32. A computer with a microphone and speakers can be used for video conferencing.
33. Webcams are used for video conferencing and as security cameras.
34. Soft copy output can be seen even the computer is switched off.
35. Hard copy output cannot be used by people who do not have a computer.
36. Searching data is faster in a soft copy output.
37. Electronic distribution of a hard copy is cheaper, faster and easier than soft copy.
38. You can change the brightness, sharpness and color settings of the image when using a projector.

39. Non-impact printers create characters by striking an inked ribbon against the paper.
40. Dot-matrix printers and daisywheel printers are examples of impact printer.
41. Laser printer cannot print text of different fonts.
42. Critical programs which are used to start the computer when it is turned on are stored in RAM.
43. Hard disk drive is an example of ROM.
44. CD uses laser technology to read and write data on the disc.
45. CDs can store data on both the sides of the disc.
46. Application software provides a general programming environment in which programmers can create specific applications to suit their needs.
47. Compiler and operating system are examples of application software.
48. MS-WORD and PAINT are examples of application software.
49. Compiler translates one statement of high-level language program into machine language and executes it.
50. A compiled program executes slower than an interpreted program.
51. Microsoft Excel is a word-processing software.
52. Binary language programs can be written to efficiently utilize memory.
53. Labels are optional in assembly language.
54. Assembly language code is machine-dependent.
55. A byte consists of 16 binary digits.
56. The main aim of data processing is to transform data into information.
57. Multimedia includes only text.
58. Animation involves displaying at least 30 still images in a fraction of a second.

ANSWER KEYS

Multiple Choice Questions

1. (c)	2. (d)	3. (c)	4. (a)	5. (b)	6. (d)	7. (b)	8. (b)
9. (a)	10. (d)	11. (b)	12. (a)	13. (d)	14. (d)	15. (b)	16. (c)
17. (d)	18. (c)	19. (b)	20. (c)	21. (a)	22. (b)	23. (c)	24. (d)
25. (c)	26. (a)	27. (d)	28. (c)	29. (a)	30. (b)	31. (d)	32. (c)
33. (a)	34. (b)	35. (c)	36. (d)	37. (c)	38. (c)	39. (b)	40. (c)
41. (c)	42. (a)	43. (d)	44. (b)	45. (d)	46. (c)	47. (d)	48. (d)
49. (b)	50. (d)	51. (a)	52. (b)	53. (c)	54. (d)	55. (a)	56. (b)
57. (c)	58. (b)	59. (d)	60. (b)	61. (b)			

State True or False

1. True	2. True	3. False	4. True	5. False	6. False	7. True	8. True
9. True	10. False	11. True	12. True	13. False	14. False	15. False	16. True
17. True	18. False	19. True	20. True	21. False	22. True	23. False	24. False
25. False	26. False	27. False	28. False	29. True	30. True	31. False	32. True
33. True	34. False	35. False	36. True	37. False	38. True	39. False	40. True
41. False	42. False	43. False	44. True	45. False	46. False	47. False	48. True
49. False	50. False	51. False	52. True	53. True	54. True	55. False	56. True
57. False	58. False						

CHAPTER 2
GUI-based Operating Systems

KEY POINTS

- A program that has to be executed must be loaded in the main memory along with its data. To improve CPU utilization and provide better response time to the users, a computer usually stores more than one program in the memory.
- The operating system keeps a track of location, access time, modified time, and other details of files and directories (folders) saved on the computer disk.
- Multiprocessing means using two or more processors (CPUs) within a single computer system.
- In Real Time Operating System (RTOS), the time interval required to process and respond to inputs is very small and highly critical. It has well-defined, fixed time constraints.
- The command interpretation module (also called command interpreter) of the operating system provides a set of commands that the users can execute.
- Linux is a very powerful, free open-source operating system based on Unix.
- Each file has a name (called filename) and an extension.
- Every file has some attributes like size (space required on disk), location on disk, owner (who created the file), last access date, last modified date, etc.
- Storing a file on a persistent storage medium like hard disk ensures the availability of the file for future use.

KEYWORDS

Operating system: A group of computer programs that controls the computer's resources like CPU, memory, I/O devices, etc., and provides the users with an interface that makes it easier to use.
Booting: It is the process of starting or restarting the computer.
Process: A program in execution is called a process.
Time slice or a quantum: The short period of time during which a user gets CPU.
Pointer: A small angled arrow that enables the users to select commands and objects on the screen.
Pointing Device: A device (like mouse) that enables the user to select objects on the screen.
Icons: Small pictures that represent commands, files, or windows.
Menus: A GUI element that displays a list of available commands.
Window: A rectangular portion of the screen that displays applications, menus, icons, files, etc.
File: A collection of data.
Sub-folder: A folder within another folder.
Field: An elementary unit that stores a single fact.
Record: A collection of related data fields.
File Position: A pointer that points to the position at which the next read/write operation will be performed.
Retrieving from a File: Extracting useful data from a given file.

MODEL QUESTION PAPER

Multiple Choice Questions

1. The operating system acts as an intermediary between a user and _____.
   (a) application programs   (b) system software
   (c) computer hardware   (d) programmers

2. Which is the first program loaded into the computer during booting and remains in memory at all times?
   (a) Application programs   (b) System software
   (c) Operating system   (d) Utility software

3. In GUI, the user interacts with operating system using _____.
   (a) Icons   (b) Menus   (c) Windows   (d) All of these.

4. The operating system enables the user to execute _____ process(s) at the same time.
   (a) one   (b) ten
   (c) thousand   (d) multiple

5. Which type of operating system provides very limited or no interaction between the user and processor during the execution of work?
   (a) batch   (b) multi-processing
   (c) time sharing   (d) multi-tasking

7. Palm OS is a _____ type of operating system.
   (a) single-user   (b) single tasking
   (c) multi-user   (d) a and c

8. In _____ operating system, more than one job reside in the main memory.
   (a) batch   (b) multi-programming
   (c) time sharing   (d) b and c

9. _____ systems provide an interactive use of the computer system by several users.
   (a) Batch   (b) Multi-programming
   (c) Time sharing   (d) Real-time

10. Which type of operating system always uses more than one CPU?
    (a) Batch   (b) Multi-programming
    (c) Time-sharing   (d) multi-processing

11. Which type of operating system always supports parallel processing?
    (a) Batch   (b) Multi-programming
    (c) Time-sharing   (d) Multi-processing

12. Which type of operating system has rigid time requirement on data processing?
    (a) Batch   (b) Multi-programming
    (c) Time-sharing   (d) Real-time

Operating system is the interface between computer hardware and its users.

13. Which operating system will you use to control robots and in medical imaging systems?
    (a) Batch
    (b) Multi-programming
    (c) Time-sharing
    (d) Real-time

14. In a CUI, which input device will you use to give commands?
    (a) Keyboard
    (b) Mouse
    (c) Joystick
    (d) Stylus

15. Select pointing devices from the following.
    (a) Mouse
    (b) Joystick
    (c) Trackball
    (d) All of these.

16. Small pictures that represent commands are called _____.
    (a) icons
    (b) menu
    (c) pointer
    (d) window

17. Windows operating system is developed by _____.
    (a) HP
    (b) Adobe
    (c) Microsoft
    (d) Infosys

18. The latest version of Windows is _____.
    (a) Windows ME
    (b) Windows 10
    (c) Windows 8
    (d) Windows NT

19. Linux is made of which component(s)?
    (a) Kernel
    (b) Files
    (c) Processes
    (d) All of these.

20. The _____ part of Linux operating system allocates CPU time and memory to programs.
    (a) kernel
    (b) files
    (c) processes
    (d) shell

21. Which part of Linux acts as an interface between the user and the kernel?
    (a) Kernel
    (b) Files
    (c) Processes
    (d) Shell

Various operating systems

21. Linux is a _____ operating system.
    (a) multi-user
    (b) multi-programming
    (c) time-sharing
    (d) All of these.

22. Linux is a _____-based operating system.
    (a) Windows
    (b) Apple OS
    (c) Unix
    (d) Mac OS

23. Which of the following makes recent item lists of each application?
    (a) Icons
    (b) Task bar
    (c) Jump list
    (d) Start menu

24. Select the symbols which can be used in a file name.
    (a) \
    (b) :
    (c) *
    (d) None of these.

Operating system components

25. Identify the type of file specified by 🎵 icon.
    (a) Audio	(b) Video
    (c) Graphics	(d) Web

26. A file with .avi extension is a _____ file.
    (a) audio	(b) video
    (c) graphics	(d) web

27. Clicking on 🖥️ (Computer) opens the _____.
    (a) Internet Explorer	(b) C drive
    (c) Windows Explorer	(d) Control Panel

28. _____ is a tool that can be used to manage files and folders stored in the computer system.
    (a) Internet Explorer	(b) C drive
    (c) Windows Explorer	(d) Control Panel

29. To select multiple consecutive files, you will use the _____ key.
    (a) Home	(b) Shift	(c) Ctrl	(d) Alt

30. To select multiple non-consecutive files you will use the _____ key.
    (a) Home	(b) Shift	(c) Ctrl	(d) Alt

31. Files deleted from which of the following will go in Recycle Bin?
    (a) Memory Card	(b) Pen Drive
    (c) External Hard Disk	(d) None of these.

32. 🌐 (Internet Explorer) was developed by _____.
    (a) Google	(b) Microsoft	(c) Adobe	(d) Wipro

33. Choose the correct data hierarchy.
    (a) Fields, Records, Files and Database	(b) Fields, Files, Records and Database
    (c) Database, Records, Files and Fields	(d) Records, Fields, Files and Database.

34. Which of the following is an elementary unit that stores a single fact?
    (a) Record	(b) Field	(c) Data	(d) Database

35. _____ is a collection of records.
    (a) File	(b) Field	(c) Data	(d) Database

36. Updating a file means _____.
    (a) inserting data	(b) editing data	(c) deleting data	(d) All of these.

37. The best term meaning extracting data from a file would be _____.
    (a) Editing	(b) Retrieving	(c) Updating	(d) Maintaining

State True or False

1. Operating system makes a computer system easier to use.
2. Application software provides users an environment in which a user can execute programs conveniently and efficiently.

3. Warm booting is done when a completely turned off computer is turned on.
4. Cold booting takes place when the operating system is used to restart the computer.
5. A computer system can have only one CPU.
6. The operating system enables the users to easily interact with the computer hardware.
7. Icons help users to interact with the computer system.
8. DOS is a GUI based operating system.
9. A computer stores only one program in the memory.
10. A quantum is usually between 10–100 milliseconds.
11. Multi-programming means using more than one processor to execute a complex task.
12. RTOS has flexible time constraints.
13. Time sharing operating system is used for traffic control.
14. In GUI, users can interact with a program only by typing commands at the prompt.
15. In command line interface, users need to memorize commands to interact with the programs.
16. Users can work in multiple windows simultaneously.
17. Cell phones and ATMs work on CUI.
18. Windows is a multi-tasking operating system.
19. Windows is based on CUI.
20. Linux is a free operating system.
21. Linux supports GUI.
22. Linux shell provides memory, file, device and security management features.
23. Everything in UNIX is either considered to be a file or a process.
24. A process is a collection of data.
25. Linux is an unstable operating system.
26. Linux is a multi-user operating system.
27. Linux can be used for networking.
28. Linux can run all common UNIX software packages and can process all common file formats.
29. Linux can be installed on mobile phones, tablets and video game consoles.
30. You should pin frequently used applications on the task bar.
31. Icons give quick access to applications.
32. You can resize the icons on your desktop.
33. It is possible to change the icon of a program.
34. It is possible to specify a descriptive file name of 233 characters.
35. You can open a file by doing a single click on its icon.
36. It is not possible to know the last access date of a file.
37. One or more files in a folder can have the same extension.
38. One or more files in a folder can have the same name.
39. All the files deleted permanently from the computer will go in the Recycle Bin.
40. Files deleted from within the Windows command prompt are not sent to the Recycle Bin.

41. You can restore files from Recycle Bin.
42. Chrome is a web browser given by Microsoft.
43. The right pane of Start Menu displays list of programs on the computer.
44. The left pane of Start Menu provides access to commonly used folders, files, settings, and features.
45. You can change the clock settings of your computer system.
46. It is not possible to change the color depth and screen resolution of your computer
47. It is possible to swap the functions of mouse buttons.
48. A collection of files is called a record.
49. Directory is a combination of one or more files.
50. A read-only file cannot be opened for viewing.
51. Hidden files are not displayed during directory listing.
52. Multi-tasking allows only one program to execute at a time.

ANSWER KEYS

Multiple Choice Questions

1. (c)	2. (c)	3. (d)	4. (d)	5. (a)	6. (d)	7. (d)	8. (b)
9. (d)	10. (d)	11. (d)	12. (d)	13. (a)	14. (d)	15. (a)	16. (c)
17. (b)	18. (d)	19. (a)	20. (d)	21. (d)	22. (c)	23. (c)	24. (d)
25. (a)	26. (b)	27. (c)	28. (c)	29. (b)	30. (c)	31. (d)	32. (b)
33. (a)	34. (c)	35. (a)	36. (d)	37. (b)			

State True or False

1. True	2. False	3. False	4. False	5. False	6. False	7. True	8. False
9. False	10. True	11. False	12. False	13. False	14. False	15. True	16. True
17. False	18. True	19. False	20. True	21. True	22. False	23. True	24. False
25. False	26. True	27. True	28. True	29. True	30. True	31. True	32. True
33. True	34. True	35. False	36. False	37. True	38. False	39. False	40. True
41. True	42. False	43. False	44. False	45. True	46. False	47. True	48. False
49. True	50. False	51. True	52. False				

CHAPTER 3
Data Organization and Database Management System

KEY POINTS

- When computers were first used for business applications, a related group of records were stored in a file.
- In batch processing systems, requests, jobs, or transactions to be performed by the computer are submitted to the computer and the results are obtained after some time.
- Online data processing is used in systems that need to provide interactive computations.
- In serial processing, transactions are performed sequentially.
- An effective database system comprises of four main components – data, hardware, software, and users.
- In real-time processing, which is a subset of online processing, users submit requests to perform some transaction(s) that must be completed before the specified deadline (which is usually very near).
- In centralized data processing, all data processing operations and calculations are performed by the central computer and different terminals (computers) are connected to the central computer for sending requests and receiving outputs.
- In decentralized data processing (DDP), relatively smaller computers located at different places in an organization are connected to each other with or without a central authority.
- A sequentially organized file stores records in the order in which they were entered.
- Relative file organization provides direct access to individual records.
- The main concern of database management system (DBMS) is to help users retrieve data efficiently from the database.
- The database administrator enforces data abstraction in database systems by defining data views at three levels – logical view, external view, and internal or physical view.
- A database model describes three things – data, the relationships that exist between data, and the constraints on that data.
- The data definition module provides functions to define the structure of the data and the data manipulation module provides functions to perform operations such as inserting, searching, and deleting data in the database.
- Database users can easily retrieve data from the database using structured query language (SQL).
- The SELECT statement of SQL allows users to query or retrieve data from a table in the database.
- The query processor accepts users' queries and transforms them into a series of low-level instructions.
- The report writer utilizes the output of query execution to display it in an easy-to-understand and interpretable format.

- The hierarchical data model supports 1 to N mapping while the network model supports a many-to-many data mapping.
- A data dictionary is a vital component of databases as it stores the metadata, that is, data about data.
- Data warehouse is an information delivery system that integrates and transforms the organization's data into information to make it suitable for making strategic decisions.
- Data mining is a technology that applies sophisticated and complex algorithms to analyze data and expose interesting information for analysis by decision-makers.
- Big Data analytics can help organizations to better understand the information contained within the data.

KEYWORDS

Alternate key: If a table has more than one candidate key, then one of them is chosen as the primary key and all the other candidate keys are called alternate keys of that table.

Batch: A set of requests that are processed together, often long after the requests are submitted.

Big Data analytics: The process of collecting, organizing, and analyzing large sets of data (called Big Data) to discover patterns and other useful information.

Candidate key: A key that is eligible to become the primary key.

Central computer: A large computer that manages resources of an organization and shares it with other computers in the system.

Composite key: A composite key is a key made up of two or more attributes within a table to uniquely identify a record.

Database: A collection of related data organized in a way that allows users to easily access, update and maintain the data.

Database schema: A layout of the database.

DBMS: A collection of interrelated data and a set of programs that enables multiple users to access, modify, share, and process the data simultaneously.

Directory: A collection of related files.

Field: An elementary unit that stores a single fact.

File: A collection of records.

Foreign key: An attribute of a table that matches the primary key of another table.

Index table: A table that stores record number and the address of the record in the file.

Link: An association between two or more records.

Logical data independence: The ability to change the logical schema of the database without affecting its external schemas or application programs.

Mapping: The process of transforming the requests and results between the three levels of schema architecture.

Metadata: Data about data.

Physical data independence: The ability to change the internal schema without affecting the logical or external schema.

Query: The statement written to retrieve information.

Query language: The part of the DML that retrieves the information from the database.

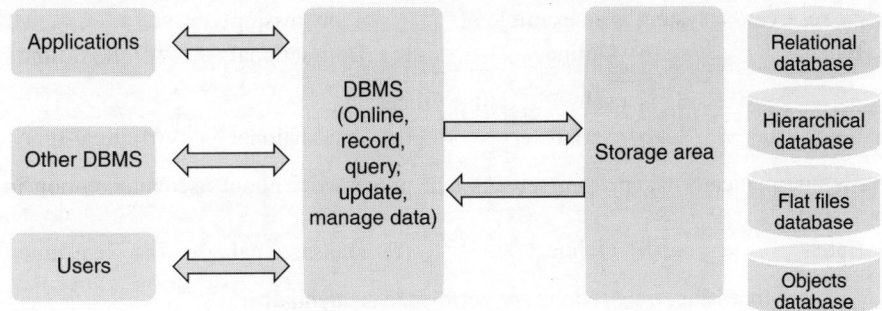

Database Management System

Record: A collection of related data fields that is seen as a single unit from the application point of view.

Relational database: A collection of related tables also known as relations. Therefore, databases that support the concept of relations are called relational databases.

Table: A collection of data records where each record contains the same fields.

MODEL QUESTION PAPER

Multiple Choice Questions

1. Which of the following is an elementary unit that stores a single fact?
   (a) Field   (b) Record   (c) File   (d) Directory

2. A collection of related data fields is known as _____.
   (a) Data Fields   (b) Record   (c) File   (d) Directory

3. A collection of related records is known as _____.
   (a) File System   (b) Field   (c) File   (d) Directory

4. A directory stores information of related_____.
   (a) Fields   (b) Records   (c) Files   (d) File System

5. The term that defines the fraction of time a system is up and running for processing is _____.
   (a) Availability   (b) Readability   (c) Accessibility (d) Usability

6. _____ is a set of requests that are processed together, often long after the requests are submitted.
   (a) Set   (b) Batch   (c) Transaction   (d) Record

7. Calculating the value of a stock market portfolio is an example of _____ processing.
   (a) Batch   (b) Online   (c) Transactional (d) Real-time

8. _____ processing is best in cases where quick response time is not desirable.
   (a) Batch   (b) Online   (c) Transactional (d) Real-time

9. _____ processing is best in cases where interactive communication is desirable.
   (a) Batch   (b) Online   (c) Transactional (d) Real-time

10. Airline reservation system is an example of _____ processing.
    (a) Batch   (b) Online   (c) Transactional   (d) Real-time

11. _____ processing is a subset of online processing.
    (a) Batch   (b) Serial   (c) Transactional   (d) Real-time

12. Data is automatically taken from sensors and processed without user intervention in _____ processing.
    (a) Batch   (b) Online   (c) Transactional   (d) Real-time

13. In _____ processing, transactions are performed sequentially.
    (a) Transactional (b) Online   (c) Serial   (d) Real-time

14. Efficient utilization of resources and effective implementation of security and privacy measures is difficult in _____ processing.
    (a) Centralized   (b) Decentralized   (c) Batch   (d) None of these

15. Processing in bank branches and airline reservation are categorized as _____ processing.
    (a) Centralized, Decentralized   (b) Centralized, Centralized
    (c) Decentralized, Decentralized   (d) Decentralized, Centralized

16. Which of the following is not a file organization technique?
    (a) Indexed   (b) Sequential   (c) Parallel   (d) Relative

17. _____ file organization stores records in the order in which they are entered.
    (a) Indexed   (b) Sequential   (c) Multi-key   (d) Relative

18. Deleting and updating records in which kind of file requires replacing an old file with the new one?
    (a) Indexed   (b) Sequential   (c) Multi-key   (d) Relative

19. All records have the same size and the same field format, and every field has a fixed size, is a characteristic of which file organization?
    (a) Indexed   (b) Sequential   (c) Multi-key   (d) Relative

20. In a sequential file, all records are sorted based on the _____ field.
    (a) Name   (b) ID   (c) Key   (d) None of these.

21. Payroll processing of all the employees of an organization can be done using a _____ file.
    (a) Indexed   (b) Sequential
    (c) Multi-key   (d) Relative

22. A _____ file does not support random access.
    (a) Indexed   (b) Sequential
    (c) Multi-key   (d) Relative

23. A _____ file does not support interactive applications.
    (a) Indexed   (b) Sequential
    (c) Multi-key   (d) Relative

Levels of data abstraction in DBMS

24. A _____ file can be used for both random accesses of data as well as for sequential access.
    (a) Indexed　　(b) Relative　　(c) Both of these.　　(d) None of these.

25. The record number represents the location of the record relative to the beginning of the file in which type of file?
    (a) Indexed　　(b) Sequential　　(c) Multi-key　　(d) Relative

26. _____ type of file is well-suited for interactive applications.
    (a) Indexed　　(b) Sequential　　(c) Multi-key　　(d) Relative

27. Records are of equal size in _____ type of file organization.
    (a) Indexed　　(b) Sequential　　(c) Relative　　(d) All of these.

28. In file-oriented approach, temporary file is also known as _____ file.
    (a) Transaction　　(b) Master　　(c) Backup　　(d) Output

29. _____ file is used to update master file.
    (a) Transaction　　(b) Master　　(c) Backup　　(d) Output

30. In file-oriented approach, _____ file contains all data relevant data for an application.
    (a) Transaction　　(b) Master　　(c) Backup　　(d) Output

31. In case of data loss, the original file can be restored from the _____ file.
    (a) Transaction　　(b) Master　　(c) Backup　　(d) Output

32. _____ is a collection of the related data organized in a way that allows users to easily access, update, and maintain the data.
    (a) Field　　(b) Record　　(c) File　　(d) Database

33. A database does stores _____ data.
    (a) Organized　　(b) Redundant　　(c) Inconsistent　　(d) All of these.

34. Separating physical storage of data from application programs that access it means _____.
    (a) Organized　　(b) Redundant
    (c) Inconsistent　　(d) Data Independence

35. World Wide Web stores _____ data.
    (a) Textual　　(b) Multi-media　　(c) Both of these.　　(d) None of these

36. Data about data in the database is stored in _____.
    (a) File　　(b) Directory　　(c) Data dictionary　　(d) Master File

37. Data in a database is searched using _____.
    (a) Words　　(b) Keywords　　(c) Fields　　(d) Records

38. Data accessibility is easiest and most efficient in _____.
    (a) Master File　　(b) Transaction File　　(c) Output File　　(d) Database

39. Data stored in files must satisfy certain types of consistency constraints. This ensures data _____.
    (a) Dependency　　(b) Consistency　　(c) Integrity　　(d) Isolation

40. Data must be restored to the correct state that existed prior to the failure. This ensures _____.
    (a) Atomicity　　(b) Consistency　　(c) Integrity　　(d) Isolation

41. Not every user should be able to access all the data. This ensures _____.
    (a) Atomicity   (b) Consistency   (c) Integrity   (d) Security

42. When a transaction is performed, either all or none of its operations must be completed. This ensures _____.
    (a) Atomicity   (b) Consistency   (c) Integrity   (d) Security

43. After the transaction is complete, the database should have the correct information. This ensures _____.
    (a) Atomicity   (b) Consistency   (c) Integrity   (d) Security

44. Committed transactions are permanently stored on a storage device. This ensures _____.
    (a) Atomicity   (b) Consistency   (c) Integrity   (d) Durability

45. The result of running a set of transactions is the same as running one transaction at a time. This feature is ensured by the property of Data _____.
    (a) Isolation   (b) Consistency   (c) Integrity   (d) Durability

46. Which of the following is not a database software?
    (a) MS Access   (b) SQL Server   (c) MS Excel   (d) Oracle

47. Application programs to access, retrieve, update, delete, or add new data to the database is written using which language?
    (a) C   (b) C++   (c) SQL   (d) Java

48. Technical details of databases may not be known by _____.
    (a) End-users   (b) Application programmers
    (c) System Analyst   (d) DBA

49. People working at railways reservation counters are an example of _____.
    (a) Sophisticated End-users   (b) Application programmers
    (c) Unsophisticated End-users   (d) DBA

50. Who makes strategic and policy decisions regarding the data?
    (a) End-users   (b) Application programmers
    (c) System Analyst   (d) DBA

51. Who provides technical support for implementing strategic and policy decisions related to data and is responsible for overall control of the system at the technical level?
    (a) End-users   (b) Application programmers
    (c) System Analyst   (d) DBA

52. Training employees in database management and use is the work of _____.
    (a) End-users   (b) Application programmers
    (c) System Analyst   (d) DBA

53. _____ monitors and performs all activities related to database design, implementation, maintenance, and security.
    (a) End-users   (b) Application programmers
    (c) System Analyst   (d) DBA

54. _____ identifies end-users' requirements and plans solutions.
    (a) End-users   (b) Application programmers
    (c) System Analyst   (d) DBA

55. _____ is a collection of interrelated data and a set of programs that enable multiple users to access, modify, share, and process the data.
    (a) File   (b) Database   (c) DBMS   (d) Directory

56. There are _____ levels of data view.
    (a) one   (b) two   (c) three   (d) four

57. Which of the following is not a type of data view?
    (a) Tabular   (b) Internal   (c) External   (d) Physical

58. Which data view focuses on how data is actually stored?
    (a) Tabular   (b) Internal   (c) External   (d) Physical

59. Which view describes data that is stored in database and the relationships that exist among that data?
    (a) Logical   (b) Internal   (c) External   (d) Physical

60. End-users are interested in which data view?
    (a) Logical   (b) Internal   (c) External   (d) Physical

61. _____ view hides all complexities to deal with the user's view of the database.
    (a) Logical   (b) Internal   (c) External   (d) Physical

62. _____ view enables customization of data according to users' needs.
    (a) Logical   (b) Internal
    (c) External   (d) Physical

63. _____ describes the structure of a database in a formal language supported by the DBMS.
    (a) View   (b) Schema
    (c) Architecture (d) Template

64. There can be _____ number of external schema.
    (a) 1   (b) 2
    (c) 3   (d) any

65. There can be ____ number of logical and physical schema.
    (a) 1   (b) 2   (c) 3   (d) any

66. There are _____ levels of database schema.
    (a) 1   (b) 2   (c) 3   (d) any

67. _____ schema can be easily implemented without affecting the application programs that are using the data.
    (a) Logical   (b) Internal   (c) External   (d) Physical

68. _____ schema is managed by the operating system under the direction of the DBMS.
    (a) Logical   (b) Internal   (c) External   (d) Physical

Tables - Attributes and Tuples

69. _____ schema is often used by the application developers and programmers to develop applications.
    (a) Logical   (b) Internal   (c) External   (d) Physical

70. _____ schema describes a part of the database as per the user's requirements and hides the rest of the database from that user.
    (a) Logical   (b) Internal   (c) External   (d) Physical

71. In three-schema architecture, each user group has its own _____ view.
    (a) Logical   (b) Internal   (c) External   (d) Physical

72. DBMS transforms the requests from _____ level.
    (a) External, Physical, Logical   (b) External, Logical, Physical
    (c) Physical, Logical, External   (d) External, Logical, Physical

73. The three-schema architecture ensures _____.
    (a) Data Isolation   (b) Data Dependence
    (c) Data Independence   (d) Data Atomicity

74. _____ is the ability to modify the database schema at one level without affecting or without changing the schema at the other levels.
    (a) Data Isolation   (b) Data Dependence
    (c) Data Independence   (d) Data Atomicity

75. The logical schema may be changed due to _____.
    (a) Addition of fields   (b) Addition of constraints
    (c) Deletion of constraints   (d) All of these.

76. _____ schema is changed to improve the performance of database.
    (a) Logical   (b) Internal   (c) External   (d) Physical

77. _____ is the ability to change the internal schema without affecting the logical or external schema.
    (a) Data Dependence   (b) Physical Data Independence
    (c) Logical Data Independence (d) External Data Independence

78. Physical schema of the database may be changed due to _____.
    (a) changing storage structure   (b) addition of indexes
    (c) deletion of indexes   (d) All of these.

79. Database _____ specifies integrity rules and type of operations that can be performed.
    (a) Model   (b) View   (c) Schema   (d) All of these.

80. Integrity rules ensure that the data is _____.
    (a) Accurate   (b) Current   (c) Complete   (d) All of these.

81. _____ data model organizes data in a tree structure.
    (a) Network   (b) Hierarchical   (c) Relational   (d) Object-oriented

82. _____ data model organizes data in a parent–child relationship.
    (a) Network   (b) Hierarchical   (c) Relational   (d) Object-oriented

83. A parent can have _____ children in a hierarchical data model.
    (a) 1   (b) 2   (c) 3   (d) *n*

84. If data is organized by state, within state by city, within city by zip code, then which data model will best suit the scenario?
    (a) Network
    (b) Hierarchical
    (c) Relational
    (d) Object-oriented

85. Data is represented by links in which data model(s)?
    (a) Network   (b) Hierarchical   (c) Relational   (d) (b) and (c)

86. Which data model stores data in the form of graphs?
    (a) Network   (b) Hierarchical   (c) Relational   (d) (b) and (c)

87. Child data element can have many parent data elements in which data model?
    (a) Network   (b) Hierarchical   (c) Relational   (d) (b) and (c)

88. In relational model, each _____ stores a record.
    (a) row   (b) column   (c) field   (d) file

89. In a relational database, each row represents a _____.
    (a) attribute (b) value   (c) entity   (d) All of these.

90. Which data model is easy to expand?
    (a) Network   (b) Hierarchical   (c) Relational   (d) (b) and (c)

91. Which type of data cannot be stored in a relational data model?
    (a) Multimedia (b) Temporal   (c) Spatial   (d) All of these.

92. Which data model is used for CAD/CAM applications?
    (a) Network
    (b) Hierarchical
    (c) Relational
    (d) Object-oriented

93. Which data model is used for expert systems and multimedia systems?
    (a) Network
    (b) Hierarchical
    (c) Relational
    (d) Object-oriented

94. A set of all the objects which share the same attributes and methods is called _____.
    (a) Class   (b) Object   (c) Method   (d) Message

95. In a relational data model, rows are known as _____.
    (a) Tuples   (b) Entities   (c) Attributes   (d) Table

96. When designing a relation, an employee will be treated as _____.
    (a) Attribute (b) Tuple   (c) Relation   (d) Key

97. An entity is described using _____.
    (a) Attribute (b) Tuple   (c) Relation   (d) Key

98. Which key uniquely identifies a row?
    (a) Primary key
    (b) Candidate key
    (c) Alternate Key
    (d) All of these.

itemid	orderid	item	amount
5	1	Chair	200.00
6	1	Table	200.00
7	1	Lamp	123.12

customerid	name	e-mail
5	Rosalyn Rivera	rosalyn@adatum.com
6	Jayne Sargent	jayne@contoso.com
7	Dean Luong	dean@contoso.com

orderid	customerid	date	amount
1	4	11/1/17	523.12
2	3	11/15/17	32.99
3	1	11/21/17	23.99

99. _____ is an attribute or a combination of attributes that uniquely identifies an entity.
    (a) Primary key
    (b) Candidate key
    (c) Alternate key
    (d) All of these.

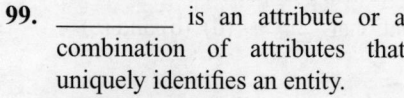

Roll_No	Name	Branch	City
01	Deepak	Computers	Bhiwani
02	Mukesh	Electronics	Rohtak
03	Teena	Mechanical	Bhiwani
04	Deepti	Chemical	Rohtak
05	Monika	Civil	Delhi

100. Every table must have at least _____ candidate key.
     (a) 1   (b) 2
     (c) 3   (d) n

101. If a table has more than one candidate key, then one of them is chosen as the primary key and all the other are called _____ keys.
     (a) Primary   (b) Candidate   (c) Alternate   (d) Composite

102. Primary key is also a _____ .
     (a) Candidate Key   (b) Alternate Key
     (c) Both (a) and (b).   (d) None of these.

103. _____ is a key made up of two or more attributes within a table to uniquely identify a record.
     (a) Primary key   (b) Candidate key   (c) Alternate key   (d) Composite key

104. _____ key is used to cross-reference tables.
     (a) Primary   (b) Foreign   (c) Alternate   (d) Composite

105. _____ key acts as primary key of another table.
     (a) Foreign   (b) Candidate   (c) Alternate   (d) Composite

106. _____ integrity checks are made when records are added, deleted or updated in the table having the foreign key.
     (a) Data   (b) Relational   (c) Referential   (d) Hierarchical

107. Name of table, attributes, primary key, foreign key, etc., are stored in _____.
   (a) Table   (b) Database   (c) Data Dictionary   (d) Directory

108. Data dictionary is shared by _____ application(s).
   (a) 1   (b) 2   (c) 3   (d) all

109. Data dictionary is usually hidden from the users so that it is not _____ by the users.
   (a) destroyed   (b) modified   (c) accessed   (d) All of these.

110. Documentation on database design process and information about data ownership is stored in _____.
   (a) Table   (b) Database   (c) Data Dictionary   (d) Directory

111. The _____ statement of the SQL allows users to query or retrieve data from a table in the database.
   (a) Select   (b) Query   (c) Retrieve   (d) Get

112. To select only specific data from the table, we use the _____ statement.
   (a) Select – where   (b) Select – having
   (c) Get – where   (d) Get – having

113. _____ is an information delivery system.
   (a) Table   (b) Database   (c) File   (d) Data Warehouse

114. In a data warehouse, data is stored by _____.
   (a) Attributes   (b) Fields   (c) Subjects   (d) Applications

115. In a transactional system, data is stored by _____.
   (a) Attributes   (b) Fields   (c) Subjects   (d) Applications

116. Before storing data in the data warehouse, it must be _____.
   (a) cleansed   (b) transformed   (c) filtered   (d) Both a and b.

117. Standardizing data means making _____ uniform.
   (a) field names   (b) character code
   (c) data layout   (d) All of these.

118. Business transactions do not update the data in the data warehouse. This means that data in the data warehouse is _____.
   (a) subject-oriented   (b) non-volatile   (c) time-variant   (d) integrated

119. Data in the data warehouse is meant for analysis and decision-making. This requires that the data should be _____.
   (a) subject-oriented   (b) non-volatile   (c) time-variant   (d) integrated

120. Time-variant data allow users to _____.
   (a) analyze the past   (b) forecast the future
   (c) relate information to the present   (d) All of these.

121. Data warehouse stores _____ data.
   (a) archived   (b) current   (c) transactional   (d) highly detailed

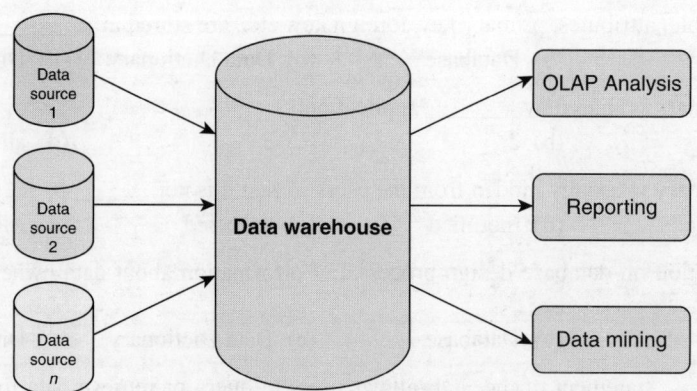

Data warehouse - Structure and functions

122. _____ refers to using a variety of techniques to identify nuggets of information in the database.
    (a) Data warehousing (b) SQL (c) Data mining (d) IoT

123. Data mining is a _____ discovery process.
    (a) Data   (b) Information   (c) Knowledge   (d) Results

124. Data _____ means summarizing general features of objects in a target class.
    (a) Characterization (b) Discrimination
    (c) Association Analysis (d) Prediction

125. Data _____ produces rules that are used to compare general features of objects between two classes.
    (a) Characterization (b) Discrimination (c) Association Analysis (d) Prediction

126. _____ technique studies the frequent item set.
    (a) Characterization (b) Discrimination (c) Association Analysis (d) Prediction

127. _____ organizes data in given classes.
    (a) Characterization (b) Discrimination (c) Classification (d) Prediction

128. Forecast of missing numerical values is done using _____.
    (a) Characterization (b) Discrimination (c) Classification (d) Prediction

129. _____ is based on the principle of maximizing the similarity between objects in a same class and minimizing the similarity between objects of different classes.
    (a) Characterization (b) Clustering (c) Classification (d) Prediction

130. _____ is also known as unsupervised classification.
    (a) Characterization (b) Clustering (c) Classification (d) Prediction

131. Outlier analysis finds out the _____ in data.
    (a) Outliers (b) Exceptions (c) Surprises (d) All of these.

132. Study of trends in data is called _____.
    (a) Evolution (b) Deviation Analysis (c) Classification (d) Prediction

133. Study of differences between measured values and expected values is called_____.
    (a) Evolution (b) Deviation Analysis (c) Classification (d) Prediction

134. Data Mining is best applied on _____.
    (a) Table
    (b) Database
    (c) Data Warehouse
    (d) Transactional systems

135. Customer segmentation uses the _____ technique.
    (a) Characterization (b) Clustering (c) Classification (d) Prediction

136. Market basket analysis uses _____ technique.
    (a) Characterization
    (b) Discrimination
    (c) Association Analysis
    (d) Prediction

137. Risk management uses _____ technique.
    (a) Outlier Analysis (b) Clustering (c) Classification (d) Prediction

138. Delinquency tracking uses _____ technique.
    (a) Outlier Analysis (b) Clustering (c) Classification (d) Prediction

139. _____ is the process of collecting, organizing and analyzing large sets of data (called Big Data) to discover patterns and other useful information.
    (a) Data Mining
    (b) Big Data Analysis
    (c) Both (a) and (b).
    (d) None of these.

140. Big data can be obtained from _____.
    (a) sensors (b) video/audio (c) social media (d) All of these.

Velocity
Speed at which data is emanating and changes are occuring between the diverse datasets

Volume
This refers to the sheer volume of data being generated every second.

Value
Having access to Big Data is all well and good but that's only useful if we can turn it into a value.

5 V's OF BIG DATA

Veracity
Data reliability and trust. Verifying and validating the data.

Variety
Can use structured as well as unstructured data.

141. Hadoop is a tool for _____.
    (a) Data Warehousing
    (b) Big Data Analysis
    (c) Data Mining
    (d) Operational Analysis

142. Zettabytes of data is analyzed using _____.
    (a) Data Warehousing
    (b) Big Data Analysis
    (c) Data Mining
    (d) Operational Analysis

143. Data Warehouse can analyze _____ of data.
    (a) Megabytes
    (b) Terabytes
    (c) Gigabytes
    (d) Zettabytes

144. Cloud-based analytics is used in _____.
    (a) Data Warehousing
    (b) Big Data Analysis
    (c) Data Mining
    (d) Operational Analysis

145. Identify the latest breakthrough in discovering knowledge from data.
    (a) Data Warehousing
    (b) Big Data Analysis
    (c) Data Mining
    (d) Operational Analysis

146. Data hierarchy includes _____.
    (a) fields, records, files, and database
    (b) records, files, fields and database
    (c) files, fields, records, and database
    (d) database, fields, records, files, and database

147. A student's roll number can be represented as his _____.
    (a) Field
    (b) Record
    (c) Database
    (d) File

148. A set of requests that are processed together is called _____.
    (a) Block
    (b) Batch
    (c) Program
    (d) Software

149. Amount of work performed per unit of time is called _____.
    (a) Response time
    (b) Performance
    (c) Throughput
    (d) Speed

150. Which of the following is not a type of processing?
    (a) Batch
    (b) Serial
    (c) Decentralized
    (d) None of these.

151. Identify the incorrect statement.
    (a) Batch processing is done without user intervention.
    (b) Batch processing is used to perform repetitive tasks on large volumes of data.
    (c) Batch processing is used in systems that need to provide interactive computation.
    (d) None of these.

152. _____ processing is used for processing continuous data.
    (a) Batch
    (b) Serial
    (c) Decentralized
    (d) Online

153. _____ processing is also called interactive processing.
    (a) Batch
    (b) Serial
    (c) Decentralized
    (d) Online

154. Users working with _____ systems expect a response in one or two seconds.
    (a) Batch
    (b) Serial
    (c) Real-time
    (d) Online

155. _____ processing automatically takes data from sensors and processes it without user intervention.
    (a) Batch
    (b) Serial
    (c) Real-time
    (d) Online

156. In _____ processing, one transaction must be completed before the next one begins.
    (a) Batch   (b) Serial   (c) Real-time   (d) Online

157. Identify the incorrect statement.
    (a) Centralized systems are easy to manage and require less personnel costs.
    (b) A central computer is a large computer that manages the resources of an organization and shares it with other computers in the system.
    (c) In decentralized processing, all applications and data are managed by a system administrator.
    (d) None of these.

158. Efficient utilization of resources takes place in _____ processing.
    (a) Batch   (b) Serial   (c) Decentralized   (d) Online

159. Lack of standardization of data structures, incompatibility and duplication of data are problems experienced in which type of processing?
    (a) Batch   (b) Serial   (c) Decentralized   (d) Online

160. File organization depends on _____.
    (a) external storage
    (b) types of queries
    (c) mode of retrieval and update
    (d) All of these.

161. Identify the incorrect statement.
    (a) A sequentially organized file stores records in the order in which they are entered.
    (b) Sequential files can be read only sequentially, starting with the first record in the file.
    (c) We cannot change the size of the records stored in a sequential file.
    (d) We can delete the records from a sequential file without using another file.

162. Identify the incorrect statement.
    (a) Updating records necessitates the creation of a new file.
    (b) All updates to data stored in a sequential file are batched.
    (c) In sequential file organization, all records may not be of the same size.
    (d) In a sequential file, records are sorted based on the value of one or more fields.

163. Identify the incorrect statement.
    (a) Sequential file can be used for interactive applications.
    (b) In relative file organization, record number represents the location of the record relative to the beginning of the file.
    (c) Relative files cannot be used for sequential access.
    (d) Relative files provide support for only one key.

164. Identify the incorrect statement.
    (a) Use of relative files is restricted to disk devices.
    (b) The records in a relative file may be of different sizes.
    (c) Relative files allow deletions and updates in the same file.
    (d) Relative files are well-suited for interactive applications.

165. Identify the incorrect statement.
    (a) Indexed sequential is not meant for interactive applications.
    (b) Records in an indexed sequential file may be stored anywhere physically.
    (c) The index table stores the record number and the address of the record in the file.
    (d) The index table is read sequentially to find the address of the desired record.

166. Identify the incorrect statement.
   (a) Indexed sequential files can be stored only on disks.
   (b) In an indexed sequential file, direct access is made to the address of the specified record.
   (c) Data is permanently stored in the transaction file.
   (d) The transaction file is used to update the master file.

167. Identify the correct statement.
   (a) The output of one program cannot go as an input of another program.
   (b) A master file contains all data relevant data for an application.
   (c) The original file can be restored from the transaction file.
   (d) Database stores redundant data.

168. Separating physical storage of data from application programs that access it is called _____.
   (a) Data Independence   (b) Data Dependence
   (c) Application Dependence   (d) Application independence

169. Which of the following does not store information in a database?
   (a) WWW   (b) Online shopping website
   (c) Tele-communications department   (d) None of these.

170. Databases cannot have _____.
   (a) Redundancy   (b) Inconsistency   (c) Integrity issues   (d) Security

171. Identify the correct statement.
   (a) Databases have data dependency.
   (b) In a database, data and programs are strongly coupled.
   (c) Databases can respond to un-anticipatory queries.
   (d) In a database, data is isolated in different applications.

172. Data must be restored to the correct state that existed prior to the failure, to ensure data _____.
   (a) Integrity   (b) Atomicity
   (c) Flexibility (d) Security

173. A successful transaction incorporates data _____.
   (a) Atomicity   (b) Isolation   (c) Consistency   (d) All of these.

174. When a transaction is performed, either all or none of its operations must be completed, this ensures _____.
   (a) Atomicity   (b) Isolation   (c) Consistency   (d) Durability

175. Committed transactions are permanently stored on a storage device. This ensures _____.
   (a) Atomicity   (b) Isolation   (c) Consistency   (d) Durability

176. _____ describes the structure of the database.
   (a) Data   (b) Metadata   (c) Hardware   (d) Software

177. _____ interacts with the user's application programs and database.
   (a) DBMS   (b) Metadata   (c) Hardware   (d) Data

178. Which of the following is not a DBMS software?
   (a) SQL Server   (b) MS PowerPoint
   (c) MS Excel   (d) Oracle

179. Users of database do not include _____.
    (a) database administrator
    (b) system analyst
    (c) application programmers
    (d) None of these.

180. Identify the incorrect statement.
    (a) An application programmer writes application programs to access, retrieve, update, delete, or add new data to the database.
    (b) SQL is a fourth generation language.
    (c) Sophisticated end-users write their own queries.
    (d) Sophisticated end-users interact with the system through an already written application program.

181. Who monitors and performs all activities related to database design, implementation, maintenance, and security?
    (a) Database administrator
    (b) System analyst
    (c) Application programmers
    (d) Sophisticated end-user

182. Who writes end-users' requirements in a technical requirements definition document after conducting a technical and economic feasibility analysis of the identified requirements?
    (a) Database administrator
    (b) System analyst
    (c) Application programmers
    (d) Sophisticated end-user

183. Identify the incorrect statement.
    (a) DBMS is a collection of interrelated data and a set of programs.
    (b) DBMS is to help users to efficiently retrieve data from the database.
    (c) System analyst enforces data abstraction in database systems by defining data views at three levels.
    (d) DBMS is to provide users with an abstract view of the data to hide certain details of how the data is stored and maintained.

184. Identify the correct statement.
    (a) Physical level is the lowest level of abstractions that focus on how data is actually stored.
    (b) Physical level describes what data is stored in the database and what relationships exist among the data.
    (c) The logical level is the highest level of abstraction that hides all complexities to deal with the user's view of the database.
    (d) The external level describes a part of the database for a particular group of users.

185. Which level supports customization of data according to the user's needs?
    (a) Internal
    (b) External
    (c) Physical
    (d) Logical

186. Identify the incorrect statement.
    (a) There is only 1 physical schema.
    (b) There is only 1 logical schema.
    (c) There can be any number of external schemas.
    (d) None of these.

187. Which schema is managed by the operating system under the direction of the DBMS?
    (a) Physical
    (b) Logical
    (c) External
    (d) User

188. Identify the correct statement.
    (a) The three-schema architecture ensures data independence.
    (b) Physical schema may get changed by adding new fields.
    (c) Logical schema gets changed if you change the storage structure.
    (d) Physical schema gets changed if you add/delete indexes.

189. _____ is the ability to modify the database schema at one level without affecting or without changing the schema at the other levels
    (a) Data dependence
    (b) Data independence
    (c) Data atomicity
    (d) Data isolation

190. Integrity rules to ensure that the data is _____.
    (a) accurate
    (b) complete
    (c) relevant
    (d) atomic

191. Identify the incorrect statement.
    (a) The hierarchical model can have any number of levels.
    (b) Hierarchical model organizes records in the form of graphs.
    (c) In the network model, a child can have multiple parents.
    (d) In a table, each column represents an attribute of that entity.

192. Identify the incorrect statement.
    (a) An object may belong to any number of classes.
    (b) Methods of an object can be accessed or invoked from outside the object by explicitly passing messages to it.
    (c) An object is a real-world entity.
    (d) Table is also known as a relation.

193. _____ are also known as tuples.
    (a) Tables
    (b) Rows
    (c) Columns
    (d) Attributes

194. Entities are described using _____.
    (a) Tables
    (b) Rows
    (c) Columns
    (d) Attributes

195. Identify the incorrect statement.
    (a) A candidate key is a key that is eligible to become the primary key.
    (b) A candidate key can be just one column or a combination of multiple columns.
    (c) A foreign key is an attribute of a table that matches the primary key of another table.
    (d) The alternate key is used to identify a record uniquely.

196. Identify the incorrect statement.
    (a) Referential integrity ensures that relationships between tables remain consistent.
    (b) A record in a table with a foreign key can be added even if there is no corresponding record in the linked table.
    (c) A record in a table with a foreign key is deleted if the primary key of the other table is deleted.
    (d) A record in a table with a foreign key is updated if the foreign key, that is, the primary key of the other table is changed.

197. Identify the correct statement.
    (a) Data dictionary can be shared by several applications.
    (b) Data dictionary is hidden from the users.

(c) Data dictionary can be manipulated only by the system administrator.
(d) All of these.

198. Data dictionary does not include _____.
    (a) type of attributes.
    (b) source of data in the table.
    (c) Both of them.
    (d) None of them.

199. The _____ clause can be used to restrict the data that has to be retrieved.
    (a) SELECT
    (b) WHERE
    (c) *
    (d) All of these.

200. Identify the incorrect statement.
    (a) In transactional systems, we store data by individual applications.
    (b) In the data warehouse, data is stored by subjects.
    (c) In a data warehouse, a particular subject may be involved in different types of transactions.
    (d) Integration of data includes data cleansing but not data transformation.

201. Identify the incorrect statement.
    (a) Data is not deleted in the data warehouse in real-time.
    (b) Data warehouse contains only current data values.
    (c) Data warehouse is used for operational processing.
    (d) The response time of operational systems is sub-seconds.

202. Identify the incorrect statement.
    (a) Data mining centers on the automated discovery of new facts and relationships in data.
    (b) Data classification is a summarization of general features of objects in a target class and produces characteristic rules.
    (c) Data discrimination draws a comparison between the general features of objects and between two classes referred to as the target class and the contrasting class.
    (d) All of these.

203. Identify the incorrect statement.
    (a) Association analysis studies the frequency of items occurring together in transactional databases.
    (b) Support identifies the frequent item sets.
    (c) Support is the conditional probability that an item appears in a transaction when another item appears.
    (d) Association analysis is commonly used for market basket analysis.

204. Identify the incorrect statement.
    (a) The classification algorithm learns from the training set and builds a model to classify new objects.
    (b) Characterization is the organization of data in classes.
    (c) Outliers are data elements that cannot be grouped in a given class or cluster.
    (d) Evolution and deviation analysis studies time-related data that changes in time.

205. Data mining cannot be used for _____.
    (a) customer segmentation
    (b) risk management
    (c) demand prediction
    (d) None of these.

206. Big data analytics uses advanced analytics techniques like _____.
    (a) text mining
    (b) machine learning
    (c) data optimization
    (d) All of these.

207. Identify the incorrect statement.
    (a) Big data analytics is the process of collecting, organizing, and analyzing large sets of data.
    (b) Big data analysis outperforms data warehousing as it can easily handle large amount of unstructured and semi-structured data efficiently.
    (c) Big data analysis techniques can analyze large data sets of size ranging from few terabytes to zettabytes.
    (d) Big data cannot be used to decode human DNA.

ANSWER KEYS

Multiple Choice Questions

1. (a) 2. (b) 3. (c) 4. (c) 5. (a) 6. (b) 7. (a) 8. (a)
9. (b) 10. (b) 11. (d) 12. (d) 13. (b) 14. (b) 15. (d) 16. (c)
17. (b) 18. (b) 19. (b) 20. (c) 21. (b) 22. (b) 23. (b) 24. (c)
25. (d) 26. (d) 27. (D) 28. (a) 29. (a) 30. (b) 31. (c) 32. (d)
33. (a) 34. (d) 35. (c) 36. (c) 37. (b) 38. (d) 39. (c) 40. (a)
41. (d) 42. (a) 43. (b) 44. (d) 45. (a) 46. (c) 47. (c) 48. (a)
49. (b) 50. (d) 51. (d) 52. (d) 53. (d) 54. (c) 55. (c) 56. (c)
57. (a) 58. (D) 59. (A) 60. (c) 61. (c) 62. (c) 63. (b) 64. (d)
65. (a) 66. (c) 67. (d) 68. (d) 69. (a) 70. (c) 71. (c) 72. (b)
73. (c) 74. (c) 75. (d) 76. (d) 77. (b) 78. (d) 79. (a) 80. (a)
81. (b) 82. (b) 83. (d) 84. (b) 85. (d) 86. (a) 87. (a) 88. (a)
89. (c) 90. (c) 91. (d) 92. (d) 93. (d) 94. (a) 95. (a) 96. (c)
97. (a) 98. (a) 99. (b) 100. (a) 101. (c) 102. (a) 103. (d) 104. (b)
105. (a) 106. (c) 107. (c) 108. (d) 109. (d) 110. (c) 111. (a) 112. (a)
113. (d) 114. (c) 115. (d) 116. (d) 117. (d) 118. (b) 119. (c) 120. (d)
121. (a) 122. (c) 123. (c) 124. (a) 125. (b) 126. (c) 127. (c) 128. (d)
129. (d) 130. (d) 131. (d) 132. (a) 133. (b) 134. (c) 135. (b) 136. (c)
137. (a) 138. (a) 139. (c) 140. (d) 141. (b) 142. (b) 143. (c) 144. (b)
145. (b) 146. (a) 147. (a) 148. (b) 149. (c) 150. (d) 151. (c) 152. (d)
153. (d) 154. (c) 155. (c) 156. (a) 157. (c) 158. (c) 159. (c) 160. (d)
161. (d) 162. (c) 163. (c) 164. (b) 165. (a) 166. (c) 167. (b) 168. (a)
169. (d) 170. (c) 171. (c) 172. (b) 173. (d) 174. (a) 175. (d) 176. (b)
177. (a) 178. (b) 179. (d) 180. (d) 181. (a) 182. (b) 183. (c) 184. (a)
185. (b) 186. (d) 187. (a) 188. (d) 189. (b) 190. (a) 191. (b) 192. (a)
193. (b) 194. (d) 195. (d) 196. (b) 197. (d) 198. (d) 199. (b) 200. (d)
201. (c) 202. (b) 203. (c) 204. (b) 205. (d) 206. (d) 207. (d)

CHAPTER 4
Internet, WWW and Web Browsers

KEY POINTS

- Owing to limited scope and cost of operation, LANs are typically owned, controlled, and managed by a single person or organization.
- WANs span a large geographic area such as a city, country, or even intercontinental distances, using a communications channel that combines many types of media such as telephone lines, cables, and air waves.
- When individual networks connect together to form a larger network (or a bigger WAN), the resulting network is called an internetwork.
- Most WANs (like the Internet) are not owned by any one individual or organization but rather exist under collective or distributed ownership and management.
- To connect to the Internet the user must gain access through a commercial Internet Service Provider (ISP).
- A Uniform Resource Locator (URL) specifies the addresses for World Wide Web pages.
- Internet Protocol Address (or IP Address) is a unique address allotted to computing devices.
- The web browser is actually the seventh layer of the OSI Model, i.e., the application layer.
- Internet is based on a client–server model.
- Web browsers must download the pages in less than two seconds.
- The World Wide Web stores enormous amount of information on an amazing variety of topics in hundreds of millions of pages.
- The search engines use automated software called robots, bots or spiders that travel along the Web searching all documents and files to create a searchable index of the flies and documents containing the keyword.
- The default shortcuts included as Favorites are: *Desktop, Downloads and Recent Places*.
- The Internet is a global network that connects billions of computers all over of the world.
- Electronic mail (e-mail) means the transmission of messages over communication networks.
- Internet chat allows two or more online users to come together to talk using an instant messenger.
- With online newspaper, users can read the full coverage of breaking news in a timely manner.
- Online shopping means buying goods and/or services from merchants who sell on the Internet.
- The contents hosted on the Intranet can be accessed only by members within the organization who have appropriate access control rights.
- Internet protocol address is a unique address allotted to computing devices such as computers, routers, printers, scanners, modems, smartphones and tablets that are connected to the Internet.
- The term 'protocol' means a set of rules that must be followed to facilitate communication.
- Domain name system (DNS) is a service that automatically converts domain names into IP addresses.
- Transmission control protocol (TCP) is a protocol that works at the transport layer and is used with the IP protocol to send data packets between sender and receiver devices.

- While an absolute uniform resource locator (URL) specifies the complete URL containing all three fields – protocol, domain, and path, relative URLs, on the other hand, contain only one field – the domain name.
- Dynamic HTML is a combination of technologies – HTML, Java Script and Cascading Style Sheets and is used to create dynamic, interactive, and animated web pages.
- Extensible markup language (XML) is a markup language that defines a set of rules for encoding documents in a format that is readable by humans as well as computers. It is used to share information in a consistent way.

KEYWORDS

Network: A collection of computers and devices interconnected to facilitate sharing of resources.

Internet: A global network that connects billions of computers all over of the world.

Host: Computer on the internet.

Client: A program that requests information from another computer on the network.

Web browser: Software that is used to find, retrieve and display web pages on the World Wide Web.

Chat: An Internet service that enables users to communicate with other people in real time. The user types his message using the keyboard. The message then appears on the screen of the other person. Similarly, the message typed by the other person appears on the user's screen.

Download: Making a copy of a file from another computer to your computer. For example, users may copy a song from another computer on the Internet to their computer.

Electronic mail: An e-mail system designed to enable the users to send and receive messages across a network.

FTP: Short form of file transfer protocol, it is basically a program that enables users to transfer files from one computer to another.

Gopher: A program that organizes information on the Internet using a system of menus. Items in the menus can be links to other documents or to other information services.

Host: Any computer on a network.

HTML: HTML stands for hypertext markup language and is used to create hypertext documents for use on the World Wide Web.

HTTP: Hypertext transfer protocol (HTTP) is a protocol that defines a set of rules to exchange documents on the World Wide Web.

Hypertext: A hypertext document is one that includes links to other documents on the World Wide Web.

Internet: A network of networks. It connects several networks all around the world to enable them to exchange information with each other. For this purpose, all the computers on the Internet use a common set of rules (protocols) for communication. Therefore, the Internet uses a set of protocols called transmission control protocol/internet protocol.

Internet service provider: A commercial service that sells access to the Internet to individuals. Users connect to the ISP through a modem. While some ISPs only offer a basic connection to the Internet, others, on the other hand, sell a variety of value-added services such as discussion forums, tech support, software libraries, news, weather reports, stock prices, plane reservations, and even electronic shopping malls.

Link: A word, picture, or other area of a web page that users can click on to move to another spot in the same document or to another document. Links (words) may be underlined and usually appear in a contrasting coloured text. When the user clicks on the link, the colour of the text changes.

Newsgroup: An Internet service in which readers can post messages or articles for other people to read. Other people can also reply to articles that they read on a newsgroup. It enables people with similar interests to communicate with each other.

Node: Computer connected to a network.

Protocol: A set of standardized rules that should be followed to exchange information among computers. There are different protocols for different kinds of communication. For example, HTTP specifies the rules for exchanging information on the World Wide Web. FTP defines the rules to copy files from one computer to another across a network.

Server: A program that provides information or services to other programs. For example, the web browser is a client that uses services like e-mail from the server.

Upload: The opposite of download – that means transferring a file, picture, document, or an audio/video clip from your computer to another computer.

URL: A uniform resource locator specifies the addresses for World Wide Web pages. A URL uniquely identifies a Web page. URLs have three parts—protocol name, server name, and a directory path. For example, consider the URL http://wings.avkids.com/SPIT/index.html. Here, http:// is the name of the protocol, wings.avkids.com is the server's name, and /SPIT/index.html is the location of the file on the server.

Web page: A document on the World Wide Web that can contain text, pictures, movies, sounds, or links to other pages.

Website: A collection of web pages on the World Wide Web having to do with a particular topic or organization.

World Wide Web: An interconnected set of hypertext documents located throughout the Internet

MODEL QUESTION PAPER

Multiple Choice Questions

1. Which method is most flexible for sharing files?
   - (a) Pen drive
   - (b) Blu-ray disk
   - (c) CD
   - (d) Network

2. LANs are based on _____ technology.
   - (a) WAN
   - (b) Internet
   - (c) Ethernet
   - (d) Intranet

3. Wireless LANs use _____ waves.
   - (a) wireless
   - (b) radio
   - (c) infrared
   - (d) light

4. Identify the type of network which spans two continents.
   - (a) LAN
   - (b) MAN
   - (c) WAN
   - (d) PAN

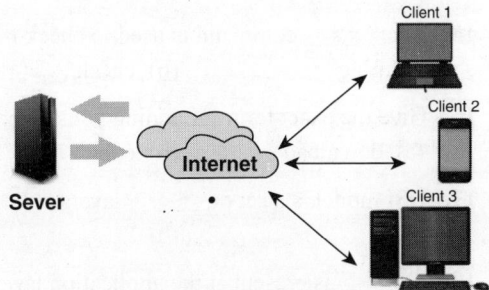

Clients connected to servers through the Internet

5. _____ is the largest WAN.
   (a) Ethernet (b) Internet
   (c) MAN (d) LAN

6. With the help of a device called _____ LAN can be connected to a WAN.
   (a) modem
   (b) switch
   (c) router
   (d) Ethernet card

7. Internet is managed by _____.
   (a) Microsoft
   (b) Google
   (c) Yahoo
   (d) None of these.

8. Data transmission of LAN is _____.
   (a) 1 Mbps to 10 Mbps (b) 10 Mbps to 100 Mbps
   (c) 10 Mbps to 1 Gbps (d) 100 Mbps to 10 Gbps

9. To transfer files over the network, you will use _____.
   (a) HTTP (b) FTP (c) e-mail (d) gopher

10. _____ is a program that organizes information on the Internet using a system of menus.
    (a) HTTP (b) Newsgroup (c) Gopher (d) Web browser

11. _____ is a protocol that defines a set of rules to exchange documents on the World Wide Web.
    (a) HTTP (b) FTP (c) SMTP (d) TFTP

12. Users connect to the ISP through a device called _____.
    (a) modem (b) switch (c) router (d) Ethernet card

13. _____ is a program that provides information or services to other programs.
    (a) Host (b) Client (c) Server (d) Service

14. A document on the World Wide Web is called a _____.
    (a) web browser (b) web page (c) website (d) web browser

15. The _____ command is used to check if the server is running.
    (a) ping (b) check (c) cmd (d) run

16. Give the exact term for adding your video on YouTube.
    (a) download (b) copy (c) upload (d) transfer

17. OSI model is a set of _____ layers.
    (a) 6 (b) 7 (c) 8 (d) 9

18. _____ is present at the application layer.
    (a) Web browser (b) Client (c) Server (d) Protocol

19. The _____ layer is also called the syntax layer.
    (a) Network (b) Physical (c) Transport (d) Presentation

20. Data encryption is done by _____ layer.
    (a) Network   (b) Presentation   (c) Transport   (d) Application
21. Which layer is known as the dialog controller?
    (a) Network   (b) Presentation   (c) Session   (d) Transport
22. Which layer is responsible for reliable data transfer between two systems?
    (a) Network   (b) Presentation   (c) Transport   (d) Application
23. Best path selection is a job of _____ layer.
    (a) Network   (b) Presentation   (c) Transport   (d) Application
24. The World Wide Web was created by _____.
    (a) Charles Babbage   (b) Ada Lovelace   (c) Tim Berners-Lee   (d) Alan Turing
25. E-mail address of recipients can be entered in _____ field(s).
    (a) To   (b) CC   (c) BCC   (d) All of these.
26. Modem converts _____.
    (a) digital data to analog signals   (b) analog signals to digital data
    (c) Both   (d) None
27. Cable modem connection uses _____ wires to provide Internet access.
    (a) twisted pair   (b) coaxial   (c) fiber optic   (d) Any of these.
28. _____ cables can easily pick up noise.
    (a) Twisted pair   (b) Coaxial   (c) Fiber optic   (d) Any of these.

Twisted pair cable   Coaxial cable   Fiber optic cable

29. Fiber optic cables use _____ waves to transmit data.
    (a) heat   (b) light   (c) radio   (d) infrared
30. Web browser works at the _____ layer of OSI model.
    (a) Physical   (b) Application   (c) Network   (d) Internet
31. Internet is based on _____ model.
    (a) client–server   (b) host program   (c) request response   (d) get post
32. Web browser acts as a _____.
    (a) server   (b) client   (c) host   (d) user
33. Web browser requests information from the server using _____ protocol.
    (a) FTP   (b) SMTP   (c) HTTP   (d) TFTP
34. _____ button is used to reload the current web page.
    (a) Back   (b) Home   (c) Forward   (d) Refresh

35. _____ is entered in the address bar.
    (a) IP address   (b) DNS   (c) URL   (d) Home page
36. _____ bar is to display progress in loading the web page.
    (a) Address   (b) Status   (c) Title   (d) Menu
37. Complete the name of the web browser: Apple _____.
    (a) Firefox   (b) Chrome   (c) Explorer   (d) Safari
38. _____ is a text-only web browser.
    (a) Mozilla Firefox   (b) Google Chrome   (c) Lynx   (d) Apple Safari
39. A good web browser must display pages in less than _____ seconds.
    (a) 1   (b) 2   (c) 3   (d) 4
40. _____ is a pre-installed web browser in Windows.
    (a) Mozilla Firefox   (b) Google Chrome   (c) Internet Explorer   (d) Apple Safari
41. Identify the web browser ◯.
    (a) Mozilla Firefox   (b) Google Chrome   (c) Opera   (d) Apple Safari
42. _____ was the first search engine.
    (a) Google   (b) Yahoo   (c) MSN Search   (d) Archie
43. Search engines use _____ to search documents on the World Wide Web.
    (a) spiders   (b) bugs   (c) virus   (d) worms
44. If the user has multiple keywords and all of them does not form a phrase, then specify the keywords using a _____ sign.
    (a) –   (b) +   (c) ,   (d) –
45. If there are multiple keywords and users want information on any of the keywords, then he must use _____ in parentheses.
    (a) OR   (b) +   (c) AND   (d) –
46. If the user wants to limit the search result by indicating keywords that should be and that should not be a part of result must, then he must use the _____ symbol.
    (a) –   (b) +   (c) ,   (d) –
47. _____ was the first text-based search engine.
    (a) Veronica   (b) Yahoo   (c) MSN Search   (d) Archie
48. Commands to import or export information from the Internet to other applications or to a file on your computer are present in _____ menu.
    (a) File   (b) Edit   (c) Mailings   (d) View
49. _____ has commands to add or organize URLs the user views frequently and wishes to save for further reference.
    (a) View   (b) Favorites   (c) Tools   (d) Edit
50. You can add _____ in Favorites.
    (a) Desktop   (b) Shortcuts of programs
    (c) Shortcuts to files   (d) Libraries

51. To print a web page you should press _____ keys.
    (a) Shift + P   (b) Alt + P   (c) Ctrl + P   (d) Enter + P

52. Tick the incorrect statement.
    (a) Internet is a global network connecting billions of computers all over the world.
    (b) Internet is a network of networks.
    (c) Each computer on the Internet is called a server.
    (d) To connect to the Internet, the user must gain access through ISP.

53. Identify the correct statement.
    (a) The first network was the internet.
    (b) An e-mail is fast, flexible, and reliable way of exchanging messages.
    (c) Anyone with or without an e-mail account can send an email to any other person who may or may not an e-mail account.
    (d) The structure of the e-mail can be given as *domainname@username*.

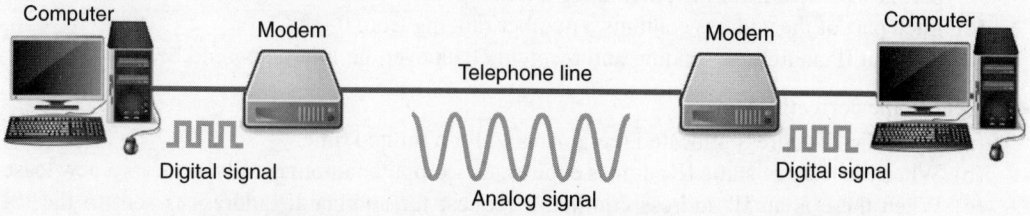

Modem performing Modulation at Sender and Demodulation at receiver

54. Identify the correct statement.
    (a) In the Subject field, type anything illustrating the content of the message.
    (b) Content of the message is written in the Subject field.
    (c) Filling up CC and BCC fields is mandatory.
    (d) In case of multiple recipients, each address is separated by a semi-colon.

55. Identify the incorrect statement.
    (a) FTP is used to upload/download files from a user's PC to a web server.
    (b) After reading the message, the receiver may save it, delete it, forward it to someone else, or reply to it.
    (c) E-mail is sent through instant messenger.
    (d) For chatting, every user must have an account with a username and password on the chatting website.

56. Identify the incorrect statement.
    (a) The chatting program allows users to talk privately as well as in a group.
    (b) Instant chatting can be used to arrange business meetings.
    (c) Any number of users can participate in a web meeting.
    (d) Businesses provide online support to customers through chatting.

57. Identify the incorrect statement.
    (a) To start an Internet conference call, users need a computer with an Internet connection, related software, a webcam, and a microphone.
    (b) During the conference, users can share files, video, and audio clips.

(c) Seminars can be arranged through Internet conferencing.
(d) Online newspapers have no legal boundaries as a hard copy newspaper.

58. Identify the incorrect statement.
    (a) When the user positions the cursor on a hyperlink, the cursor changes to a circle-shaped figure.
    (b) WWW was created in 1989 by Tim Berners-Lee.
    (c) Web browsers are used to access the web.
    (d) Mozilla Firefox, Opera, Google Chrome, Safari and Edge are popularly used web browsers.

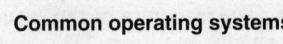

Opera   Google Chrome   Safari

Mozilla Firefox   Microsoft Edge

Common operating systems

59. Identify the correct statement.
    (a) IP address facilitates unique identification of devices for communication to take place.
    (b) An IP address is divided into six parts where each part is separated from the other using a dot.
    (c) Each part of the address contains a number ranging from 0–128.
    (d) Without IP addresses, sending and receiving data over the Internet would be very slow.

60. Identify the correct statement.
    (a) Dynamic IP address allocated remains valid for a limited time.
    (b) When the lease of static IP address expires, the computer automatically requests a new lease.
    (c) When there is an IP address conflict, a request for another IP address is sent to the ISP manually.
    (d) Dynamic IP address is permanent.

61. Identify the incorrect statement.
    (a) There are limited static addresses.
    (b) Dynamic IP address is safe to use.
    (c) E-mail servers and other web servers must have a dynamic IP address.
    (d) Users can configure their static IP address by themselves.

62. Identify the incorrect statement.
    (a) Dynamic IP address is preferable for applications such as voice over IP, online gaming, and other applications that need to locate and connect to a particular computer on the Internet.
    (b) Private IP addresses are allocated to devices that do not require public access.
    (c) Every time we use the Internet, we always use the DNS.
    (d) All of these.

63. Identify the incorrect statement.
    (a) The DNS system works as a network of DNS servers.
    (b) DNS is a service that automatically converts IP addresses to domain names.
    (c) DNS assumes that IP addresses are assigned statically and will not change.
    (d) ISPs maintain their own DNS servers to resolve name-to-IP address mapping.

64. Identify the correct statement.
    (a) Org is the domain name for international organizations.
    (b) In is the domain name for Indonesia.
    (c) URL specifies the unique address for a file that is accessible on the Internet.
    (d) News, gopher and mailto are protocols that cannot be specified in the URL.

65. Identify the correct statement.
    (a) Absolute URL contains only one field, which is the domain name.
    (b) Relative URL specifies the complete URL containing all three fields.
    (c) Spaces are written as a + sign in the URL.
    (d) Multiple variables are separated with ? in a URL.

66. Identify the correct statement.
    (a) A domain name same as URL.
    (b) IPv6 address can support 2^{32} devices.
    (c) There are 32 bits in IPv4 address which are divided into four groups of eight bits.
    (d) The IPv4 address has 128 bits.

67. Identify the incorrect statement.
    (a) TCP works at the transport layer.
    (b) IP works at the transport layer.
    (c) The main responsibility of the TCP is to establish a connection between the sender and the receiver so that reliable and error-free data transmission can take place.
    (d) TCP deals with segmentation and reassembly of data packets.

68. Identify the incorrect statement.
    (a) UDP is a transport layer protocol.
    (b) UDP offers limited service as compared to TCP.
    (c) Video conferencing and online computer games prefer to use TCP.
    (d) TCP is slower as compared to UDP.

69. Identify the correct statement.
    (a) TCP is preferable when data to be exchanged is large.
    (b) TCP does nothing to correct errors and supports unreliable data transfer.
    (c) TCP is a connection-less protocol.
    (d) TCP does not send any acknowledgment.

70. Identify the incorrect statement.
    (a) FTP provides authentication and security to stored files and programs.
    (b) FTP users cannot update files on a server.
    (c) Copying files from a client to a server is called uploading.
    (d) Using FTP, files can be easily transferred by simply dragging and dropping.

71. Identify the correct statement.
    (a) In case of an anonymous FTP site, enter anonymous as username and e-mail address as password.
    (b) In block mode, files are transferred as a continuous stream with no intervention.
    (c) FTP uses two connections for data exchange – one for sending commands and the other for sending or receiving data.
    (d) In passive-mode FTP, the client initiates the connection.

72. Identify the incorrect statement.
    (a) Telnet is a text-based protocol.
    (b) Telnet is used to access specific applications or data located at a remote compute.
    (c) Telnet is an interactive protocol.
    (d) Telnet is available only for Unix and Linux operating systems.

73. Identify the incorrect statement.
    (a) Telnet allows users to log in as users of the remote host.
    (b) Even a dumb terminal can use the applications hosted on the world's most powerful computer.
    (c) Users cannot transfer files using Telnet.
    (d) HTTP is said to be the mother tongue of web browsers.

74. Identify the incorrect statement.
    (a) All the tags opened must be closed in HTML.
    (b) With HTML, web page designers can embed text, images, audio, video, and interactive forms in a web page.
    (c) HTML allow designers to embed scripts within a web page to design interactive pages.
    (d) None of these.

75. Identify the incorrect statement.
    (a) DHTML is a combination of technologies – HTML, Java Script, and Cascading Style Sheets that are used to create dynamic, interactive, and animated web pages.
    (b) DHTML a scripting language.
    (c) DHTML facilitates web pages to change at any time, without returning to the web server first.
    (d) DHTML is used for creating games.

76. Identify the incorrect statement.
    (a) XML is a markup language that defines a set of rules for encoding documents in a format that is readable by humans as well as computers.
    (b) XML is used to share information in a consistent way.
    (c) XML is designed to be self-descriptive.
    (d) XML does not support the use of nested tags to represent hierarchical data.

77. Identify the correct statement.
    (a) XML tags are not predefined.
    (b) In web applications, XML and HTML cannot be used together.
    (c) HTML is used to describe data but XML is used to format and display that data.
    (d) HTML is extensible since it allows designers to define their own tags.

78. Identify the incorrect statement.
    (a) Hacking means gaining unauthorized access to a computer system or its network either to harm it or to steal sensitive information available on the computer.
    (b) Ethical hacking is considered legal activity.
    (c) Hacking is an important method of ensuring the security of a computer system and its network.
    (d) Ethical hackers, also known as white-hat hackers, use the same tools and techniques that the criminal hackers (or black-hat hackers) use.

79. Identify the incorrect statement about using ethical hacking.
    (a) To recover lost information
    (b) To find out any holes in computer and network security
    (c) To deploy sound measures to prevent security breaches
    (d) To facilitate malicious hackers from gaining access to the computer system.

80. Benefits of ethical hacking does not include _____
    (a) fight against terrorism
    (b) preventing loss of confidential data
    (c) preventing national security breaches.
    (d) None of these.

81. Identify the correct statement.
    (a) Mobile computing allows transmission of data, voice, and video using computer or any other wireless device.
    (b) Mobile computing involves the use of mobile communication, mobile hardware, and mobile software.
    (c) Mobile communication uses radio wave signals and devices use wireless network
    (d) All of these.

82. Advantages of mobile computing does not include _____.
    (a) entertainment
    (b) location flexibility
    (c) increased productivity
    (d) None of these.

83. Identify the incorrect statement.
    (a) IoT helps in connectivity among people only.
    (b) A big challenge in mobile computing is identity verification.
    (c) The huge availability of address space in IPv6 has led to the development of the IoT.
    (d) IoT is the concept of connecting any device over the Internet.

84. The information collected by IoT devices can be used to _____.
    (a) detect patterns
    (b) make recommendations
    (c) detect possible problems before they occur
    (d) All of these.

85. Identify the incorrect statement.
    (a) IoT can solve traffic congestion issues and reduce noise, crime, and pollution.
    (b) Security is the biggest issue while talking about IoT.
    (c) Users use Facebook to build social relations organized around professional lives.
    (d) Users use SNS to share news, interest, opinions, insights, and experiences within their groups of communities.

86. Identify the incorrect SNS and its utility match.
    (a) LinkedIn to build social relations organized around professional lives.
    (b) Facebook for creating lines of communication between ordinary individuals and public figures.
    (c) MySpace for musicians to promote themselves and communicate with their fans.
    (d) Facebook used to connect with family, friends, and business customers.

87. Identify the correct statement.
    (a) On SNS, identity thefts are being done either by creating a fake account or stealing and hacking the password of another SNS user.
    (b) Data leakage, code of conduct and copyrights are major concerns of SNS.
    (c) Giving wrong affiliations, credentials or expertise, is an unethical behavior on SNS.
    (d) All of these.

State True or False

1. If your computer is connected with your friend's computer then you can copy files from his computer.
2. Computer networks increase storage capacity and efficiency.
3. E-mail has been made possible only because of computer networks.
4. WAN has limited scope than LAN.
5. WANs are typically owned, controlled, and managed by a single person.
6. You can create a wireless LAN.
7. LANs have higher data transfer rates than WANs.
8. WAN can be created by linking LANs together.
9. You can connect two or more networks.
10. LAN cannot be connected to a WAN.
11. Internet has a distributed ownership and management.
12. You can create a private WAN.
13. Internet is a private WAN.
14. Error rate is higher in LAN than in WAN.
15. Conferencing is an Internet service in which readers can post messages, or articles for other people to read.
16. Web pages are created using markup languages.
17. When your computer is connected to the Internet through a broadband connection, it is said to be offline.
18. You can use any shareware software without buying license for it.
19. OSI model layers are functionally dependent on each other.
20. Data compression is done in the physical layer.
21. Checkpoints during data transmission are inserted by the network layer.
22. Transport layer eliminates data duplication.
23. Data link layer performs flow control and error control functions.
24. You can enter a group chat or a personal chat.
25. During Internet conferencing, users can talk but not share files with each other.
26. You can shop 24 × 7 on the Internet.
27. A dial-up connection is very fast.
28. DSL connections support high bandwidth for data transmission and is cheap.

29. The infrared technology enables computing devices to communicate via long-range wireless signals.
30. Web browser can display only text and images.
31. Web browser can send as well as receive information from the server.
32. In a web browser, you can open multiple web pages simultaneously.
33. To go to the home page, you must use the Back button.
34. You can view the source code of a web page in the web browser.
35. Lynx web browser can display videos.
36. Pop ups may compromise your personal data.
37. ◉ is the icon of Google Chrome.
38. You can enhance privacy and security features of your web browser.
39. You cannot manage how your browser handles cookies.
40. You can block pop-ups of some sites and allow for others.
41. Search engine is a special website.
42. All search engines give the same results.
43. All search engines follow the same algorithm.
44. Searching for same information using different search engines gives better results.
45. When there are multiple keywords that form a phrase, then enclose the keywords in parenthesis.
46. Commands like Cut, Copy, Paste are present in the View Menu.
47. Favorites are a series of icons.
48. Desktop is present in Favorites by default.
49. Shortcuts to programs or files can be added in Favorites.
50. While printing, every page can be printed on a single A4 size paper.

ANSWER KEYS

Multiple Choice Questions

1. (d)	2. (c)	3. (b)	4. (c)	5. (b)	6. (c)	7. (d)	8. (c)	
9. (b)	10. (c)	11. (a)	12. (a)	13. (c)	14. (b)	15. (a)	16. (c)	
17. (b)	18. (a)	19. (d)	20. (b)	21. (c)	22. (c)	23. (a)	24. (c)	
25. (d)	26. (c)	27. (b)	28. (a)	29. (b)	30. (b)	31. (a)	32. (b)	
33. (c)	34. (d)	35. (c)	36. (b)	37. (d)	38. (c)	39. (b)	40. (c)	
41. (c)	42. (d)	43. (a)	44. (b)	45. (a)	46. (d)	47. (a)	48. (a)	
49. (b)	50. (d)	51. (c)	52. (c)	53. (b)	54. (a)	55. (c)	56. (c)	
57. (d)	58. (a)	59. (a)	60. (a)	61. (c)	62. (d)	63. (b)	64. (c)	
65. (c)	66. (c)	67. (b)	68. (c)	69. (a)	70. (b)	71. (c)	72. (d)	
73. (d)	74. (d)	75. (b)	76. (d)	77. (a)	78. (c)	79. (a)	80. (d)	
81. (d)	82. (d)	83. (a)	84. (d)	85. (c)	86. (b)	87. (d)		

State True or False

1. True
2. True
3. True
4. False
5. False
6. True
7. True
8. True
9. True
10. False
11. True
12. True
13. False
14. False
15. False
16. True
17. False
18. True
19. False
20. False
21. False
22. True
23. True
24. True
25. False
26. True
27. False
28. False
29. False
30. False
31. True
32. True
33. False
34. True
35. False
36. True
37. True
38. True
39. False
40. True
41. True
42. False
43. False
44. True
45. False
46. False
47. False
48. True
49. False
50. False

CHAPTER 5
Communication and Collaboration

KEY POINTS

- Internet is mostly used for communication and collaboration.
- While communicating over the Internet, you must not share your personal information with strangers.
- E-mail is a client application that is used to send and receive information.
- To send and receive e-mail messages, a user must have a valid e-mail address.
- The user connects to the ISP's network, send his messages and collect his new e-mails from the server.
- The first part of the address identifies the user and the second part consists of the webmail or the ISP that has provided you the e-mail facility.

KEYWORDS

Inbox: Folder in which all the incoming e-mails (e-mails that are received) are stored.
Outbox: Folder in which all the e-mails sent are stored temporarily when it is not fully sent.
Draft: Folder in which e-mail messages that are composed but not sent and even not queued to be sent are stored.
Junk: Folder in which all fake and spam kinds of e-mail messages are stored.
Sent Items: Folder that stores all the e-mail messages that were successfully delivered.
Spam e-mail: Also known as junk e-mail, it is an unsolicited mail that is sent in bulk by the sender whom we do not know.
Deleted Items: Folder that stores all the e-mail messages that have been deleted.
Instant messaging: Exchange of real-time messages through a software application.
Emoticons or smilies: Small facial expressions used to add a specific feeling or emotion in the text.
Netiquette, Network Etiquette or Internet Etiquette: Set of rules that should be followed when one goes online.

MODEL QUESTION PAPER

Multiple Choice Questions

1. Internet can be used for communication using _____ technologies.
   (a) e-mail   (b) conferencing   (c) telephony   (d) All of these.
2. While communicating over the Internet, you should not share your personal information with _____.
   (a) strangers   (b) friends   (c) relatives   (d) All of these.

3. E-mail is a _____ application.
   (a) host   (b) server   (c) client   (d) user

4. You can send an e-mail to _____ users.
   (a) 1   (b) 4   (c) 8   (d) None of these

5. To download e-mail, you must download it from the _____.
   (a) host   (b) server   (c) client   (d) user

6. Which e-mail service is now known as Outlook.com?
   (a) Hotmail   (b) Gmail   (c) Yahoo   (d) Rediff

7. A _____ is responsible for maintaining the mail server and the list of user accounts.
   (a) mail master (b) postmaster   (c) client master (d) e-mail master

8. A home user's computer is connected to the Internet through the _____.
   (a) telephone   (b) modem   (c) ISP   (d) fax

9. Every e-mail address is divided into two parts, separated by _____ symbol
   (a) &   (b) @   (c) #   (d) %

10. Which part of the e-mail address identifies the webmail or the ISP?
    (a) first   (b) second   (c) @   (d) None of these.

11. In an e-mail address, username field cannot be larger than _____ characters.
    (a) 62   (b) 63   (c) 64   (d) None of these.

12. The domain name cannot be longer than _____ characters.
    (a) 252   (b) 254   (c) 64   (d) 128

13. Which character (s) can you use in an e-mail address?
    (a) ((b) /   (c) Both of these. (d) None of these.

14. All received emails will go to your _____.
    (a) Inbox   (b) Outbox   (c) Sentbox   (d) Mailbox

15. All important emails are marked with a _____ symbol.
    (a) sun   (b) moon   (c) star   (d) diamond

16. Composed emails that have to be stored for future use are saved in _____ folder.
    (a) Outbox   (b) Inbox   (c) Drafts   (d) Sent

17. Which folder stores all the e-mail messages that were successfully delivered?
    (a) Outbox   (b) Inbox   (c) Drafts   (d) Sent

18. Which field helps you to hide other recipient's names and addresses from each other?
    (a) To   (b) CC   (c) BCC   (d) All of these.

19. All e-mail messages in your inbox are by default arranged by _____.
    (a) date   (b) name of the sender (c) subject (d) size

20. The size of the file being sent as an attachment should not exceed _____ MB.
    (a) 5   (b) 15   (c) 25   (d) 35

21. Address from the Address Book can be copied into which field(s)?
    (a) To   (b) CC   (c) BCC   (d) All of these.

22. To e-mail an advertisement on paper you would need a _____.
    (a) printer   (b) scanner   (c) projector   (d) plotter
23. Yahoo! Messenger is a/an _____.
    (a) instant messaging software   (b) e-mail client
    (c) social networking website   (d) All of these.
24. Choose the characters which will show that you are happy.
    (a) O:-)   (b) >:o   (c) :-P   (d) :-)
25. _____ is a global network that connects billions of computers all over the world.
26. LAN   (b) MAN   (c) WAN   (d) Internet
27. _____ is a network of networks.
    (a) Internet   (b) Intranet   (c) Extranet   (d) All of these.
28. Each computer on the Internet is called a _____.
    (a) Server   (b) Computer   (c) Device   (d) Host
29. _____ provides internet service.
    (a) ASP   (b) ISP   (c) JSP   (d) IPS
30. ISP stands for _____.
    (a) Internet Service Provider   (b) Internet Service Program
    (c) Intranet Service Provider   (d) Intranet Service Program
31. You can share _____ using Internet.
    (a) voice messages   (b) text messages
    (c) video messages   (d) All of these.
32. Mozilla Firefox and Opera are examples of _____.
    (a) ISPs   (b) Web browsers
    (c) E-mail applications   (d) Social networking sites
33. _____ allow users to browse the Internet.
    (a) ISPs   (b) Web browsers
    (c) E-mail applications   (d) Social networking sites
34. The first ever network of computers was created for _____.
    (a) military purposes   (b) business purposes
    (c) research organization and universities   (d) All of these.
34. The first network of computers was known as _____.
    (a) ARPANET   (b) APARNET   (c) PICONET   (d) Internet
35. _____ means of transmission of messages electronically over communication networks.
    (a) Courier services   (b) RTGS   (c) Email   (d) SMS
36. The address of the email recipient is written in the _____ field.
    (a) From   (b) To   (c) Subject   (d) Body
37. Content of the message is written in the _____ field of email.
    (a) From   (b) To   (c) Subject   (d) Body
38. The two optional fields of a message are _____.
    (a) To and From   (b) CC and BCC   (c) Subject and Body   (d) None of these.

39. When you have to send the same message to multiple recipients then you should mention all the email addresses (except one) in the _____ field.
    (a) To   (b) CC   (c) BCC   (d) From

40. The _____ option allows users to make a copy of a message received from a person and then e-mail it to someone else.
    (a) Send   (b) Reply   (c) Forward   (d) Post

41. _____ application allows users to exchange files.
    (a) SMTP   (b) FTP   (c) UDP   (d) IP

42. _____ is the application using which two users can talk instantly.
    (a) E-mail   (b) Chatting   (c) Browsing   (d) Transferring

43. Identify which of the following is not a reason for business to use instant chatting.
    (a) Answer user queries   (b) Provide online support
    (c) Conduct business meetings   (d) None of these.

44. During Internet conferencing, users cannot share _____.
    (a) Information (b) Files   (c) Video   (d) None of these.

45. _____ is not required for Internet conferencing.
    (a) Webcam   (b) Microphone   (c) Chatting software (d) None of these.

46. Newspaper on the Internet is also known as _____.
    (a) online newspaper   (b) electronic newspaper
    (c) Web newspaper   (d) All of these.

47. HTML is a _____.
    (a) Language   (b) Protocol   (c) Application (d) Website

48. _____ allows users to add links to other documents, graphics, audio, and/or video files.
    (a) FTP   (b) Telnet   (c) HTML   (d) HTTP

49. The text on which the mouse pointer changes to hand-shape is known as _____.
    (a) High text   (b) Hypertext   (c) Link text   (d) Anchor text

50. WWW was created by _____.
    (a) Larry Page   (b) Bill Gates   (c) Tim Berners-Lee (d) Steve Jobs

51. Which of the following is not correct about online shopping?
    (a) You can make the payment through debit/credit card.
    (b) You can touch and feel the products sold online.
    (c) There is always a chance of getting our confidential information being compromised.
    (d) It can be done 24 × 7.

52. IP address is allotted to _____.
    (a) Computers   (b) Smartphones (c) Printers   (d) All of these.

53. _____ facilitates unique identification of devices for communication over the Internet.
    (a) IP address   (b) Sequence Number (c) MAC address (d) Port Number

54. The IP address has _____ parts.
    (a) 1   (b) 2   (c) 3   (d) 4

55. Each part of the IP address has a number ranging from _____.
    (a) 0 – 999   (b) 0 – 128   (c) 0 – 255   (d) 0 – 256

56. _____ address is issued using a leasing system.
    (a) Static IP   (b) Dynamic IP   (c) Fixed IP   (d) Permanent IP

57. _____ address reveals technical information about the continent, country and city in which the computer is located.
    (a) Static IP   (b) Dynamic IP   (c) Temporary IP   (d) Momentary IP

58. There are limited _____ IP addresses.
    (a) Static   (b) Dynamic   (c) Temporary   (d) Momentary

59. Web servers are allotted _____ IP addresses.
    (a) Static   (b) Dynamic   (c) Temporary   (d) Momentary

60. _____ service translates domain names into IP addresses.
    (a) TCP   (b) IP   (c) DNS   (d) UDP

61. DNS stands for _____.
    (a) Domain Name System   (b) Data Name Server
    (c) Data Number System   (d) Domain Number System

62. TCP stands for _____.
    (a) Transmission Carrier Protocol   (b) Transmission Control Protocol
    (c) Transmission Control Program   (d) Transmission Carrier Program

63. Which of the following statement is not true about DNS?
    (a) IP addresses should be assigned statically.   (b) Name and address pair can be cached.
    (c) ISPs have their own DNS server.   (d) None of these.

64. The domain .in belongs to which country?
    (a) Indonesia   (b) India   (c) Iceland   (d) Iran

65. Which of the following is true about domain names?
    (a) .org is used for non-profit organizations.
    (b) Domain names are also organized from right to left.
    (c) .mobl is a valid domain name for mobile communication network.
    (d) All of these.

66. _____ specifies the unique address for a file that is accessible on the Internet.
    (a) URL   (b) TCP/IP   (c) UDP/IP   (d) DNS

67. The syntax for specifying the URL is _____.
    (a) Protocol://domain-name/path   (b) path://domain-name/protocol
    (c) domain-name://Protocol/path   (d) Protocol/domain-name/path

68. Relative URL contains only the _____ field.
    (a) Protocol   (b) Path   (c) Domain name   (d) None of these.

69. Anything following the question mark (?) in a URL is _____.
    (a) domain-name   (b) protocol   (c) variable-value pair   (d) path

70. In a URL, two variable-value pairs are separated with a _____ symbol.
    (a) !   (b) &   (c) @   (d) +
71. The current version of IP is ___.
    (a) 4   (b) 5   (c) 6   (d) 7
72. IPv6 has _____ bit address.
    (a) 32   (b) 64   (c) 128   (d) 256
73. _____ protocol establishes a connection between the sender and the receiver so that reliable and error-free data transmission can take place.
    (a) TCP   (b) IP   (c) UDP   (d) SMTP
74. Segmentation and reassembly is done by which protocol?
    (a) TCP   (b) IP   (c) UDP   (d) SMTP
75. _____ is an alternative protocol to TCP.
    (a) FTP   (b) IP   (c) UDP   (d) SMTP
76. Which transmission protocol is best-suited for online computer games, watching videos online, and listening to audio online?
    (a) FTP   (b) IP   (c) UDP   (d) SMTP
77. Identify the incorrect statement about UDP.
    (a) Preferable for small data exchanges
    (b) Does nothing to correct errors and supports unreliable data transfer
    (c) Is a connection-oriented protocol
    (d) Does not break the message into smaller segments.
78. FTP is not _____.
    (a) fast   (b) reliable   (c) efficient   (d) connection-less
79. FTP allow users to _____ files.
    (a) rename   (b) copy   (c) delete   (d) All of these.
80. In which mode the client initiates the connection?
    (a) Active connection mode   (b) Passive connection mode
    (c) Block mode   (d) Stream mode
81. In which mode, the server is always waiting for any request from the client?
    (a) Active connection mode   (b) Passive connection mode
    (c) Block mode   (d) Stream mode
82. In which mode, files are transferred as a continuous stream with no intervention?
    (a) Active connection mode   (b) Passive connection mode
    (c) Block mode   (d) Stream mode
83. _____ is a text-based protocol that is used for accessing a remote computer's (called host) data and application programs.
    (a) FTP   (b) Telnet   (c) UDP   (d) SMTP
84. _____ enables research scholars and professors to log in to the university's computer from any terminal.
    (a) FTP   (b) Telnet   (c) UDP   (d) SMTP

85. Which of the following is incorrect about Telnet?
    (a) It is a text-based computer protocol.
    (b) It is insecure because it transfers all data in clear text.
    (c) Users cannot transfer files using Telnet.
    (d) None of these.
86. _____ is a code embedded in a file that instructs the web browser how to display the page.
    (a) Hyperlink   (b) Hypertext   (c) Markup   (d) Image
87. _____ interprets the meaning of Markups.
    (a) HTML   (b) Web browser   (c) Web server   (d) Web client
88. Which of the following cannot be embedded in a HTML page?
    (a) JavaScript   (b) VBScript   (c) Visual Basic   (d) Form
89. Which of the following is best-suited for creating an interactive game?
    (a) HTML   (b) JavaScript   (c) CSS   (d) DHTML
90. You can create your own tags using which language?
    (a) HTML   (b) DHTM   (c) XML   (d) All of these.
91. Arbitrary data structures can be easily represented using which language?
    (a) HTML   (b) DHTM   (c) XML   (d) All of these.
92. Nested tags to represent hierarchical data are used in which language?
    (a) HTML   (b) DHTM   (c) XML   (d) All of these.
93. Tags are not pre-defined in which language?
    (a) HTML   (b) DHTM   (c) XML   (d) All of these.
94. _____ means finding possible entry points in a computer system or a computer network to break into it.
    (a) Hacking   (b) Ethical hacking   (c) Cracking   (d) Ethical Cracking
95. _____ is done to steal sensitive information available on the computer.
    (a) Hacking   (b) Ethical hacking   (c) Cracking   (d) Ethical Cracking
96. Hacking does not involve _____.
    (a) breaking passwords
    (b) recovering passwords
    (c) illegal use of someone else's e-mail account
    (d) harming a computer system
97. _____ means finding weaknesses in a computer or network system for testing purpose.
    (a) Hacking   (b) Ethical hacking   (c) Cracking   (d) Ethical Cracking
98. _____ are known as black-hat hackers.
    (a) Ethical hackers   (b) Hackers   (c) Crackers   (d) Ethical Crackers
99. Ethical hackers are also known as _____ hackers.
    (a) white-hat   (b) red-hat   (c) black-hat   (d) grey-hat
100. Vulnerabilities are present in the computer due to _____.
    (a) improper system configuration
    (b) hardware or software flaws
    (c) operational weaknesses in a process
    (d) All of these.

101. When the organization does not reveal that their information security team has hired ethical hackers to test the effectiveness of the measures taken by them, then this is called _____ environment.
    (a) blind
    (b) single blind
    (c) double blind
    (d) All of these.

102. Which of the following statement is true about ethical hackers?
    (a) Ethical hackers must be provided complete details of the assets.
    (b) Hiring an ethical hacker and trusting him may lead to a massive security breach.
    (c) The ethical hacker may place malicious code, viruses, malware and other destructive and harmful software on a computer system.
    (d) All of these.

103. Mobile communication uses _____ that are carried over the air to intended devices.
    (a) ultraviolet waves
    (b) infrared waves
    (c) radio waves
    (d) microwaves

104. The main components of mobile computing are _____.
    (a) mobile hardware
    (b) mobile software
    (c) mobile communication
    (d) All of these.

105. Which of the following is not an advantage of mobile computing?
    (a) Highly secure
    (b) Enhances productivity
    (c) Location flexibility
    (d) Entertainment

106. IoT connects different _____.
    (a) objects
    (b) machines
    (c) animals
    (d) All of these.

107. _____ is the concept of connecting any devices over the Internet.
    (a) Mobile computing
    (b) IoT
    (c) Internet
    (d) Social networking site

108. The technology used in self-driving cars, smart watch, smart football and smart refrigerator is _____.
    (a) mobile computing
    (b) IoT
    (c) Internet
    (d) Android

109. Google+, Foursquare, Pinterset and Twitter are all examples of _____.
    (a) search engines
    (b) social networking sites
    (c) video conferencing sites
    (d) instant messaging sites

110. _____ sites are used to share news, interest, opinions, insights and experiences.
    (a) Search engines
    (b) Social networking sites
    (c) Video conferencing sites
    (d) Instant messaging sites

111. Challenge(s) in SNS include _____.
    (a) free speech
    (b) data leakage
    (c) code of conduct
    (d) All of these.

112. Which SNS is used to build social relations organized around professional lives?
    (a) LinkedIn
    (b) MySpace
    (c) Facebook
    (d) Twitter

113. _____ is used for creating lines of communication between ordinary individuals and figures of public interest.
    (a) LinkedIn
    (b) MySpace
    (c) Facebook
    (d) Twitter

114. If anyone misbehaves on SNS, then it means _____.
    (a) misusing free speech
    (b) data leakage
    (c) violation of code of conduct
    (d) violating code of conduct

115. Not providing the sources of their information when posting on SNS results in _____.
    (a) misusing free speech
    (b) data leakage
    (c) violation of code of conduct
    (d) violating code of conduct

116. Giving any form of compensation to a blogger or tweeter is considered as _____.
    (a) unreported endorsements
    (b) compromising privacy
    (c) effecting company's brand value
    (d) violating code of conduct

117. The term UGC refers to _____.
    (a) User Generated Content
    (b) getting creative ideas
    (c) holding online contests allowing its customers to submit designs
    (d) All of these.

118. Giving anonymous and fake feedback just to cause damage to a company's reputation is known as _____.
    (a) improper anonymity
    (b) distorted endorsements
    (c) cybercrime
    (d) identity theft

State True or False

1. Internet is used by users to work on a project simultaneously.
2. Video conferencing is the most widely used technique for communication over the Internet.
3. You must respect all netizens.
4. Internet is a local network.
5. E-mail is based on client–server architecture.
6. You can send a video through an e-mail.
7. All e-mail addresses on the Internet must be unique.
8. You need to pay to Gmail for setting up an e-mail account.
9. ISPs provide a free e-mail account to customers.
10. An e-mail is delivered instantly.
11. Sending an e-mail saves our Nature.
12. E-mail service has a text editor.
13. You cannot print your e-mail.
14. Accessing a webmail does not require any authentication.
15. Mail server is present in every user's computer.
16. E-mails are stored temporarily in the email server.
17. The second part of the address identifies the user.
18. SiYa12@live.com is an invalid e-mail address.
19. A person can have only one e-mail address.
20. Usernames can begin with a dot.
21. All the unread e-mails will appear in italics.

22. Every e-mail address has a mailbox.
23. Outbox stores all pending unsent e-mails.
24. Junk mails may harm your computer.
25. It is possible to forward an e-mail that has been recently deleted.
26. E-mail reply is sent to the person other than the sender of the message.
27. You can send a pdf file as an e-mail attachment.
28. You can check for any spelling mistakes in your e-mail.
29. Every Gmail account has an address book.
30. A video being played on the computer is a hard copy.
31. Lottery winning e-mails are spam mails.
32. You should unblock unknown senders.
33. You should not open, read, forward or reply a spam e-mail.
34. Using IM software you can chat with all offline users.
35. IM is used for collaboration and communication.
36. IM software can be used to send large files.
37. Smiley is used to exhibit your various moods.
38. You should write e-mails using capital letters.
39. You should make extensive use of emoticons to exhibit your mood.

ANSWER KEYS

Multiple Choice Questions

1. (d)	2. (d)	3. (c)	4. (d)	5. (b)	6. (a)	7. (b)	8. (c)
9. (b)	10. (b)	11. (c)	12. (b)	13. (c)	14. (a)	15. (c)	16. (c)
17. (d)	18. (c)	19. (a)	20. (c)	21. (d)	22. (b)	23. (a)	24. (d)
25. (d)	26. (a)	27. (d)	28. (b)	29. (a)	30. (d)	31. (b)	32. (b)
33. (c)	34. (a)	35. (c)	36. (b)	37. (d)	38. (b)	39. (b)	40. (c)
41. (b)	42. (b)	43. (d)	44. (d)	45. (d)	46. (d)	47. (a)	48. (c)
49. (b)	50. (c)	51. (c)	52. (d)	53. (a)	54. (d)	55. (c)	56. (b)
57. (a)	58. (a)	59. (a)	60. (c)	61. (a)	62. (b)	63. (d)	64. (b)
65. (d)	66. (a)	67. (a)	68. (c)	69. (c)	70. (b)	71. (c)	72. (c)
73. (a)	74. (a)	75. (c)	76. (c)	77. (c)	78. (d)	79. (d)	80. (a)
81. (b)	82. (d)	83. (b)	84. (b)	85. (d)	86. (c)	87. (b)	88. (c)
89. (d)	90. (c)	91. (c)	92. (c)	93. (c)	94. (a)	95. (a)	96. (b)
97. (b)	98. (b)	99. (a)	100. (d)	101. (c)	102. (d)	103. (c)	104. (d)
105. (a)	106. (d)	107. (b)	108. (b)	109. (b)	110. (b)	111. (d)	112. (a)
113. (d)	114. (c)	115. (d)	116. (a)	117. (d)	118. (b)		

State True or False

1. True	2. False	3. True	4. False	5. True	6. True	7. True	8. False
9. True	10. True	11. True	12. True	13. False	14. False	15. False	16. True
17. False	18. False	19. False	20. False	21. False	22. True	23. True	24. True
25. True	26. False	27. True	28. True	29. True	30. False	31. True	32. False
33. True	34. False	35. True	36. True	37. True	38. False	39. False	

CHAPTER 6
Application of Digital Financial Services

KEY POINTS

- Digital financial services provide a variety of affordable, convenient and secure banking services to poor people in developing countries.
- Money should be saved to pay for unexpected events or emergencies.
- Ideally, one's emergency fund should be about three to six months of his expenses.
- Banks play a crucial role in the socio-economic matters of the country.
- To have control over your financial life, you must not have EMI more than 60% of your monthly income. Otherwise you may be in a financial mess. You must avoid taking loans, especially personal loans.
- In the banking sector, Alternate Delivery Channels (ADCs) are channels and methods for providing banking services directly to the customers.
- A POS System has a computer that runs the POS software, a receipt printer, barcode scanner, credit card reader and an on-site server for legacy-based point-of-sale systems.
- Life Insurance is the key to good financial planning. It not only safeguards your money but also ensures its growth.
- Under PMJDY scheme, any individual irrespective of his area (rural or urban), can get a bank account without depositing any amount, provided he fulfills other eligibility criteria. It is a very beneficial scheme, especially for the rural population where banking services and other financial institutions are rarely available.

KEYWORDS

Savings: That part of the income which is not spent on current expenditures.

Remittance: The process by which a bank accepts money from its customer and makes arrangement for payment of the same amount of money to another person at the same place or a different place.

Chit funds: Indigenous saving mechanism that is unorganized and is usually run between friends, families and known persons.

Loan: An arrangement in which a borrower takes money from a bank or a financial institution and promises to return it within a fixed period of time and at a fixed ROI.

Overdraft: The act of overdrawing from a bank account.

KYC: It stands for Know Your Customer. It is the process of a business verifying the identity of its clients.

Automated Teller Machine (ATM): An electronic banking outlet or a computerized machine that allows bank customers to gain access to their accounts with a card and a PIN code.

PoS or swipe machine: A device to carry out the sales of goods or service to customers in a cashless environment.

Internet banking: Also known as online banking or web banking, it allows people to perform banking operations using the Internet.

NEFT: A payment system facilitating one-to-one funds transfer.

Non-life Insurance: An insurance policy that protects an individual against losses and damages other than those covered by life insurance.

Mobile banking: The act of doing financial transactions on a mobile device like cell phone, tablet, etc.

MODEL QUESTION PAPER

Multiple Choice Questions

1. Digital financial services have become popular with the use of _____.
   (a) TV   (b) Camera   (c) Mobile Phones   (d) Laptops
2. _____ is that part of the income which is not spent on current expenditure
   (a) Savings   (b) Fixed Income   (c) Variable Income (d) Interest
3. Examples of emergency include _____.
   (a) job layoff   (b) death in family (c) medical expenses (d) All of these
4. To transfer money to other people, banks use _____.
   (a) DD   (b) Money Order   (c) Cheques   (d) All of these.
5. Banks can electronically transfer money in a few ____.
   (a) days   (b) minutes   (c) hours   (d) seconds
6. _____ are indigenous saving mechanisms that are unorganized.
   (a) Banks
   (b) Financial institutions
   (c) Chit funds
   (d) All of these
7. _____ implement monetary policy to stabilize financial system of the country from the dangers of inflation, deflation, crisis, etc.
   (a) Chit Funds
   (b) Private Lenders
   (c) Financial Institutions
   (d) Banks
8. _____ account is used by businessmen to conduct their business transactions smoothly.
   (a) Current   (b) Fixed Deposit (c) Savings   (d) Recurring
9. On which type of account, does the bank not pay any interest on amount?
   (a) Current   (b) Fixed Deposit (c) Savings   (d) Recurring
10. People who do not have a big amount to save must open a _____ account.
    (a) Current   (b) Fixed Deposit (c) Savings   (d) Recurring
11. Which account has a fixed period of maturity?
    (a) Current   (b) Fixed Deposit (c) Savings   (d) Recurring
12. Which loan would you take to bear the expenses of marriage in your family?
    (a) Home   (b) Car   (c) Personal   (d) Education
13. ROI is highest on which type of loan?
    (a) Home   (b) Car   (c) Personal   (d) Education

14. In _____ loans, the amount is provided for a fixed tenure at an applicable interest rate.
    (a) term   (b) bank overdraft   (c) bill discounting   (d) business

15. KYC was made a norm laid by _____.
    (a) Banks   (b) Financial institutions
    (c) Chit Funds   (d) RBI

16. _____ are biometric authentication enabled hand-held devices for performing banking operations.
    (a) ATMs   (b) Macro ATMs
    (c) Micro-ATMs   (d) All of these.

17. Mirco ATMs are installed at every _____.
    (a) bank
    (b) Bank Mitra
    (c) Chit fund
    (d) Private Financial Institution

18. The merchant applying for PoS must have a _____.
    (a) bank account   (b) turnover of Rs 1 Lakh per month
    (c) fixed landline connection (d) All of these.

19. Transactions conducted through PoS are authorized by _____.
    (a) Merchant   (b) Customer   (c) Bank   (d) None of these.

20. To use internet banking, a bank customer must have a computer with _____ software installed in it to access the bank's website.
    (a) web browser (b) bank   (c) MS Office   (d) PDF

21. Maximum Rs _____ can be transferred to Nepal through NEFT.
    (a) 5000   (b) 50000   (c) 500000   (d) Any amount

22. Using _____ funds are instantly transferred electronically.
    (a) NEFT   (b) RTGS   (c) Both of these.   (d) None of these.

23. The minimum amount of funds that can be transferred through RTGS is Rs _____.
    (a) 2000   (b) 20000   (c) 200000   (d) Any amount

24. _____ ensures some amount of compensation for any kind of loss or damage caused by events beyond the control of the insured party.
    (a) Insurance   (b) Bank Account (c) PPF   (d) PMJDY

25. _____ is used to control inflation.
    (a) Fixed Deposit (b) NEFT   (c) Insurance   (d) RTGS

26. Personal accident insurance, travel insurance, motor insurance, all come under the category of _____ insurance.
    (a) Life   (b) Non-life   (c) Car   (d) Medical

27. The coverage period for most non-life insurance policies and plans is usually _____.
    (a) 1 year   (b) life-time   (c) 5 years   (d) 10 years

28. Crores of bank accounts were opened under the _____ scheme.
    (a) PMJDY   (b) PMSBY   (c) PMJJBY   (d) APY
29. The account holder under PMJDY can take maximum loan of Rs. _____.
    (a) 5000   (b) 50000   (c) 500000   (d) any amount
30. Under the PMSBY, insurance is provided to people in _____ age group.
    (a) 20–60   (b) 18–70   (c) 20–70   (d) 18–60
31. The amount of insurance provided under PMSBY is Rs _____.
    (a) 2000   (b) 20000   (c) 200000   (d) any amount
32. Which scheme provides pension to the poor people?
    (a) PMJDY   (b) PMSBY   (c) PMJJBY   (d) APY
33. Under the APY, the subscriber can choose a monthly pension from Rs. _____
    (a) 1000 – 5000   (b) 10000 – 50000   (c) 100 – 500   (d) 2000 – 8000
34. Which scheme provides loans to small businesses?
    (a) PMJDY   (b) PMSBY   (c) PMJJBY   (d) PMMY
35. Under PMMY, which loan is provided to entrepreneurs who are either in their primitive stage or require lesser funds in order to get their businesses started.
    (a) Shishu   (b) Kishor   (c) Tarun   (d) All of these.
36. Which scheme provides loans to small businesses?
    (a) PMJDY   (b) PMJJBY   (c) NPS   (d) PMMY
37. Under the PPF scheme, investors can invest minimum Rs. _____ to maximum Rs. _____ in one financial year.
    (a) 500, 50000   (b) 500, 150000   (c) 500, 100000   (d) 500, 200000
38. In PPF, the ROI is declared by _____.
    (a) banks
    (c) government
    (b) chit funds
    (d) financial Institutions
39. In PPF, money can be deposited in maximum _____ transactions.
    (a) 3   (b) 4   (c) 6   (d) 12
40. For mobile banking, you can use your _____.
    (a) mobile phone   (b) smart phone   (c) tablet   (d) All of these.
41. Which of the following wallet sends credit or debit card information to the merchants?
    (a) NFC   (b) Google   (c) PayPal   (d) Square

State True or False

1. Digital financial services offer affordable banking services to poor people.
2. Money should not be saved to pay for emergencies.
3. Savings cannot ensure financial security of the family.
4. It is possible to gain interest on savings.

Credit and debit cards

5. The sooner one starts to save for retirement, the more he will have to save in the future.
6. Keeping cash at home is safer than keeping the money in banks.
7. Banks pay their customers interest on their savings.
8. Banks can transfer money to accounts only within the country.
9. Faster the mode of transfer, lower the charges.
10. You can electronically transfer money through bank.
11. Chit funds are based purely only on mutual trust between its members.
12. Lot of paper work is involved in chit funds.
13. Private lenders charge very high interest rate.
14. Current account is used for making investments and savings.
15. In a current account, the account holder can perform only a limited number of transactions in a day.
16. The rate of interest (ROI) of RD account is higher than that offered on Savings Account.
17. Every bank has a fixed ROI.
18. It is possible to take loan against insurance policy.
19. Bill discounting enable businessmen to withdraw more money than what is deposited.
20. You should leave some space between the name, surname and PAY while writing down the name.
21. You should sign in the MICR band.
22. KYC norms are used to prevent financial frauds.
23. College ID Card can be submitted as the Identity Proof in a bank.
24. Electricity bill is not a valid Address Proof.
25. ATM machine is an Alternate Delivery Channel for a bank.
26. ADCs are used for smooth flow of regular transactions with higher profits at lower operational expenses and transaction costs.
27. Micro ATM is used to carry out the sales of goods or service to customers in a cashless environment.
28. While making a purchase using PoS, the customer must enter his PIN number.
29. The bank does charge an extra amount for making online transactions.
30. You can book local train tickets also through Internet Banking.
31. Only those people who have a bank account can transfer the funds electronically using NEFT.
32. Beneficiary of the funds transfer may or may not have an account with the NEFT enabled bank branch in the country.
33. NEFT does not allow cross-border fund transfer.
34. RTGS funds transfer is irrevocable.
35. In RTGS, funds are transferred in batches.
36. Customers doing online baking can themselves transfer funds through RTGS and NEFT.
37. Insurance provides protection against tangible losses.
38. You can insure your business as well as property against fire or any other damage.

39. Insurance does not provide safety and security.
40. Insurance premium is invested in government securities and stock so that it can be used for industrial and economic development of the country.
41. You can withdraw the deposited insurance premium easily before the expiry of the term of the policy.
42. Insurance policies are exempted from income-tax.
43. Agriculture can also be protected against losses of cattle, machines, tools and crop with insurance.
44. Employers pay for the group insurance of the employees.
45. For life insurance, the premiums are paid on a one-time basis.
46. The account holder under PMJDY is given a RuPay debit card which can be used at all ATMs for cash withdrawal.
47. The amount received from PPF is fully exempted from tax.
48. It is not possible to take loan against PPF.
49. In PPF, loan can be taken only between 3rd and the 6th financial year.
50. In PPF, tenure of investment is 15 years. Therefore, the account cannot be continued after this period.
51. You can have joint accounts in PPF.
52. Grandparents can also open a PPF account in the names of their minor grandchildren.
53. You should store sensitive information in your mobile phone.

ANSWER KEYS

Multiple Choice Questions

1. (c) 2. (a) 3. (d) 4. (d) 5. (b) 6. (c) 7. (d) 8. (a)
9. (a) 10. (d) 11. (b) 12. (c) 13. (c) 14. (a) 15. (d) 16. (c)
17. (b) 18. (d) 19. (c) 20. (a) 21. (b) 22. (b) 23. (c) 24. (a)
25. (a) 26. (b) 27. (a) 28. (a) 29. (a) 30. (b) 31. (c) 32. (d)
33. (a) 34. (d) 35. (a) 36. (c) 37. (b) 38. (c) 39. (d) 40. (d)
41. (a)

State True or False

1. True 2. False 3. False 4. True 5. False 6. False 7. True 8. False
9. False 10. True 11. True 12. False 13. True 14. False 15. False 16. True
17. False 18. True 19. False 20. False 21. False 22. True 23. True 24. False
25. True 26. True 27. False 28. True 29. False 30. True 31. False 32. False
33. False 34. True 35. False 36. True 37. True 38. True 39. False 40. True
41. False 42. True 43. True 44. True 45. False 46. True 47. True 48. False
49. True 50. False 51. False 52. False 53. False

CHAPTER 7
IT and Its Applications in Business

KEY POINTS

- Information must be relevant, accurate, complete, current, and economical.
- These days, almost every business is conducted over computers and communication devices to organize large databases, personal schedules, and various other forms of essential information.
- Breakthrough in information technology (IT) has resulted in better or automated solutions that have not only increased the productivity, but also lowered operational costs, improved speed and ease of sharing and storing information, decreased the probability of human error through automation and contributed to an increase in revenue.
- All businesses today are moving towards marking their presence on the Internet. Whether big or small, all businesses have a website to advertise their products, take orders, buy merchandise, and sell excess products.
- Outsourcing is done as a cost-saving measure by big companies that want to focus on their key business area, rather than focusing on routine business tasks.
- An office information system (OIS) or office automation system (OAS) uses hardware, software and networks to enhance work flow and facilitate communication among employees.
- MIS is an information system that generates accurate, timely, and organized information. This helps business managers make decisions, solve problems, supervise activities and track progress by generating useful reports on a regular basis.
- Decision support system (DSS) not only uses data from its internal information systems, but also makes use of data from external sources such as business magazines, surveys of competitors available on the Internet, interest rates, population trends, customer demographics and spending behaviour of a group of customers.
- Knowledge exists in the form of documents, policies, procedures, expertise, and experience.

KEYWORDS

Artificial intelligence (AI): A branch of computer science that works on making computers intelligent like humans.

Back-office outsourcing: Outsourcing of internal business functions such as payroll, billing, purchasing, accounting, and HR.

Business data processing (BDP): Performing operations to convert business data into useful information

Data: A collection of raw facts or figures.

Expert system: A branch of AI that designs intelligent machines, which solve real-world problems by using deductive logic.

Front-office outsourcing: Outsourcing of customer-related services such as marketing and technical support.

Information: Processed data to provide answers to *who, what, where,* and *when* type of questions.

Information system: A collection of hardware, software, data, people, and procedures that are designed to generate information to support routine activities.

Information technology (IT): A comprehensive term that includes all types of technology used to exchange, store, use, or create information.

Knowledge: Application of data and information to answer the *how* part of the question.

Knowledge management system (KMS): A system that manages knowledge in an organization (in the form of documents, policies, procedures, expertise, and experience) to support identification, creation, capture, evaluation, storage retrieval, sharing and dissemination of information.

Mobile application (app): Software application that runs on smartphones, tablets, and other mobile devices.

Natural language processing (NLP): A branch of AI that involves programming computers to understand natural human languages.

Nearshore outsourcing: Outsourcing to a neighbouring country.

Offshore outsourcing: Outsourcing to another country.

Onshore outsourcing: Outsourcing in the same country.

Outsourcing: Hiring employees who work outside the company.

Robotics: A branch of AI that programs computers to see, hear, and react to sensory input.

MODEL QUESTION PAPER

Multiple Choice Questions

1. Collection of raw facts or figures is called _____.
   (a) Data   (b) Information   (c) Knowledge

2. Processed data is known as _____.
   (a) Input   (b) Information   (c) Knowledge   (d) Output

3. 'How' part of a question answered by _____.
   (a) Data   (b) Information   (c) Knowledge

4. Information should be _____.
   (a) Economical   (b) Relevant
   (c) Both of these. (d) Only b

5. If the employee works hard and is skilled with the latest technology, then his promotion is guaranteed.
   (a) Data
   (b) Information
   (c) Knowledge

The data pyramid

6. Monthly salary of the parliament member is an example of _____.
   (a) Data   (b) Information   (c) Knowledge

7. _____ means performing operations in order to convert business data into useful information.
   (a) Business Data Processing
   (b) Built-in Data Process
   (c) Business Digital Processing

8. _____ software is widely used by business to analyze and summarize data and draw charts.
   (a) Word Processing   (b) Spreadsheet   (c) Database   (d) Presentation

9. BDP cannot be used for _____.
   (a) Accounting
   (b) Payroll
   (c) Inventory Management
   (d) None of these.

10. Microsoft Money and QuickBooks are examples of _____ software.
    (a) Accounting and Payroll
    (b) only Payroll
    (c) Inventory Management
    (d) only Accounting

11. Inventory management can be done on _____ software.
    (a) Microsoft Word   (b) Microsoft Excel   (c) OpenOffice Calc   (d) b and c

12. QuickBooks is a software used for _____.
    (a) Accounting   (b) Payroll   (c) Book-keeping   (d) All of these.

13. Flipkart, Snapdeal, Amazon are _____ websites.
    (a) online shopping   (b) social networking   (c) e-mail   (d) search engine

14. Online marketing is done through _____.
    (a) E-mail
    (b) Google AdWords
    (c) Both (a) and (b).
    (d) None of these.

15. _____ was the bank which first started mobile face-to-face banking.
    (a) ICICI   (b) HDFC   (c) IndusInd   (d) SBI

16. CRM stands for _____.
    (a) Call Record Management
    (b) Customer Record Management
    (c) Customer Relationship Management
    (d) All of these.

17. Web cameras and microphones are together used in _____.
    (a) Tele conferencing   (b) Tele commuting   (c) Video conferencing

18. Outsourcing is mainly done to _____.
    (a) Reduce costs
    (b) Save time
    (c) Increase productivity
    (d) Automation

19. Payroll processing, if outsourced, will be a part of _____.
    (a) BPO   (b) KPO   (c) PPO   (d) LPO

20. BPO service that is outsourced within the same country is called _____.
    (a) Outsourcing
    (b) Onsourcing
    (c) Nearshore Outsourcing
    (d) Onshore Outsourcing

21. In which type of outsourcing payroll, billing and HR are outsourced?
    (a) Internal Outsourcing
    (b) External Outsourcing
    (c) Front-office Outsourcing
    (d) Back-office Outsourcing

22. In which type of outsourcing customer service is outsourced?
    (a) Internal Outsourcing
    (b) External Outsourcing
    (c) Front-office Outsourcing
    (d) Back-Office Outsourcing

23. Which of these is not a valid reason for outsourcing?
    (a) Reduce costs
    (b) Efficiency of tasks
    (c) Both of these.
    (d) None of these.

24. Equity research is done in _____.
    (a) BPO
    (b) BDP
    (c) BPO
    (d) PPO

25. Identify the disadvantages of KPOs and BPOs.
    (a) Inferior quality of outputs
    (b) Increased complexities
    (c) Both (a) and (b)
    (d) None of these.

26. Select the most preferred countries for voice-based KPOs.
    (a) India
    (b) Chile
    (c) Mexico
    (d) All of these.

27. Select the most preferred countries (after India) for BPOs.
    (a) Sri Lanka
    (b) Bangladesh
    (c) Philippines
    (d) All of these.

28. Information systems include _____.
    (a) information and software
    (b) hardware and data
    (c) people
    (d) All of these.

29. Small organizations will usually not have which type of Information System?
    (a) TPS
    (b) MIS
    (c) OAS
    (d) DSS

30. Senior managers work at which level of Information System?
    (a) EIS
    (b) DSS
    (c) TPS
    (d) KMS

31. Operational decisions are taken at which level of Information System?
    (a) EIS
    (b) DSS
    (c) TPS
    (d) KMS

32. Which of the following is not a part of OAS?
    (a) EDI
    (b) Voice e-mail
    (c) Hardware
    (d) Office building

33. Electronic Data Interchange is a type of _____.
    (a) Hardware
    (b) Software
    (c) Technology
    (d) None of these.

34. Collect customers' feedback is done at which level of Information System?
    (a) EIS
    (b) DSS
    (c) TPS
    (d) KMS

35. Different types of reports are generated at which level of Information System?
    (a) MIS
    (b) DSS
    (c) TPS
    (d) KMS

36. Aggregated data is displayed in which type of report?
    (a) Detailed
    (b) Summarized
    (c) Exception
    (d) All of these.

37. Filtered data used to take corrective measures are available in which type of report?
    (a) Detailed
    (b) Summarized
    (c) Exception
    (d) All of these.

38. Which type of system has least analytical capability?
    (a) MIS
    (b) DSS
    (c) EIS
    (d) KMS

39. Data from internal sources as well as external sources is analyzed at which level of IS?
    (a) MIS   (b) DSS   (c) OIS   (d) TPS

40. What-if analysis is done at which level of Information System?
    (a) MIS   (b) DSS   (c) EIS   (d) Both (b) and (c).

41. Experience, feedback and sharing of project files are features of which type of Information System?
    (a) MIS   (b) DSS   (c) OIS   (d) KMS

42. Open Source Software can be associated with which type of information system?
    (a) MIS   (b) DSS   (c) OIS   (d) KMS

43. Tick the incorrect statement.
    (a) Data is a collection of raw facts or figures.
    (b) Information comprises of processed data to provide answers to the 'who', 'what', 'where', and 'when' type of questions.
    (c) Knowledge is the application of data and information to answer the 'how' part of the question.
    (d) Data makes the information more usable.

44. Which of the following is not a characteristic of information?
    (a) Irrelevant   (b) Complete   (c) Current   (d) Economical

45. _____ software allows users to draw a variety of charts to interpret the data from different angles.
    (a) Word Processing   (b) Spreadsheet   (c) Database   (d) PowerPoint

46. Identify the incorrect statement.
    (a) CRM system is used to track a customer throughout his experience or interaction with the business.
    (b) Outsourcing means hiring employees who work outside the company but in the same country.
    (c) In back-office outsourcing, internal business functions such as payroll, billing, purchasing, accounting, and HR are outsourced.
    (d) In front-office outsourcing, customer-related services such as marketing and technical support are outsourced.

47. Identify the incorrect statement.
    (a) Call center jobs are BPO jobs.
    (b) Data privacy breaches can take place in outsourcing jobs.
    (c) KPO jobs require advanced analytical and technical skills.
    (d) Equity research, business and market research, legal and medical services are examples of BPO jobs.

48. Knowledge is obtained by _____ the data.
    (a) processing   (b) collecting   (c) applying   (d) All of these.

49. The information must be latest, means that it should be _____.
    (a) Accurate   (b) Complete   (c) Current   (d) Economical

50. Information should be applicable in that context, means that information should be _____.
    (a) Accurate   (b) Complete   (c) Current   (d) Relevant

51. Business Data Processing include _____.
    (a) Accounting
    (b) Inventory Management
    (c) Automation
    (d) All of these.

52. Enhanced communication does not facilitate _____.
    (a) Internet Marketing
    (b) Stay competitive
    (c) CRM
    (d) None of these.

53. Services provided by BPO does not include _____.
    (a) Tech support
    (b) Data entry
    (c) Insurance processing
    (d) None of these.

54. Services provided by KPO does not include _____.
    (a) Analytics
    (b) Legal process
    (c) Marketing services
    (d) None of these.

55. Identify the incorrect statement.
    (a) A KPO extends the work of a BPO.
    (b) KPOs offer low-cost expertise.
    (c) Political and economic instability has no effect on KPO.
    (d) Losing out on key talent at home is a major threat to the company.

56. Chartered accountants, engineers, doctors, architects, lawyers, economists, biotechnologists all work for a _____.
    (a) KPO
    (b) BPO
    (c) CPO
    (d) BDP

KPO
- Engineering service outsourcing
- Financial research outsourcing
- Business research
- Design and animation
- Analysis
- Marketing services
- Publishing outsourcing
- Legal process outsourcing
- Market research outsourcing

57. Which country has more number of KPOs?
    (a) Philippines
    (b) India
    (c) Bangladesh
    (d) None of these.

58. Identify the correct statement.
    (a) Information system is a collection of hardware, software, data, people, and procedures.
    (b) Information system is a collection of hardware, software and data.
    (c) Information system is a collection of hardware, software, data and people.
    (d) Information system is a collection of hardware and software, data.

59. Arrange the Information Systems from lower level of pyramid to higher level.
    (a) KMS, DSS, MIS, TPS
    (b) DSS, KMS, MIS, TPS
    (c) DSS, KMS, TPS, MIS
    (d) TPS, MIS, DSS, KMS

60. Data entry operators work with _____ information system.
    (a) DSS
    (b) KMS
    (c) TPS
    (d) MIS

61. _____ information system is used to make tactical decisions.
    (a) DSS
    (b) KMS
    (c) TPS
    (d) MIS

62. Collecting customers' feedback and generating employees' paycheck is done by _____ information system.
    (a) DSS
    (b) KMS
    (c) TPS
    (d) MIS

63. Detailed, summary and exception reports are created using _____ information systems.
    (a) DSS   (b) KMS   (c) TPS   (d) MIS

64. Which report gives quick overview of a business activity?
    (a) Detailed   (b) Summary   (c) Exception   (d) Inventory

65. Executive information system is a special type of _____.
    (a) DSS   (b) KMS   (c) TPS   (d) MIS

66. _____ information system is used to perform what-if analysis.
    (a) DSS   (b) KMS   (c) TPS   (d) MIS

67. Types of knowledge do not include _____.
    (a) Experience   (b) feedback   (c) shared files (d) None of these.

68. Identify the incorrect statement.
    (a) KMS ensures speedy responses to user queries.
    (b) KMS avoids training of new employees.
    (c) KMS solves problems faster.
    (d) KMS improves performance.

ANSWER KEYS

Multiple Choice Questions

1. (a)	2. (b)	3. (c)	4. (c)	5. (c)	6. (a)	7. (a)	8. (b)		
9. (d)	10. (a)	11. (d)	12. (d)	13. (a)	14. (c)	15. (c)	16. (c)		
17. (c)	18. (a)	19. (a)	20. (d)	21. (d)	22. (c)	23. (c)	24. (c)		
25. (c)	26. (d)	27. (d)	28. (d)	29. (c)	30. (b)	31. (c)	32. (d)		
33. (c)	34. (c)	35. (a)	36. (b)	37. (c)	38. (a)	39. (b)	40. (d)		
41. (d)	42. (d)	43. (d)	44. (a)	45. (b)	46. (b)	47. (d)	48. (d)		
49. (c)	50. (d)	51. (d)	52. (d)	53. (d)	54. (d)	55. (c)	56. (a)		
57. (d)	58. (a)	59. (d)	60. (c)	61. (d)	62. (c)	63. (d)	64. (a)		
65. (a)	66. (a)	67. (d)	68. (b)						

CHAPTER 8
Data Security and Encryption

KEY POINTS

- As the Internet is an insecure channel for exchanging private data or messages and intrusion or frauds like phishing are very common, some methods must be implemented to protect the data.
- Internet security ensures authenticated access of data that is exchanged over the Internet.
- Authorized or unauthorized users may modify the existing data, add wrong data, or delete some important data.
- The most common threats to data security come either from use of malwares or through frauds like phishing.
- A worm, once installed, can connect to a remote computer over the Internet to download a more substantial piece of malicious software.
- Users must always use the latest operating system and antivirus software.
- In a man-in-the-middle (MIM) attack or network spoofing attack, the attacker intentionally inserts himself into a conversation between two persons.
- A good symmetric encryption algorithm is one that makes it very difficult, if not impossible, for attackers to decrypt the generated cipher text without knowing the key used for encryption.
- Ransomware is a subset of malware that locks the data (usually by encryption) on the victim's computer and asks for payment to decrypt that data and return access to the victim.
- Sniffing means monitoring and capturing data that is being transmitted over a network.
- Phishing is done to acquire sensitive information such as passwords, account numbers, and credit card details. In this technique, the fraudster constructs a fake website that looks similar to the legitimate website.
- Secure socket layer (SSL) is a security protocol that uses encryption of messages exchanged between a web server and a browser in an online communication.
- HTTPS ensures secure communication between a user's browser and a web server. A website supporting the HTTPS protocol has its URL beginning with https://.
- A website audit includes all activities to review the forms, information, content, graphics, evaluation of ranking, and the quality of a website. It is especially done to identify and improve any shortcomings that might have otherwise been ignored.
- During a website audit, factors like traffic are also monitored as it plays a key role in the success of a website and generation of sales.

KEYWORDS

Accountability: The activities of the authorized persons are documented to deter employees from wrong-doing.

Antivirus: A software that prevents, detects, and removes malicious software programs such as virus, worms, Trojan horses, spywares, adwares, and so on that are harmful to computer systems.

Authentication: Confirming the identity of the person requesting to gain access to a resource. This can be done by validating a username and password.

Authorization: Determining the set of actions that an authenticated person can perform on a resource. For example, an employee working in the Accounts department is not authorized to access the files of the Sales and Marketing department.

Cookie: Small-sized files that store information about an Internet user on his or her own computer.

Cracker: A person who breaks into the system by password cracking or by cracking the security measures implemented to protect the data.

Cybercrime: Any crime or illegal activity that involves a computer and a network.

Cyberstalking: Use of the Internet to stalk or harass an individual, an organization, or a specific group. Cyberstalking also includes monitoring someone's online activity.

Cyberterrorism: Disruptive use of IT by terrorists to attack networks, computer systems and telecommunication infrastructures.

Cyberwarfare: Nations using IT to penetrate another nation's networks to cause damage or disruption.

Cyberespionage: The practice of using IT to obtain secret information without seeking permission from its owners. It is usually done using cracking techniques and malware.

Decryption: The process of converting encrypted data back into its original form so that the receiver can correctly interpret its meaning.

Denial of service: An attempt to make a computer resource unavailable to its intended users.

Encryption: The process of converting data into a cipher text.

Firewall: A piece or hardware, software, or both that is installed to prevent unauthorized access to computers or networks.

Hacking: The practice of identifying weaknesses or loopholes in a computer system, or a computer application, or a network to exploit its weaknesses to gain unauthorized access.

Hacker: A person who either breaks into the system for which he/she has no authorization or goes beyond the limits of legitimate access.

Malware: Software designed with wrong intentions, usually embedded within legitimate software that is either useful or attractive.

Spamming: The process of flooding the Internet with many copies of the same message for commercial advertising, usually for dubious products like get-rich schemes or loan at low interest rates.

Spyware: A malicious program that surreptitiously monitors activity on a computer and reports that information to others without the user's consent.

Trojan horse: A non-self-replicating malicious software that pretends to be harmless so that users can easily download it on the computer.

Virus: A small program that gets loaded in the computer without the user's knowledge and replicates itself repeatedly.

Vulnerability assessment: An audit or a check that is performed to identify potential vulnerabilities in a computer system or network.

MODEL QUESTION PAPER

Multiple Choice Questions

1. The term data security includes security of _____.
   (a) Data
   (b) Information
   (c) Transactions
   (d) All of these.

2. Data security does not include _____.
   (a) Authenticated access
   (b) Privacy
   (c) Integrity
   (d) None of these.

Hackers

White Hat — People who specialize in hacking check the faults of the system

Grey Hat — Exploit security to attract the attention of the owners

Black Hat — People who break into networks and cause harm to the network and property

White-hat people are known as Ethical Hackers

3. Which is not true about a hacker?
   (a) He breaks into security.
   (b) He is an authorized user.
   (c) He crosses the boundary of legitimate access.
   (d) He is always a person outside of the organization.

4. Who is a cracker?
   (a) A hacker
   (b) One who cracks passwords
   (c) One who bypasses security mechanism
   (d) All of these.

5. Which of the following is not a threat to data security?
   (a) Humans
   (b) Malware
   (c) Natural Disaster
   (d) None of these.

6. Confidential data can be tampered by _____ it.
   (a) deleting
   (b) modifying
   (c) stealing
   (d) All of these.

7. Protecting confidential data includes _____.
   (a) preventing it from being altered
   (b) detecting any attempt to damage, modify or steal it
   (c) recovery of lost or damaged data
   (d) All of these.

8. The generic term for all types of software designed with bad intentions to cause a threat to data security is _____.
   (a) Virus
   (b) Malware
   (c) Worm
   (d) Trojan Horse

9. The generic term used for a piece of code that is usually embedded within legitimate software is _____.
   (a) Virus
   (b) Malware
   (c) Worm
   (d) Trojan Horse

10. _____ replicates itself.
    (a) Virus
    (b) Spyware
    (c) Adware
    (d) Trojan Horse

11. Identify the malware which can delete files or consume all the memory space.
    (a) Virus
    (b) Spyware
    (c) Adware
    (d) Trojan Horse

12. Identify the malware which needs a host file to spread itself.
    (a) Virus
    (b) Spyware
    (c) Adware
    (d) Trojan Horse

13. The _____ is loaded in memory from the bot record.
    (a) MS Office
    (b) Operating System
    (c) Application Software
    (d) Utility Software

14. _____ viruses infect only executable files.
    (a) Boot record
    (b) Program
    (c) Stealth
    (d) Macro

15. _____ viruses are a combination of boot viruses and program viruses.
    (a) Multipartite
    (b) Polymorphic
    (c) Stealth
    (d) Macro

16. _____ virus will remove the virus code from an infected file when antivirus software is run.
    (a) Multipartite   (b) Polymorphic   (c) Stealth   (d) Macro
17. _____ viruses create copies during replication.
    (a) Multipartite   (b) Polymorphic   (c) Stealth   (d) Macro
18. _____ virus inserts itself in the computer's memory.
    (a) Multipartite   (b) Resident   (c) Stealth   (d) Macro
19. _____ virus is dormant when the file is not being executed.
    (a) Direct Action   (b) Resident   (c) Stealth   (d) Macro
20. _____ virus changes the paths that indicate the location of a file.
    (a) Overwrite   (b) Directory   (c) Network   (d) Cavity
21. _____ virus multiplies through shared resources such as shared drives and files.
    (a) Overwrite   (b) Directory   (c) Network   (d) Cavity
22. When a file gets infected with a _____ virus, it seems missing or inaccessible to the users.
    (a) Overwrite   (b) Directory   (c) Network   (d) FAT
23. _____ replicates itself.
    (a) Worms   (b) Spyware   (c) Adware   (d) Trojan Horse
24. _____ is a malicious code that locates vulnerabilities on a computer to exploit them.
    (a) Worms   (b) Spyware   (c) Virus   (d) Trojan Horse
25. _____ is a non-self-replicating malicious code that can even install a virus.
    (a) Worms   (b) Spyware   (c) Adware   (d) Trojan Horse
26. _____ may allow the computer to be accessed from a remote machine.
    (a) Worms   (b) Spyware   (c) Adware   (d) Trojan Horse
27. _____ Trojan Horse floods the target server with traffic to make it impossible for users to access certain websites.
    (a) Denial-of-Service attack   (b) File serving
    (c) Keylogging   (d) Password stealing
28. Antivirus can detect _____.
    (a) Virus   (b) Trojan Horse   (c) Ransomware   (d) All of these.

Pop-up advertisements on the screen

Changed computer settings that the user cannot switch back

Additional applications installed on the computer

The computer becomes slow in executing tasks

The antivirus is unexpectedly disabled

Unexpected crashes

Common signs of a malware infection

29. _____ is usually used for tracking and storing the user's Internet browsing patterns.
    (a) Worms   (b) Spyware   (c) Virus   (d) Trojan Horse
30. _____ does not transfer the user's personal information to another location.
    (a) Worms   (b) Spyware   (c) Adware   (d) Trojan Horse
31. _____ slows down the computer's speed.
    (a) Virus   (b) Spyware   (c) Adware   (d) All of these.
32. In _____, the attacker modifies the browser to permanently change the home page.
    (a) Denial-of-Service   (b) Spoofing
    (c) Browser Hijacking   (d) Sniffing
33. In _____, the attacker sends numerous external communication requests to the target machine.
    (a) Ping of flood (b) Ping of death (c) Teardrop attack (d) Mail bombs
34. A ping packet in the network that exceeds 65,535 bytes is sent in _____ attack.
    (a) Ping of flood (b) Ping of death (c) Teardrop attack (d) Mail bombs
35. In _____, the attacker puts a confusing sequence number in the packets.
    (a) Ping of flood (b) Ping of death (c) Teardrop attack (d) Mail bombs
36. In _____, unauthorized users send a large number of messages with large attachments to a particular server to fill its disk space.
    (a) Ping of flood (b) Ping of death (c) Teardrop attack (d) Mail bombs
37. In a _____ attack, the attacker inserts himself into a conversation between two persons.
    (a) Man-in-the-Middle (b) Ping of death (c) Teardrop attack (d) Mail bombs
38. In a _____ attack, the attacker impersonates the people in the conversation.
    (a) Ping of flood   (b) Ping of death
    (c) Man-in-the-Middle   (d) Mail bombs
39. Man-in-the-Middle attack can be prevented by _____.
    (a) using an anti-spoofing software (b) using HTTPS
    (c) using packet filters   (d) All of these.
40. In _____, the fraudster constructs a fake website that looks similar to the legitimate site and asks for the user's personal information to steal it.
    (a) online auction fraud   (b) online purchase fraud
    (c) phishing   (d) online intellectual property theft
41. Copy–pasting content from a website without taking permissions from the author is _____.
    (a) phishing   (b) violation of intellectual property
    (c) work-from-home scam   (d) None of these.
42. Link in a spam e-mail may have _____.
    (a) virus   (b) worm   (c) bugs   (d) All of these.
43. A password cannot contain _____.
    (a) Characters   (b) Digits
    (c) Special Characters   (d) None of these.

44. Which of the following is not necessary while working on the Internet?
    (a) To go to a website, type its address in the address bar. Do not click on any link or cut and paste its address
    (b) Delete cookies and history of web pages browsed.
    (c) Do not use an obsolete operating system.
    (d) None of these.

45. Antivirus does the following to protect the computer from malware.
    (a) Deletes the file
    (b) Quarantine the file
    (c) Deletes the virus code
    (d) All of these.

46. Signature-based antivirus software examines files when they are _____.
    (a) created
    (b) opened
    (c) attached with an e-mail
    (d) All of these.

47. In _____ type of antivirus, virus code is detected by searching for matches in a virus dictionary.
    (a) signature-based
    (b) heuristic-based
    (c) Both of these.
    (d) None of these.

48. The _____ type of antivirus protects the computer from brand-new viruses.
    (a) signature-based
    (b) heuristic-based
    (c) Both of these.
    (d) None of these.

49. Antivirus does not use which of the following approach?
    (a) Emulate the beginning of the code of each executable
    (b) Emulate the operating system and run the executable programs
    (c) Work in the background and monitor the computer's activity
    (d) None of these.

50. Identify the incorrect statement.
    (a) Web-based antivirus scans should not be done as they are either spyware or Trojan horses.
    (b) If there are more than one antivirus software installed, then only one of them should work in the interactive.
    (c) Firewall exercises full control over data packets coming in and going out of the computer to the Internet.
    (d) Antivirus is configured with a set of rules that decides the packets to be accepted, that to be transmitted or received across the network.

51. Firewall can be a _____.
    (a) Hardware
    (b) Software
    (c) Both of these.
    (d) None of these

52. _____ type of firewall examines each data packet that either enters or leaves the network.
    (a) Packet filtering
    (b) Stateful
    (c) Circuit-level gateway
    (d) Proxy

53. _____ type of firewall records all connections passing through it.
    (a) Packet filtering
    (b) Stateful
    (c) Circuit-level gateway
    (d) Proxy

Anti-malware software

54. _____ firewall acts as an intermediary for requests from one network to another.
    (a) Packet filtering   (b) Stateful
    (c) Circuit-level gateway   (d) Proxy

55. Firewalls can be implemented to block traffic for one or more _____.
    (a) protocol   (b) IP address   (c) domain name   (d) All of these.

56. _____ is the process of converting data into a cipher text.
    (a) Encryption   (b) Decryption   (c) Translation   (d) Compression

57. Which property is to ensure that the sender cannot deny sending the message?
    (a) Authentication   (b) Non-repudiation   (c) Integrity   (d) Consistency

58. Which property ensures that the message has not been modified or tampered with during transmission?
    (a) Authentication   (b) Non-repudiation   (c) Integrity   (d) Consistency

59. Which property verifies the originator of the message?
    (a) Authentication   (b) Non-repudiation   (c) Integrity   (d) Consistency

60. _____ is the process of converting encrypted data back into its original form.
    (a) Encryption   (b) Decryption   (c) Translation   (d) Compression

61. Which encryption algorithm uses a single key to encrypt messages?
    (a) Symmetric   (b) Asymmetric   (c) Both of these.   (d) None of these.

62. Who knows the secret symmetric key?
    (a) Sender   (b) Receiver   (c) Both of them.   (d) None of them.

63. Which of the following is not a disadvantage of symmetric key algorithm?
    (a) The key may get into the hands of attackers.
    (b) There is no provision for authenticating the sender.
    (c) Data integrity cannot be assured.
    (d) The secret key can be a number, a word, or just a string of random letters.

64. In asymmetric key encryption algorithm, the original message is encrypted using _____ key.
    (a) public key   (b) private key   (c) symmetric key   (d) None of these.

65. The encrypted message is decrypted with _____ .
    (a) public key   (b) private key   (c) symmetric key   (d) None of these.

66. Which of the following is not a feature of asymmetric encryption algorithm?
    (a) Both the sender and the receiver know about the secret key.
    (b) The two keys are mathematically related to each other.
    (c) The algorithm used for encryption is universally known.
    (d) It is impossible to compute the private key if the public key is known.

67. In a digital signature, the sender signs the message with his _____ .
    (a) public key   (b) private key   (c) symmetric key   (d) None of these.

68. In a digital envelope, the original message is encrypted with _____ .
    (a) public key   (b) private key   (c) symmetric key   (d) None of these.

69. In a digital envelope, symmetric key is encrypted with _____ of the receiver.
    (a) public key   (b) private key   (c) symmetric key   (d) None of these.

70. A digital certificate has _____.
    (a) digital signature of the certificate-issuing authority
    (b) public key of the owner of the certificate
    (c) the owner's identity
    (d) All of these.

71. The job of certificate authority is to _____ certificates.
    (a) issue   (b) revoke   (c) Both of these.   (d) None of these.

72. _____ defines degree to which data and other resources are accessible for use when required.
    (a) Reliability   (b) Availability   (c) Accessibility   (d) Readability

73. Confirming the identity of the person requesting to gain access to a resource means _____.
    (a) Authentication (b) Authorization   (c) Reliable   (d) Accountable

74. Determining the set of actions that an authenticated person can perform on a resource.
    (a) Authentication (b) Authorization   (c) Reliable   (d) Accountable

75. A nation is using IT to penetrate another nation's networks to cause damage or disruption. This is known as _____.
    (a) Cyber-terrorism (b) Cyber-warfare (c) Cyber-crime   (d) Cyber-espionage

76. The practice of using IT to obtain secret information without seeking permission from its owners is known as _____.
    (a) Cyber-terrorism (b) Cyber-warfare (c) Cyber-crime   (d) Cyber-espionage

77. _____ is a subset of malware which locks the data on the victim's computer and asks for payment to decrypt that data.
    (a) Ransomware   (b) Virus   (c) Spyware   (d) Adware

78. Ransomware works by _____
    (a) changing user's credentials
    (b) encrypting user's files and data
    (c) Both of these.
    (d) None of these.

79. Which of the following demands money after attacking the computer?
    (a) Ransomware   (b) Virus   (c) Spyware   (d) Adware

80. Payment in case of a ransomware attack is demanded in _____.
    (a) Dollars   (b) Yen   (c) Euro   (d) Bitcoin

81. Ransomware can get installed through _____.
    (a) spam e-mails
    (b) infected apps
    (c) clicking pop-up messages
    (d) All of these.

82. _____ is a popular currency among cybercriminals because it is decentralised, unregulated and practically impossible to trace.
    (a) Dollars   (b) Yen   (c) Euro   (d) Bitcoin

83. Which of the following is not a good way to control ransomware attacks?
    (a) Download a good anti-virus software
    (b) Being extra cautious while clicking on links in e-mails
    (c) Installing a pop-up blocker on your computing device
    (d) Taking back-up of computing devices on a regular basis

84. Which of the following is not correct?
    (a) It is possible to delete a ransomware if the computer is not locked.
    (b) Anti-virus tools can detect and delete ransomware.
    (c) There are decryption tools that can be used in case of a ransomware attack.
    (d) Paying ransom guarantees that your files will be reusable.
85. _____ means tricking or deceiving computer systems or users.
    (a) Spoofing   (b) Sniffing   (c) Hacking   (d) Tracking
86. Spoofing is done by _____.
    (a) hiding one's identity
    (b) faking the identity of another user on the Internet
    (c) DoS attack
    (d) Both (a) and (b).
87. Identify the attack in which messages are either sent using a bogus e-mail address, IP address of a certain computer is masked or a cyber-criminal fakes an identity.
    (a) Spoofing   (b) Sniffing   (c) Hacking   (d) Tracking
88. Avoid trust relationship on Internet to prevent _____.
    (a) Spoofing   (b) Sniffing   (c) Hacking   (d) Tracking
89. _____ means monitoring and capturing data that is being transmitted over a network.
    (a) Spoofing   (b) Sniffing   (c) Hacking   (d) Tracking
90. Legitimate use of sniffing does not involve _____.
    (a) diagnosing network issues
    (b) troubleshooting network related issues
    (c) analyzing network usage
    (d) extracting confidential data
91. Sniffing cannot be done by _____.
    (a) internal user   (b) external user   (c) wireless user   (d) None of these.
92. In _____ sniffing, the sniffer just monitors and captures the data.
    (a) active   (b) passive   (c) Both of these.   (d) None of these.
93. In _____ sniffing, the sniffer alters the data.
    (a) active   (b) passive   (c) Both of these.   (d) None of these.
94. _____ sniffing is more difficult to detect and hence it is more dangerous.
    (a) Active   (b) Passive   (c) Both of these.   (d) None of these.
95. Identify the protocol which protects computers and users from sniffing attack.
    (a) HTTPS   (b) SSL   (c) TLS   (d) All of these.
96. E-mails can be encrypted using _____ protocol which uses _____ encryption.
    (a) PGP, symmetric
    (b) PGP, asymmetric
    (c) DES, symmetric
    (d) DES, asymmetric
97. _____ software can detect sniffing.
    (a) Anti-sniffing   (b) Antivirus   (c) Anti-spyware   (d) All of these.
98. Identify the incorrect statement.
    (a) Computers that need not communicate directly with the Internet are placed in the DMZ.
    (b) Computers in DMZ are protected by firewalls.

(c) A DMZ can also be set up on home networks.
(d) DMZ can be a logical or a physical network.

99. SSL uses _____ of messages.
    (a) encryption
    (b) decryption
    (c) translation
    (d) compression

100. To create an SSL connection, one must have SSL _____.
    (a) signature
    (b) certificate
    (c) degree
    (d) password

101. The SSL certificate contains _____.
    (a) domain name
    (b) details of CA
    (c) the applicant's address
    (d) All of these.

102. The existence of an encrypted session is indicated by the presence of _____.
    (a) lock icon in the address bar
    (b) green address bar
    (c) secured protocol
    (d) All of these.

103. When browsing a website over an SSL connection, the URL begins with _____ protocol.
    (a) HTTP   (b) HTTPS   (c) TLS   (d) SFTP

104. SSL works with _____ encryption algorithm.
    (a) symmetric   (b) asymmetric   (c) Both of these.   (d) None of these.

105. Identify the incorrect statement.
    (a) SSL protects from phishing attack.
    (b) SEO gives higher ranking to websites using HTTPS.
    (c) Performance of a website degrades when it uses SSL.
    (d) HTTPS uses SSL certificates.

HTTP + SSL = HTTPS

(Hypertext Transfer Protocol) — Defines how messages are transmitted between visitor's browser and website server.

(Security Socket Layer) — Protects and encrypts information sent across the internet.

(Hypertext Transfer Protocol Secure) — Encrypts information sent between browser and server.

HTTPS makes it harder for hackers to break the connection and steal personal information such as credit card numbers, addresses, passwords, etc.

106. HTTPS provides _____.
    (a) authentication   (b) security   (c) confidentiality   (d) All of these.

107. Identify the incorrect statement.
    (a) Without HTTPS, a government censor can choose to block certain pages of a site.
    (b) With HTTPS, ISPs can no longer insert ads or inject code in the website.

Software piracy is the act of **stealing software that is legally protected.** This stealing includes selling, distributing, modifying or copying the software.

(c) On a website supporting HTTP, confidential data can be intercepted, spied on and even altered by anyone.
(d) HTTPS exchanges data in an unencrypted form.

108. HTTPS encryption mechanism requires ____ keys.
    (a) one (b) two (c) three (d) four

109. Identify the incorrect statement.
    (a) A website audit includes all activities to review the forms, information, content, graphics, evaluation of ranking, and the quality of a website.
    (b) During a website audit, traffic to a website is also monitored
    (c) Website audit does not reveal a website's ranking, bounce rates and search percentages.
    (d) Website audit gives an insight into new graphic and strategic ideas.

110. Website audit does not report _____.
    (a) response time (b) download time (c) 404 errors (d) None of these.

111. To control duplication, _____ is checked.
    (a) page title (b) page content (c) Keywords (d) All of these.

112. Identify the incorrect statement.
    (a) Web audit saves the website from penalization.
    (b) Web audit helps a website to discover malware infection.
    (c) Website audit should be an ongoing process that should be conducted at least once a year.
    (d) None of the above.

113. Users should not have to click more than ____ times to open a particular page.
    (a) 1 (b) 2 (c) 3 (d) 4

114. Identify the correct statement.
    (a) The homepage of a website should have detailed information.
    (b) Contact Us section must be present in every website.
    (c) Every page should have a link, button or any other way to return to the homepage.
    (d) The algorithm for ranking the websites is always the same.

115. Website audit should be done at least _____.
    (a) once in a week
    (b) once every fortnight
    (c) once in a month
    (d) once in six months

116. Identify the incorrect statement.
    (a) A hacker is someone who either breaks into the system for which he has no authorization or goes beyond his limits of legitimate access.
    (b) Confidential data may be tampered by deleting, modifying or stealing data from a database.
    (c) A hacker can be a cracker.
    (d) Cybercrime means any crime or illegal activity that involves a computer but not the network.

117. In a cybercrime, a computer can be a _____.
    (a) target (b) weapon (c) accessory (d) All of these.

118. Cybercrime does not include _____.
    (a) threatening a nation's security
    (b) copyright infringement
    (c) child pornography.
    (d) None of these

119. An attempt to gain unauthorized access or deny authorized access to a resource is called _____.
    (a) Threat   (b) Attack   (c) Vulnerability   (d) Threat

120. The degree to which data and other resources are accessible for use when required is called _____.
    (a) Availability   (b) Accountability (c) Confidentiality   (d) Authentication

121. An unauthorized access to steal, modify, or destroy confidential data:
    (a) Compromise   (b) Theft   (c) Malicious attack   (d) Threat

122. An audit or a check that is performed to identify potential weaknesses in a computer system or network.
    (a) Auditability   (b) Accountability
    (c) Vulnerability assessment   (d) All of these.

123. The practice of using IT to obtain secret information without seeking permission from its owners is known as cyber _____.
    (a) stalking   (b) terrorism   (c) warfare   (d) espionage

124. Use of the Internet to stalk or harass an individual, an organization, or a specific group is called cyber _____.
    (a) stalking   (b) terrorism   (c) warfare   (d) espionage

125. Identify the incorrect statement about malware.
    (a) Malware is specifically designed to gain access to a computer either to disrupt its operation or gather sensitive data from it.
    (b) It includes computer virus, spyware, worms, Trojan horse, etc.
    (c) Malwares are usually embedded within legitimate software that is either useful or attractive.
    (d) None of these.

126. Identify the correct statement.
    (a) Virus replicates itself repeatedly.
    (b) Virus cannot delete files from the computer.
    (c) A virus cannot be attached and sent in an e-mail.
    (d) A virus does not have any effect on the computer's performance.

127. Identify the correct statement.
    (a) Worm always require a host file to spread.
    (b) Program viruses were used to infect floppy disks or hard disks.
    (c) When the operating system is loaded in memory, the boot virus also gets loaded along with the operating system.
    (d) Boot viruses infect only executable files.

128. Identify the incorrect statement.
    (a) Multipartite viruses are a combination of two types of viruses – boot viruses and program viruses.
    (b) Stealth virus will remove the virus code from an infected file when antivirus software is examining the system
    (c) Polymorphic viruses redirect the hard disk head so that the next read operation is done from another memory sector instead of the correct one.
    (d) None of these.

129. Identify the incorrect statement.
    (a) Polymorphic viruses randomly insert superfluous instructions, each time a copy of the virus is created.
    (b) It is very difficult for antivirus software to identify, locate, and remove polymorphic viruses.
    (c) A polymorphic virus inserts itself in the computer's memory
    (d) To clean a file infected by an overwrite virus, users have no option but to delete the file completely, thereby losing all its contents.

130. Identify the incorrect statement.
    (a) Space filler does not affect or damage the contents of the actual program itself.
    (b) A directory virus changes the paths that indicate the location of a file.
    (c) Network viruses rapidly spread through a LAN or through the Internet.
    (d) The FAT virus disrupts a system completely by destroying data and forcing the user to reformat the system.

131. Identify the incorrect statement about worms.
    (a) Worms can attack applications such as Microsoft Word and Excel by inserting malicious code in documents and then use them as an attachment with e-mail.
    (b) The most destructive feature of a worm is that it can replicate itself 2,50,000 times over a period of several hours.
    (c) Worm always needs a program to replicate.
    (d) Worms can be detected and removed by antivirus software.

132. Identify the incorrect statement.
    (a) A Trojan horse is a self-replicating malicious software that pretends to be harmless.
    (b) Trojans give unauthorized access to its controller.
    (c) Trojan can ruin the FAT and install a virus.
    (d) Keyloggers record every step of the user's activity on the infected computer.

133. Identify the incorrect statement.
    (a) Antivirus software cannot detect and remove Trojan horses.
    (a) Spyware is usually used for tracking and storing the user's Internet browsing patterns.
    (b) Adware displays advertisements automatically without the user's permission.
    (c) Unlike spyware, adware does not transfer the user's personal information to another location.

134. Identify the incorrect statement.
    (a) In ping of death, the attacker sends numerous external communication requests to the target machine.
    (b) In the teardrop method of DoS, the attacker puts a confusing sequence number in the packets.
    (c) When a browser is hijacked, the attacker modifies the browser to permanently change the home page.
    (d) Spam e-mails are used to launch the DoS attack on an e-mail account.

135. Identify the incorrect statement.
    (a) In MIM attack, the attacker intentionally inserts himself into a conversation between two persons.
    (b) In MIM attack, the attacker impersonates the people in the conversation and gains access to the information that they were sending to each other.
    (c) Packet filters must be installed to prevent MIM attack.
    (d) HTTPS, SSL and TLS cannot prevent MIM attack.

136. Identify the correct statement.
    (a) In purchase fraud, the fraudster constructs a fake website that looks similar to the legitimate site and asks for the user's personal information.
    (b) Online intellectual property theft is done by violating copyright issues.
    (c) All malware lock the data on the victim's computer and ask for payment to decrypt that data and return access to the victim
    (d) All of these.

137. Ransomware does spread through _____.
    (a) malicious email attachments
    (b) spam mails
    (c) infected external storage
    (d) All of these.

138. Bitcoin is popular among cybercriminals because it is _____.
    (a) decentralized
    (b) unregulated
    (c) difficult to trace
    (d) All of these.

139. Identify the correct statement.
    (a) Ransomware can be detected by antivirus software.
    (b) Ransomware can be removed by antivirus software.
    (c) Ransomware can be detected as well as removed by antivirus software.
    (d) Ransomware can neither be detected nor removed by antivirus software.

140. Identify the incorrect statement.
    (a) Installing a pop-up blocker on your computing device can help you to prevent a ransomware attack.
    (b) To fix ransomware, you can re-install the operating system.
    (c) Grey-hat hacker hacks to check the security systems to make it more hack-proof.
    (d) E-mail and IP spooking can be used to cause DoS attack.

141. Identify the correct statement.
    (a) On Internet, you should depend on trust relationships.
    (b) HTTPS and SSL can prevent spoofing attacks.
    (c) Spoofing means monitoring and capturing data that is being transmitted over a network.
    (d) In passive sniffing, the sniffer just monitors and captures the data.

142. Identify the incorrect statement.
    (a) Disabling promiscuous mode on network interfaces can prevent sniffing.
    (b) In active sniffing, the traffic is not only monitored and captured, but it may also be altered in some way.
    (c) Passive sniffing is more difficult to detect.
    (d) Anti-virus software and anti-sniffer software can detect sniffing.

143. Features of a phishing e-mail does not include:
    (a) Phishing e-mails have fake links.
    (b) There may be a small spelling and grammar mistake in the fake e-mail.
    (c) They request an immediate response or give a specific deadline.
    (d) None of these.

144. Identify the incorrect statement about spam e-mail.
    (a) It does not have any attachment.
    (b) It floods the Internet with many copies of the same message for commercial advertising.
    (c) They are too good to be true.
    (d) The source and identity of the sender is mostly unknown.

Symmetric encryption

145. Identify the incorrect statement.
    (a) Confidentiality refers to the ability to hide information from unauthorized people.
    (b) To ensure confidentiality, data is encrypted before it is transferred from one computer to another.
    (c) Accessibility means that the information is always accessible to authorized users.
    (d) Integrity ensures that data is inaccurate.

146. Identify the incorrect statement.
    (a) Integrity verifies the originator of the message.
    (b) Non-repudiation makes sure that the sender cannot deny sending the message.
    (c) Symmetric encryption is basically done on small amount of data.
    (d) The longer the key, the more difficult it will be to decrypt the message.

147. Identify the incorrect statement.
    (a) Symmetric encryption uses a pair of keys.
    (b) The public key is given to anyone who wants to send a message.
    (c) The private key, on the other hand, is kept secret and is known only to its owner.
    (d) Public and private keys are allotted by a certificate authority.

148. Identify the incorrect statement.
    (a) Symmetric encryption is computationally faster.
    (b) Every operating system including Windows, Mac, Linux, have built-in support for maintaining and testing firewalls.
    (c) Firewall helps to screen out hackers and malicious software that tries to reach a computer.
    (d) Packet firewall does not record all connections passing through it.

149. Identify the incorrect statement.
    (a) Firewalls can block packets based on domain names.
    (b) Firewalls can be programmed to accept or block based on certain keywords.
    (c) In organizations, computers that need to communicate directly with the Internet (or any other public servers) are placed in the DMZ.
    (d) Computers in DMZ are not protected at all.

150. Identify the incorrect statement.
    (a) DMZ is considered more secure, safer than a firewall
    (b) DMZ can also work as a proxy server.
    (c) In SSL, the web server uses its private key to decrypt the symmetric session key.
    (d) SSL does not provide any protection against phishing attacks.

151. Identify the incorrect statement.
    (a) HTTPS prevents tampering of data by ISPs or hackers.
    (b) HTTPS does not provide authentication.
    (c) With HTTP, the data is exchanged in an unencrypted form.
    (d) HTTPS makes normal web browsing confidential.

152. Identify the incorrect statement about website auditing.
    (a) A website audit includes all activities to review the forms, information, content, graphics, evaluation of ranking, and the quality of a website.
    (b) It does not monitor the response time and download time.
    (c) It is especially done to identify and improve website shortcomings.
    (d) It reveals broken links and other errors.

153. Identify the incorrect statement.
    (a) Web audit saves the website from penalization.
    (b) Web audit helps the website to discover malware infection.
    (c) Web audit monitors the website optimizing process.
    (d) A user should not have to click more than once to open a particular page.

ANSWER KEYS

Multiple Choice Questions

1. (d)	2. (d)	3. (d)	4. (d)	5. (d)	6. (d)	7. (d)	8. (b)	
9. (b)	10. (a)	11. (a)	12. (a)	13. (b)	14. (b)	15. (a)	16. (c)	
17. (b)	18. (b)	19. (a)	20. (b)	21. (c)	22. (d)	23. (a)	24. (a)	
25. (d)	26. (d)	27. (a)	28. (d)	29. (b)	30. (c)	31. (d)	32. (c)	
33. (a)	34. (b)	35. (c)	36. (d)	37. (a)	38. (c)	39. (d)	40. (c)	
41. (b)	42. (d)	43. (d)	44. (d)	45. (d)	46. (d)	47. (a)	48. (b)	
49. (d)	50. (d)	51. (c)	52. (a)	53. (b)	54. (d)	55. (d)	56. (a)	
57. (b)	58. (c)	59. (a)	60. (b)	61. (a)	62. (c)	63. (d)	64. (a)	
65. (b)	66. (a)	67. (b)	68. (c)	69. (a)	70. (d)	71. (c)	72. (b)	
73. (a)	74. (b)	75. (b)	76. (d)	77. (a)	78. (c)	79. (a)	80. (d)	
81. (d)	82. (d)	83. (d)	84. (d)	85. (a)	86. (d)	87. (a)	88. (a)	
89. (b)	90. (d)	91. (d)	92. (b)	93. (a)	94. (b)	95. (d)	96. (b)	
97. (d)	98. (a)	99. (a)	100. (b)	101. (d)	102. (d)	103. (b)	104. (b)	
105. (c)	106. (d)	107. (d)	108. (b)	109. (c)	110. (d)	111. (d)	112. (d)	
113. (c)	114. (c)	115. (d)	116. (d)	117. (d)	118. (d)	119. (b)	120. (a)	
121. (a)	122. (c)	123. (d)	124. (a)	125. (d)	126. (a)	127. (c)	128. (c)	
129. (c)	130. (a)	131. (c)	132. (a)	133. (a)	134. (a)	135. (d)	136. (b)	
137. (d)	138. (d)	139. (c)	140. (c)	141. (d)	142. (a)	143. (d)	144. (a)	
145. (d)	146. (a)	147. (a)	148. (d)	149. (d)	150. (c)	151. (b)	152. (b)	
153. (d)								

CHAPTER 9
Elements of Word Processing

KEY POINTS

- MS Word is word processing application software developed by Microsoft.
- Rulers are used to align text, graphics, tables, and other elements in a document.
- Print Preview is used to see how a document would look when printed on a page.
- Editing a file means making some changes in the file. While editing a document we may insert, delete or replace some existing content.
- The simplest way to select text is to click on it and drag the mouse over the text you want to select.
- Alignment of text means how the text is displayed horizontally on the page. There are four options for text alignment – left, center, right and justified.
- WordArt is decorative text that you can add to a document.
- Microsoft Word provides bullets and numbers to maintain a list of items in a presentable order.
- Each cell can store some data.
- Microsoft Word allows you to apply beautiful borders on any or all of the four sides of a table. You can even add shading to its rows and columns to make the table more attractive.
- Headers and/or footers are added to include important information about the document.
- Adding hyperlinks to your document can help readers quickly access information, in other parts of the document or on the Internet, that you want to share.

KEYWORDS

Word processor: Also known as word processing program, it is software that processes words, paragraphs, pages, and entire papers.

Document Area: Area where the text is typed.

Cursor: The flashing vertical bar on the screen.

Page margins: Blank space around the edges of the page.

Clipboard: A small area to hold data temporarily.

Table: A structure of vertical columns and horizontal rows.

Cell: The intersection of row and a column.

Resizing the table: Changing the height and width of cells in a table.

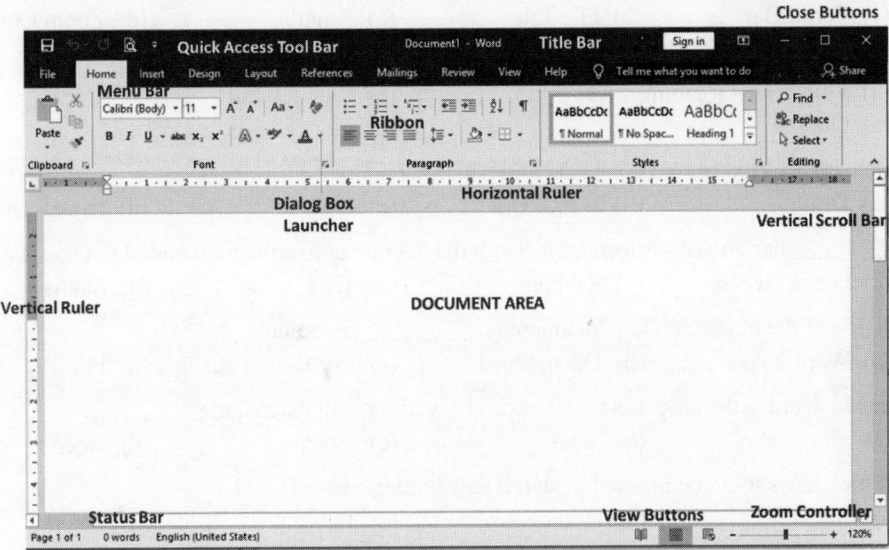

Microsoft Word Document

MODEL QUESTION PAPER

Multiple Choice Questions

1. Word is a _____ software.
   (a) Database　　　(b) Word processing　　(c) Spreadsheet　　(d) Animation

2. Select elements that cannot be inserted in MS Word.
   (a) Chart
   (b) Worksheet
   (c) PowerPoint presentation
   (d) None of these.

3. Select the most popular word processor.
   (a) Microsoft Word　(b) WordPerfect　(c) AppleWorks　(d) OpenOffice.org

4. _____ bar displays the name of the document.
   (a) Quick Access　(b) Ribbon　(c) Title　(d) Scroll

5. Title bar displays the name of the document and the _____.
   (a) program name
   (b) date of creation
   (c) date it was last accessed
   (d) name of the author

6. _____ bar contains buttons for frequently used commands.
   (a) Quick Access　(b) Ribbon　(c) Title　(d) Scroll

7. The command to print a document is present in the _____ tab.
   (a) Home　(b) File　(c) Page Layout　(d) View

8. There are _____ rulers in a document.
   (a) 1　(b) 2　(c) 3　(d) 4

9. _____ is used to align text, graphics, tables, and other elements in a document.
   (a) Scroll Bar   (b) File Tab   (c) Ruler   (d) Zoom Control
10. Which view displays pages exactly as they will appear when printed?
    (a) Full Screen Reading   (b) Web Layout
    (c) Outline   (d) Page Layout
11. Headers and footers cannot be seen in which view?
    (a) Draft   (b) Web Layout   (c) Outline   (d) Page Layout
12. _____ bar displays information about the document like the total number of pages and words.
    (a) Quick Access   (b) Ribbon   (c) Title   (d) Status
13. Name of the newly created document is _____ by default.
    (a) Word 1   (b) Document 1   (c) My Document   (d) File 1
14. In MS Word, a document is automatically saved with an extension _____.
    (a) .doc   (b) .docs   (c) .docx   (d) .docz
15. Which key should be pressed to start a new paragraph?
    (a) Insert   (b) Home   (c) Tab   (d) Enter
16. Print _____ is used to see how a document would look when printed on a page.
    (a) Preview   (b) Layout   (c) Orientation   (d) Window
17. If you want to add more than one space between two words, use the _____ Key.
    (a) Home   (b) Tab   (c) Space Bar   (d) Shift
18. Delete key is used to delete the character _____ the cursor.
    (a) in front of   (b) behind   (c) above   (d) under
19. _____ button is used to reverse the last action(s) performed.
    (a) Cut   (b) Paste   (c) Undo   (d) Redo
20. Arrow keys + _____ key is used to select text
    (a) F5   (b) F6   (c) F7   (d) F8
21. To select a paragraph, click _____ times on the paragraph.
    (a) 1   (b) 2   (c) 3   (d) 4
22. To select the whole document, press Ctrl + _____ keys on the keyboard.
    (a) A   (b) D   (c) W   (d) S
23. _____ command is used to move a text from one location to another.
    (a) Cut/Copy   (b) Copy/Paste   (c) Cut/Paste   (d) Copy/Copy
24. To paste text, press the _____ keys
    (a) Ctrl + X   (b) Ctrl + C   (c) Ctrl + P   (d) Ctrl + V
25. _____ button is used to enlarge the font size of the text.
    (a) Large   (b) Grow   (c) Big   (d) Increase
26. Each time the Shrink button is clicked, the font is reduced by ___ point(s).
    (a) 1   (b) 2   (c) 3   (d) 4
27. The default font color in MS Word 2010 is _____.
    (a) white   (b) red   (c) black   (d) gray

28. The default font in MS Word 2010 is _____.
    (a) Times New Roman   (b) Comic Sans
    (c) Arial   (d) Calibri

29. The default font size in MS Word 2010 is _____.
    (a) 10   (b) 11   (c) 12   (d) 14

30. _____ determines the blank space on each side of a paragraph.
    (a) Alignment   (b) Line Spacing   (c) Margin   (d) Paragraph Spacing

31. To get capital letter, press the letter along with _____ key.
    (a) Ctrl   (b) Alt   (c) Shift   (d) Insert

32. _____ case option reverses the case of every individual character.
    (a) Upper   (b) Lower   (c) Sentence   (d) Toggle

33. _____ stores data in a table.
    (a) Row   (b) Column   (c) Cell   (d) Grid

34. While resizing a table, you can change the cell's _____.
    (a) height   (b) width   (c) both   (d) None of these.

35. To divide a cell into multiple cells, you will use the _____ command.
    (a) merge   (b) divide   (c) split   (d) break

36. To follow a hyperlink, click the hyperlink while holding down the _____ key on your keyboard.
    (a) Alt   (b) Ctrl   (c) Shift   (d) Enter

State True or False

1. Word comes as a part of Microsoft Office suite.
2. You cannot apply themes in MS Word.
3. You can create bills in MS Word.
4. It is not possible to create flyers and letter heads in MS Word.
5. Word can process only text.
6. In Word, you can create documents meant to be printed on A4 size page only.
7. You can insert page margins in a Word document.
8. After a line is complete, you must use the Enter key to move to the next line.
9. You can customize the Quick Access Toolbar.
10. Vertical ruler is displayed on the right side of the Word window.
11. Cursor represents the location where text will be inserted when you type.
12. Status bar cannot be customized.
13. To create a new document press Ctrl + D.
14. Every time you make changes to a Word document, it must be saved.
15. To save a document every time you make changes to it, you must use Save As option.
16. Headers, footers and page numbers can be placed outside the page margins.
17. In landscape orientation, page is displayed vertically.
18. To print a page, press Alt + P keys.

19. It is possible to select which section of the document has to be printed.
20. It is possible to print only even pages of a document.
21. While editing a document, you can delete some text.
22. To delete text, you can either use the Delete key or Backspace key.
23. Delete key is pressed to delete the character behind the cursor.
24. To select a single word, right click on the text.
25. The Cut command must always be followed by the Copy command.
26. Cut–Paste is used to duplicate some content at another location.
27. When you perform Copy or Cut operations, Word stores the data temporarily in the clipboard.
28. Ctrl + C keys are pressed to cut a text.
29. To create multiple duplicate copies, you can paste as many times as you want.
30. Cut, Copy and Paste operations can be performed across multiple documents.
31. You can change the font using the Insert tab.
32. A text is said to be justified if it is aligned with both left and right margins.
33. Text created using WordArt is non-editable.
34. A numbered list is also called an unordered list.
35. Using different cases in our document makes our text more readable.
36. You can add a 3D effect to a callout.
37. It is not possible to insert text within an arrow.
38. Bevel effect adds thickness and a rounded edge to shapes.
39. A cell in a table can store a picture.
40. Once a table is created, you cannot add or delete rows or columns from it.
41. You can add only thick black border to a document.
42. The default font size of text in a header is larger than the text in the document area.
43. Headers and footers are non-editable sections in a Word document.

ANSWER KEYS

Multiple Choice Questions

1. (b)	2. (d)	3. (a)	4. (c)	5. (a)	6. (a)	7. (b)	8. (b)
9. (c)	10. (d)	11. (a)	12. (d)	13. (b)	14. (c)	15. (d)	16. (a)
17. (b)	18. (a)	19. (c)	20. (d)	21. (c)	22. (a)	23. (c)	24. (d)
25. (b)	26. (a)	27. (c)	28. (d)	29. (b)	30. (c)	31. (c)	32. (d)
33. (c)	34. (c)	35. (c)	36. (b)				

State True or False

1. True	2. False	3. True	4. False	5. False	6. False	7. True	8. False
9. True	10. False	11. True	12. False	13. False	14. True	15. False	16. False
17. True	18. False	19. True	20. True	21. True	22. True	23. False	24. False
25. False	26. False	27. True	28. False	29. True	30. True	31. False	32. True
33. False	34. False	35. True	36. True	37. False	38. False	39. True	40. False
41. False	42. False	43. False					

CHAPTER 10
Spreadsheet

KEY POINTS

- Microsoft Excel is a commercial spreadsheet application developed by Microsoft.
- In Excel, a cell is addressed using a combination of its row number and column number.
- Saving a workbook automatically saves all its worksheets.
- Microsoft Excel cell can hold data of different types like Numbers, Currency, Dates, etc.
- You can change the width of column(s) by dragging the right boundary of the column heading until the column has the desired width.
- The result of formula is displayed in the cell that has been currently selected and contains the formula.
- The name of every function is followed by brackets. In between the brackets, the arguments (range of cells) are specified.
- When the data of a cell(s) is linked to other cells, then data is dynamically pulled from the source cell(s) into the linked cell(s).
- Conditional formatting applies different formats to data that meets certain conditions.
- Add-ins provide optional commands and features for Microsoft Excel that is, by default, not available in Excel.

KEYWORDS

Cell: Intersection of a row and a column.
Formula: An expression that performs a calculation.
Function: Predefined formulas that are already available in Excel.

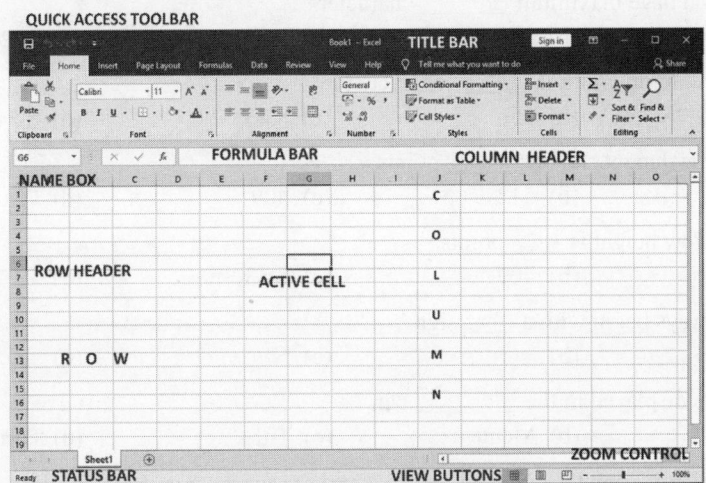

Microsoft Excel sheet

MODEL QUESTION PAPER

Multiple Choice Questions

1. Excel was developed by _____.
   - (a) Adobe
   - (b) Google
   - (c) Firefox
   - (d) Microsoft

2. Excel is a/an _____ software.
   - (a) application
   - (b) word processing
   - (c) graphics
   - (d) presentation

3. A file in Excel is saved using the _____ extension.
   - (a) .pptx
   - (b) .docx
   - (c) .xlsx
   - (d) .shtx

4. In which layout of Excel, pages are displayed as they will appear when printed?
   - (a) Normal Layout
   - (b) Page Layout
   - (c) Page Break View Layout
   - (d) None of these.

5. You can have maximum _____ columns in your Excel sheet.
   - (a) 16384
   - (b) 655356
   - (c) 1,048,576
   - (d) 12345

6. To print a page, you can press _____ keys.
   - (a) Ctrl + T
   - (b) Ctrl + P
   - (c) Alt + P
   - (d) Alt + T

7. When you open a workbook, Excel gives you ____ worksheets
   - (a) 1
   - (b) 2
   - (c) 3
   - (d) 4

8. _____ is an individual addressable location in an Excel sheet.
   - (a) Cell
   - (b) Row
   - (c) Column
   - (d) All of these.

9. A cell reference or address can also be specified as _____.
   - (a) SheetName.Cell
   - (b) SheetName&Cell
   - (c) SheetName#Cell
   - (d) SheetName!Cell

10. Pressing Shift + F11 would _____ a worksheet.
    - (a) insert
    - (b) delete
    - (c) edit
    - (d) save

11. A column can have maximum _____ characters.
    - (a) 128
    - (b) 255
    - (c) 512
    - (d) 1024

12. The default column width is _____ characters.
    - (a) 255
    - (b) 256
    - (c) 8.43
    - (d) 8.34

13. Maximum row height can be _____ points.
    - (a) 255
    - (b) 512
    - (c) 409
    - (d) 72

14. The default row height is ____ points.
    - (a) 72
    - (b) 409
    - (c) 8.43
    - (d) 12.75

15. Formulas always begin with a ____ sign.
    - (a) !
    - (b) =
    - (c) >
    - (d) –

16. Formulas are displayed in the _____ bar.
    - (a) Status
    - (b) Menu
    - (c) Title
    - (d) Formula

17. Which function is used to find the most frequently occurring number?
    - (a) Mean
    - (b) Median
    - (c) Mode
    - (d) Count

18. Which function is used to is get the current date and time?
    (a) Date   (b) Time   (c) Year   (d) Now
19. Round(123.789065, 3) will give the result _____.
    (a) 123   (b) 123.789   (c) 23.7   (d) 789
20. Excel allows you to nest up to ____ if functions.
    (a) 6   (b) 7   (c) 8   (d) 9
21. Which function returns the position of a value in the specified range?
    (a) index   (b) pos   (c) match   (d) loc
22. Which chart is used to show comparisons among individual data item?
    (a) Column   (b) Bar   (c) Pie   (d) Line
23. Which chart is used to compare the aggregate values of a number of data series?
    (a) Bubble   (b) Radar   (c) Surface   (d) Line
24. To create links between data, you should use _____ command.
    (a) Copy   (b) Paste   (c) Paste special (d) Paste link
25. Which option is used to change the orientation of the pasted entries?
    (a) Transpose   (b) Paste link   (c) Formats   (d) Values
26. _____ are defined to perform same task or action on same type of data.
    (a) Formulas   (b) Functions   (c) Macros   (d) Charts
27. ____ allow users to record different tasks and apply them over, on some another portion of the data.
    (a) Formulas   (b) Functions   (c) Macros   (d) Charts
28. _____ provides optional commands and features for Microsoft Excel that is, by default, not available in Excel.
    (a) Formulas   (b) Functions   (c) Macros   (d) Add-ins

State True or False

1. You can analyze your data in Excel.
2. Page Layout view shows a preview of where pages will break when printed.
3. The address of the first cell in Excel is A0.
4. After column Z, the address of the column would be AB.
5. In Excel, a cell is addressed using its row number only.
6. When writing the address of a cell, the column letter always precedes the row number.
7. Excel does not allow you to print only some selected sheets.
8. You must individually save all the worksheets.
9. You can insert/delete worksheets from the Excel Workbook.
10. You can insert a row or column in a worksheet.
11. Whenever a row/column is deleted, the row/column numbers have to be manually adjusted accordingly wherever they are referenced.
12. 1 point equals approximately 1/72 inch.
13. If you set the row height to 0, the column is hidden.

14. You can change the height of row(s) by dragging the boundary below the row heading until the row has the desired height.
15. Formulas can be written using cell addresses.
16. The result of formula is displayed in cell A1.
17. Formulas once entered cannot be edited.
18. You can copy a formula by clicking on the cell having the formula and then dragging the mouse across other cells.
19. OR operator requires that all the conditions must be true to give *true* result.
20. Match returns a specific value in a range.
21. An area chart is used to show the size of items that make up a data series, proportional to the sum of the items.
22. Pie chart can contain more than one data series.
23. When you save your file in another format, some of its formatting, data or features may not be saved.
24. Excel allows you to hide a row in its sheet.
25. Excel allows you to link cells that are in the worksheets of the same workbook.
26. It is possible to copy and paste only the cell width and not its content.
27. Paste special command allows you to copy every piece of information about the cell(s) except its border.
28. You can apply only one rule in conditional formatting.
29. In Excel, you can apply different sorting order for different columns in the same worksheet.
30. When data is sorted, only rows that meet the filter criteria will be displayed and others will be hidden.
31. To analyze summary data, you can use pivot tables and charts.
32. You cannot record mouse clicks while recording a macro.
33. You can download add-ins from the Internet and even create them on your own.
34. Inactivating an add-in removes it from your computer.
35. To remove an add-in from your computer you must uninstall it.

ANSWER KEYS

Multiple Choice Questions

1. (d)   2. (a)   3. (c)   4. (b)   5. (a)   6. (b)   7. (c)   8. (a)
9. (d)   10. (a) 11. (b) 12. (c) 13. (c) 14. (d) 15. (b) 16. (d)
17. (c) 18. (d) 19. (b) 20. (b) 21. (c) 22. (b) 23. (b) 24. (d)
25. (a) 26. (c) 27. (c) 28. (d)

State True or False

1. True   2. False   3. False   4. False   5. False   6. True   7. False   8. False
9. True   10. True   11. False 12. True   13. True   14. True   15. True   16. False
17. False 18. True   19. False 20. True   21. False 22. False 23. True   24. True
25. False 26. True   27. True   28. False 29. True   30. False 31. True   32. False
33. True   34. False 35. True

CHAPTER 11
Microsoft PowerPoint

KEY POINTS

- Microsoft PowerPoint is presentation software developed by Microsoft.
- Slide Views are a group of four buttons present to the left of the Zoom control, near the bottom of the screen. It helps you to switch between PowerPoint views.
- You can create PowerPoint templates to make your presentation contain thoughtful arrangement of elements and color, fonts, effects, style, and layout.
- PowerPoint allows users to create presentations containing text, images, sounds and other media objects.
- Headers and/or footers are added to include important information about the slides.

KEYWORDS

Presentation: Document prepared in Microsoft Presentation.
Slide Area: Area where the slide is created and edited.

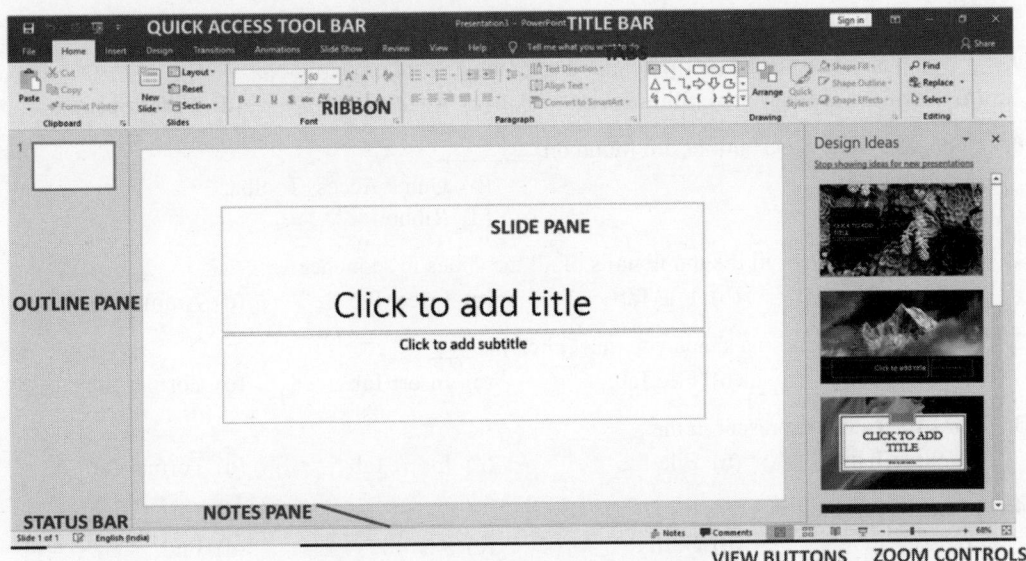

Microsoft PowerPoint application

MODEL QUESTION PAPER

Multiple Choice Questions

1. PowerPoint was developed by _____.
   (a) Microsoft   (b) Apple   (c) Google   (d) Apache

2. Presentation is saved with an extension _____.
   (a) .ppt   (b) .pptx   (c) ppts   (d) .pptd

3. _____ tab is used to create a new presentation.
   (a) File   (b) Insert   (c) Slide Show   (d) Animations

4. Tabs are present in the _____.
   (a) File   (b) Insert   (c) Ribbon   (d) Animations

5. _____ is the area where the slide is created and edited
   (a) Title bar   (b) Ribbon   (c) Tabs   (d) Slide area

6. _____ displays a list of topics which you can browse to find details about a topic of your choice.
   (a) Status Bar   (b) Search Bar   (c) Help   (d) Ribbon

7. _____ consists of a slider that can be slid left or right to zoom in or out.
   (a) Status Bar   (b) Zoom Control
   (c) View Buttons   (d) Title Bar

8. _____ view is useful while editing individual slides and rearranging them.
   (a) Normal Layout   (b) Slide Sorter   (c) Reading   (d) Notes Section

9. _____ is not displayed on the screen during the presentation.
   (a) Normal Layout   (b) Slide Sorter   (c) Reading   (d) Notes Section

10. Undo, Redo and Save buttons are found on _____.
    (a) Status Bar   (b) Quick Access Toolbar
    (c) Title Bar   (d) Ribbon

11. _____ displays all the thumbnails of all the slides in sequence.
    (a) Slide Tab   (b) File Tab   (c) Insert Tab   (d) Animations Tab

12. To apply 3D effects on a shape you must click the _____.
    (a) Slide Tab   (b) File Tab   (c) Insert Tab   (d) Format Tab

13. WordArt feature is present in the _____.
    (a) Slide Tab   (b) File Tab   (c) Insert Tab   (d) Format Tab

14. To end a presentation, press the _____ key.
    (a) Esc   (b) Shift   (c) Alt   (d) End

15. Rehearse Timing command is available in the _____.
    (a) Slide Show Tab   (b) File Tab   (c) Insert Tab   (d) Format Tab

16. _____ view displays the time of each slide in your presentation.
    (a) Normal Layout (b) Slide Sorter
    (c) Notes Section (d) Reading

17. To record narration with your presentation, you must have a _____.
    (a) speaker   (b) webcam   (c) microphone   (d) headset

State True or False

1. Microsoft PowerPoint can be used on Mac OS.
2. You can incorporate other Microsoft objects in your presentation.
3. In Normal Layout view, slides are displayed as matrix.
4. You can edit the slides in Reading View.
5. In Reading View, you can start the slide show from any slide.
6. Images are written in the placeholder.
7. A presentation can have slides with different layout.
8. You can delete slides from the Slide Sorter View.
9. You cannot create animated presentations in PowerPoint.
10. Resizing and scaling stretches or shrinks the dimensions of an object.
11. You can insert the name of the company/organization in Header section of your slides.
12. Headers and Footers buttons are present in the Format Tab.
13. There is a single Notes Page for all the slides in the presentation.
14. A presentation must be presented by a person, always.
15. You can choose not to show certain slides during a slide show.
16. In self-running presentation, automatic timing is set.
17. You can either allot same time for every slide or give each slide a different time to display during a slideshow.
18. You can apply transition effects in the Slide Sorter View.
19. The size of a narration-recorded presentation is less than the presentation without a recorded narration.
20. You can record narration from the Slide Show Tab.

ANSWER KEYS

Multiple Choice Questions

1. (a)   2. (b)   3. (a)   4. (c)   5. (d)   6. (c)   7. (b)   8. (a)
9. (d)   10. (b)   11. (a)   12. (d)   13. (c)   14. (a)   15. (a)   16. (b)
17. (c)

State True or False

1. True   2. True   3. False   4. False   5. True   6. False   7. True   8. True
9. False   10. True   11. True   12. False   13. False   14. False   15. True   16. True
17. True   18. True   19. False   20. True

CHAPTER 12
Microsoft Access

KEY POINTS

- Microsoft Access allows you to link related information easily. It can also import or link directly to data stored in other applications and databases.
- Databases in Access are composed of tables, queries, forms, and report objects.
- In Access, a field can store different types of data.
- A field name can have 1 to 64 characters.
- An auto-number field stores an integer whose value increases or decreases automatically as new records are added or deleted.
- Access uses table relationships to join tables when you need to use them in a database object.
- You can create a query using Query Wizard and Query Design.
- Forms are used often as they provide an easy way to guide people in entering data correctly.
- Access offers you the ability to create a report from any table or query.

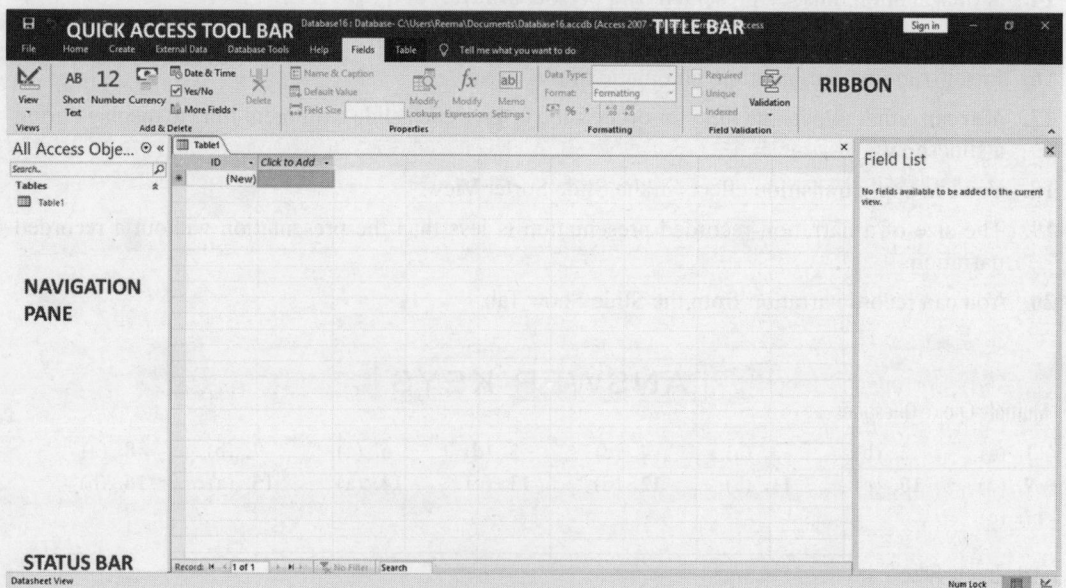

Microsoft Access Database application

KEYWORDS

Microsoft Access: A DBMS from Microsoft that combines the relational Microsoft Jet Database Engine with a graphical user interface and software development tools.

Database: An organized collection of data.

Table: An object that is used to define and store data.

Primary key Used to uniquely identify each record in a table.

Foreign key: A field (or collection of fields) in one table that uniquely identifies a row of another table or the same table.

Query: An object that provides a custom view of data from one or more tables.

Form: An object in a desktop database designed primarily for data input or display or for control of application execution.

Report: An object in desktop database designed for formatting, calculating, printing and summarizing selected data.

MODEL QUESTION PAPER

Multiple Choice Questions

1. Queries in Access can be used _____.
   (a) to view, change and analyze data in different ways
   (b) as a source of records for forms and reports
   (c) Both (a) and (b)
   (d) None of these.

2. To create queries in Access _____.
   (a) you can drag and drop fields on query builders
   (b) you can type the SQL command in SQL view
   (c) you can use query wizard or design view
   (d) All of the above.

3. Query design window has two parts. The upper part shows:
   (a) Name of fields, field type and size
   (b) Tables with fields and relationships between tables
   (c) Criteria
   (d) Sorting check boxes.

4. What does the show check box in query design window indicate?
   (a) It indicates whether the field is to be used or not.
   (b) It indicates whether the field is to be displayed in query result or not.
   (c) It indicates whether the field name is to be displayed in query result or not.
   (d) None of above.

5. What is a form in MS Access?
   (a) It is a printed page where users will write their data to fill it up.
   (b) It is an input screen designed to make the viewing and entering data easier.

> If you are unable to redeem the licence key, you may have a pirated or second-hand book. To buy an original book with a valid licence key, please go to www.orientblackswan.com or contact customercare@orientblackswan.com.

(c) This is an important part of database used by analysts to draw conclusions.
(d) All of the above.

6. Which of the following statement is true?
    (a) Reports can be used to retrieve data from tables and calculate.
    (b) Queries can be printed in a well-formatted manner and presented as information.
    (c) Queries can include calculated fields that do not exist in table.
    (d) Reports and forms are similar but forms are used to print whereas reports display on screen only.

7. Two tables can be linked with relationship so that the data integrity can be enforced. Where can you find Relationship command?
    (a) File menu (b) View menu (c) Database menu (d) Tools menu

8. To create relationship between two tables,
    (a) drag the primary key of a table into the foreign key of another table.
    (b) drag the foreign key of a table into the primary key of another table.
    (c) drag any field from parent table and drop on child table.
    (d) Any of above can be done to create relationship.

9. What happens when you release the mouse pointer after you drop the primary key of a table into foreign key of another table?
    (a) A relationship is created
    (b) Edit relationship dialog box appears
    (c) Error occurs
    (d) Nothing happens.

10. What do you mean by one-to-many relationship between Student and Class table?
    (a) One student can have many classes
    (b) One class may have many students
    (c) Many classes may have many students
    (d) Many students may have many classes.

11. Referential integrity means:
    (a) Do not enter a value in the foreign key field of a child table if that value does not exist in the primary key of the parent table.
    (b) Do not enter a value in the primary key field of child table if that value does not exist in the primary key of the parent table.
    (c) Do not enter a value in the foreign key field of a parent table if that value does not exist in the primary key of the child table.
    (d) All of the above.

12. We can remove a relationship defined between two tables:
    (a) From Edit menu, choose Delete Relationship
    (b) Select the relationship line and press Delete
    (c) Choose Delete option from Relationship menu
    (d) All of the above.

13. If you need to edit a relationship,
    (a) Right click the relationship line and choose Edit Relationship
    (b) Double click the relationship line
    (c) Both of the above.
    (d) None of the above.

14. If you write criteria values vertically (one in a row) it will mean:
    (a) OR conditions
    (b) AND conditions
    (c) NOT condition
    (d) None of above.

15. To achieve AND effect when you are entering criteria in a query design window,
    (a) write criteria values vertically, one in a row
    (b) write criteria values horizontally
    (c) write criteria values in same field separated with AND
    (d) write criteria values in same field separated with &.

16. When a picture or graphic image is placed in the report header section, it will appear____.
    (a) once at the beginning of the report
    (b) at the top of every page
    (c) every after record break
    (d) on the first and last pages of the report.

17. This data type allows alphanumeric characters and special symbols.
    (a) Text
    (b) Memo
    (c) Auto number
    (d) None of the above.

18. In a database table, the category of information is called _____.
    (a) Tuple
    (b) Field
    (c) Record
    (d) All of above.

19. To create a new table, in which method you don't need to specify the field type and size?
    (a) Create Table in Design View
    (b) Create Table using wizard
    (c) Create Table by entering data
    (d) All of above.

20. Which of the following is not a database object?
    (a) Tables
    (b) Queries
    (c) Relationships
    (d) Reports

21. The third stage in designing a database is when we analyze our tables more closely and create a _____ between tables.
    (a) Relationship
    (b) Join
    (c) Query
    (d) None of these.

22. The size of Yes/No field is always _____.
    (a) 1 bit
    (b) 1 byte
    (c) 1 character
    (d) 1 GB

23. This is the stage in database design where one gathers and lists all the necessary fields for the database project.
    (a) Data definition
    (b) Data refinement
    (c) Establishing relationship
    (d) None of the above.

24. The size of a field with Number data type cannot be _____.
    (a) 2
    (b) 4
    (c) 8
    (d) 16

25. This key uniquely identifies each record:
    (a) Primary key
    (b) Key record
    (c) Unique key
    (d) Field name

26. A database language concerned with the definition of the whole database structure and schema is _____.
    (a) DCL
    (b) DML
    (c) DDL
    (d) All of the above.

27. When creating a new table, which method can be used to choose fields from standard databases and tables?
    (a) Create table in Design View
    (b) Create table using wizard
    (c) Create table by Entering data
    (d) None of the above.

28. What happens when you release the mouse pointer after you drop the primary key of a table into the foreign key of another table?
    (a) A relationship is created
    (b) Edit relationship dialog box appears
    (c) Error occurs
    (d) Nothing happens.

29. Which field type will you select when creating a new table if you want to enter long text in that field?
    (a) Text   (b) Memo   (c) Currency   (d) Hyperlink

30. In Table Design view what are the first column of buttons used for?
    (a) Indicate Primary Key
    (b) Indicate Current Row
    (c) Both of the above.
    (d) None of the above.

31. This option allows you to build a new table by entering data directly into the datasheet.
    (a) Datasheet View
    (b) Design View
    (c) Link Table
    (d) None of the above.

32. Which is not a view to display a table in Access?
    (a) Datasheet View
    (b) Design View
    (c) Pivot Table and Pivot Chart View
    (d) None of the above.

33. Which of the following database objects hold data?
    (a) Forms   (b) Reports   (c) Queries   (d) Tables

34. A _____ enables you to view data from a table based on a specific criterion.
    (a) Form   (b) Query   (c) Macro   (d) Report

35. When entering field name, how many characters you can type in maximum?
    (a) 60
    (b) 64
    (c) 68
    (d) Any number of characters.

36. It is a database object to view, change, and analyze data in different ways:
    (a) Query   (b) Form   (c) Report   (d) None of the above.

37. Which of the following creates a drop down list of values to choose from a list?
    (a) OLE Object   (b) Hyperlink   (c) Memo   (d) Lookup Wizard

38. Which field type can store photos?
    (a) Hyperlink
    (b) OLE
    (c) Both of these can be used.
    (d) Access tables can't store photos.

39. Microsoft Access is a/an
    (a) RDBMS
    (b) OODBMS
    (c) ORDBMS
    (d) Network database model.

40. What are the columns In a Microsoft Access Table called?
    (a) Rows   (b) Records   (c) Fields   (d) Columns

41. Which of the following is not a Type of Microsoft Access Database object?
    (a) Table   (b) Form   (c) Worksheets   (d) Modules

42. Which of the fields has a width of 8 Bytes?
    (a) Memo   (b) Number   (c) Date/time   (d) Hyperlink

43. Which of the following statement is True?
    (a) Foreign key fields do not allow duplicate values
    (b) In primary key field you cannot enter duplicate value
    (c) Both (a) and (b).
    (d) None of these.

44. Which of the following is not a database model?
    (a) Network database model
    (b) Relational database model
    (c) Object-oriented database model
    (d) None of the above.

45. This is the stage in database design where one gathers and lists all the necessary fields for the database project.
    (a) Data definition
    (b) Data refinement
    (c) Establishing relationship
    (d) None of the above.

46. The third stage in designing a database is when we analyze our tables more closely and create a _____ between the tables.
    (a) Relationship
    (b) Join
    (c) Query
    (d) None of these.

47. To create primary key for a table when in design view,
    (a) type Primary in field type box when creating required field.
    (b) mark the Primary check box in field name of required field.
    (c) click the primary key button in Design ribbon when the cursor is in required field.
    (d) None of these.

48. A composite key is
    (a) required when a table does not have any unique fields in it.
    (b) the primary key with AutoNumber as the field type.
    (c) made up of two or more fields to uniquely identify records.
    (d) is a foreign key that uniquely identifies records.

49. If we create 'Student' field in 'Fees' table to store 'student_id' of 'Students' table, then this 'Student' field in 'Fees' table is called:
    (a) Foreign Key
    (b) Native Key
    (c) Composite Key
    (d) Primary Key

50. Which of the following expresses the correct order?
    (a) Characters, Fields, Records, Tables, Files, Databases
    (b) Characters, Fields, Records, Tables, Databases, Fields
    (c) Databases, Tables, Files, Records, Fields, Characters
    (d) Files, Databases, Tables, Records, Fields, Characters

51. Each record is constituted by a number of individual data items, which are called:
    (a) Fields
    (b) Data Types
    (c) Relations
    (d) Tables

52. A database object in MS-Access that stores a question about the data in database is _____.
    (a) Table
    (b) Form
    (c) Query
    (d) Report

53. The task of arranging data in order is called:
    (a) Searching
    (b) Sorting
    (c) Ordering
    (d) All of the above.

54. Collection of related records in a database is known as:
    (a) File (b) Bench (c) Table (d) Relationship
55. Both conditions display on the same row in the design grid when operator is in use:
    (a) OR (b) AND (c) LIKE (d) IN
56. In MS-Access, to open new database, press _____.
    (a) Ctrl + N (b) Ctrl + O (c) Alt + F4 (d) None of these.
57. While creating relationship, when you drag a field to drop into another table, the mouse pointer changes into:
    (a) A doctor's sign (b) Thin + sign (c) Outline rectangle (d) None of these.
58. What is the result of "Select * from customer where CustID>10 and CustID<100" query?
    (a) Display all customers with CustID from 0 to 100
    (b) Display all customers with CustID above 10
    (c) Display all customers with CustID below 100
    (d) Display all customers with CustID from 11 and 99.
59. You have field 'Sex' of type Byte Number. How to limit its value to 0 and 1 only?
    (a) By setting requires to 'Yes'
    (b) By using default value
    (c) By defining validation rule
    (d) By using format.
60. What do you call the process of restricting the display of records in a table to those matching a particular criterion?
    (a) Filtering (b) Restricting (c) Sorting (d) Shifting
61. In MS-Access, AutoNumber data type _____.
    (a) can be sequential (b) can be random (c) can be edited (d) Only (a) and (b)
62. Which of the following is an invalid field name?
    (a) Employee.Name (b) Employee\'sName (c) Employee_Name (d) Employee Name
63. Query can be used to select data from _____.
    (a) single table (b) multiple tables (c) both A and B (d) None of these.
64. Data can be imported into Access Database from _____.
    (a) Word Files (b) Excel Files (c) PowerPoint Files (d) HTML Files
65. In MS-Access, Field value may contain _____.
    (a) Text (b) Date and Time (c) Picture (d) All of the above.
66. Which of the following relationship is not valid in MS-Access?
    (a) Many to Many (b) Many to Null (c) One to One (d) One to Many
67. A(n) _____ is the default control for a Yes/No field.
    (a) Check box (b) Option button (c) Toggle button (d) List box
68. Which of the following queries modifies fields but not records?
    (a) Append (b) Delete (c) Make-Table (d) Update
69. Which type of field is incremented automatically?
    (a) Auto Elevate (b) AutoNumber (c) AutoIncrement (d) AutoValue

70. Which object is used to create a form?
    (a) Tables and Queries
    (b) Tables only
    (c) Tables and Reports
    (d) Queries and reports

71. The basic elements of a form or a report are called:
    (a) Controls
    (b) Objects
    (c) Windows
    (d) Properties

72. In MS-Access, to open an existing database, press:
    (a) Ctrl + N
    (b) Ctrl + O
    (c) Alt + F4
    (d) None of these.

73. Which Form tool creates a new form that shows both form and datasheet views?
    (a) Form
    (b) Form Wizard
    (c) Multiple Item Form
    (d) Split Form

ANSWER KEYS

Multiple Choice Questions

1. (d)	2. (d)	3. (b)	4. (b)	5. (b)	6. (c)	7. (d)	8. (a)	
9. (b)	10. (a)	11. (a)	12. (b)	13. (c)	14. (a)	15. (d)	16. (a)	
17. (a)	18. (b)	19. (c)	20. (c)	21. (a)	22. (a)	23. (a)	24. (d)	
25. (a)	26. (c)	27. (b)	28. (b)	29. (b)	30. (c)	31. (a)	32. (d)	
33. (d)	34. (b)	35. (b)	36. (a)	37. (d)	38. (b)	39. (a)	40. (c)	
41. (c)	42. (c)	43. (b)	44. (d)	45. (a)	46. (a)	47. (c)	48. (c)	
49. (a)	50. (a)	51. (a)	52. (c)	53. (b)	54. (c)	55. (b)	56. (a)	
57. (c)	58. (d)	59. (c)	60. (a)	61. (d)	62. (a)	63. (c)	64. (b)	
65. (d)	66. (b)	67. (a)	68. (d)	69. (b)	70. (a)	71. (a)	72. (b)	
73. (d)								

SOLVED PAPER – 1

Multiple Choice Questions

1. The application required to access the Internet services and resources available on the World Wide Web.
   (a) Web Browsers   (b) Web Servers   (c) ISP   (d) None of them.

2. The output of the computer's printer in known as the _____.
   (a) COM   (b) Softcopy   (c) Hardcopy   (d) None of them.

3. The result of =ROUND(2.15,1) entered in a cell shows _____.
   (a) 2.1   (b) 2.2   (c) 2   (d) None of them.

4. The result of =MOD(-3,2) entered in a cell shows _____.
   (a) –1.5   (b) 1   (c) 0   (d) 1

5. Press _____ while you drag the corner handle, to alter the size of a chart without changing its proportion.
   (a) [F11]   (b) [Shift]   (c) [Ctrl]   (d) [Alt]

6. In MS-Excel, what is the default page orientation?
   (a) Portrait   (b) Horizontal
   (c) Language   (d) None of them.

7. What happens in MS-Excel, when you click on the Gridlines and Draft Quality check box on the sheet tab of page setup dialog box?
   (a) Sometimes print   (b) Gridlines will not be printed
   (c) Gridlines will be printed   (d) None of them.

8. How can you create a new blank presentation in MS-PowerPoint.
   (a) Click on the New button   (b) Use the File New command
   (c) Both (a) and (b).   (d) None of them.

9. Change Case command appears in which Menu?
   (a) Insert   (b) Edit   (c) Slideshow   (d) Format

10. What should you do to make an inserted sound file play continuously over several slides in the presentation?
    (a) Use the Record Sound feature, press the Record button and play your music as you click through the whole slideshow
    (b) In the Custom Animation task pane, open Effects Options and set the sound to play for the desired number of slides
    (c) Using the Play CD Audio Track feature, set the CD to play for the desired number of tracks
    (d) All of them.

11. The area on the slide that holds the text to display in the presentation outline is a _____.
    (a) Bullet point   (b) Textbox   (c) Title box   (d) Placeholder

12. In MS-Excel the AutoFormat command in used to
    (a) easily apply a consistent format throughout a workbook.
    (b) choose between standard table formats that include borders, shading, font colors and other formatting options.
    (c) create a professional and consistent look for your data.
    (d) All of them.

13. Which of the following statements regarding search engines and directories is true?
    (a) A search engine does not differentiate between the good and bad sites.
    (b) A directory is someone's attempt to categorize among the best sites available for a given subject or topic.
    (c) A search engine shows all the Web pages that contains your keywords and may list thousands of unordered results.
    (d) All of them.

14. Which of the following is sent out by a search engine continuously to pursue all links, stepwise?
    (a) Spiders   (b) Packets
    (c) Cookies   (d) None of the above.

15. Which of the following option you would use for immediate and real-time communication with your friend?
    (a) Blog   (b) Usenet   (c) Instant Messaging   (d) E-mail

16. Internet uses _____.
    (a) Packet switching   (b) Hybrid switching   (c) Circuit switching   (d) None of them.

17. What is the ascending order of a data hierarchy?
    (a) Byte-bit-field-record-file-database
    (b) Bit-byte-record-field-file-database
    (c) Byte-bit-record-file-field-database
    (d) Bit-byte-field-record-file-database

18. Software instructions intended to satisfy the user's specific processing requirements is known as _____.
    (a) Application software   (b) System software
    (c) Microcomputer   (d) Documentation

19. In computer terminology, what does the word 'information' means?
    (a) Raw   (b) Data in more useful or intelligible form
    (c) Alphanumeric data program   (d) Data

20. Which of the following comprise the Central Processing Unit?
    (a) Keyboard   (b) Printer
    (c) Arithmetic Logic Unit   (d) Tape

21. What do you mean from the term 'computer literacy'?
    (a) Ability to assemble computers
    (b) Ability to write computer programs
    (c) Knowing what a computer can and cannot do
    (d) Knowing computer-related vocabulary.

22. Which software application is often used for writing business letters?
    (a) Word processing
    (b) Database
    (c) Spreadsheet
    (d) Graphical presentation

23. A floppy disk contains _____.
    (a) Circular track only
    (b) Both circular tracks and sectors
    (c) Sectors only
    (d) None of them.

Types of network topography

24. The first page that is displayed of any Web site is known as?
    (a) Banner page   (b) First page   (c) Master page   (d) Home page

25. What is the use of the justification button in the toolbar?
    (a) To display the four options for aligning text
    (b) To open the justification dialog box
    (c) To enter the current line
    (d) To display a drop-down list of justification options.

26. The base of binary number system is _____.
    (a) 16   (b) 4   (c) 2   (d) 8

27. The purpose of arithmetic/logic operators is:
    (a) Do logical comparisons, such as equal to, greater than, less than
    (b) Do calculations using addition, subtraction, multiplication and division
    (c) To check data for accuracy
    (d) Both calculations and logical comparisons.

28. How does the CPU read information from the secondary memory?
    (a) RAM   (b) Through registers   (c) Directly   (d) None of them.

29. What is a plotter?
    (a) A fast output device using camera lenses
    (b) An output device used to produce drawings and graphics
    (c) An input device used to produce good quality graphics
    (d) None of them.

30. A _____ is a collection of buttons that represent various actions that can be performed in an application.
    (a) Buttons   (b) Toolbar   (c) Menu   (d) None of them.

31. What is the name of the topmost bar of any application window that displays the name of the document?
    (a) Title bar   (b) Status bar   (c) Menu bar   (d) Toolbar

32. Supercomputers are primarily used for
    (a) data retrieval operations.
    (b) Input-Output intensive processing.

(c) mathematical intensive scientific applications.
(d) None of them.

33. E-mail
    (a) cannot provide protection given to the first class mail.
    (b) cannot address too many users.
    (c) always requires bridge to send messages to different networks.
    (d) None of them.

34. Select the graphical package from the following.
    (a) CorelDraw   (b) MS-Word   (c) MS-Excel   (d) None of them.

35. Simulation of the airflow around an entire aircraft can only be done by using _____.
    (a) Microcomputers   (b) Minicomputers
    (c) Supercomputers   (d) None of these.

36. Which of the following rules below for range names is not correct?
    (a) Range names can directly be used in formulas.
    (b) Names cannot be the same as a cell reference.
    (c) The only separators allowed are underscore characters and/or periods between words.
    (d) In the range name you are can use spaces or commas.

37. Select the first step in MS-Word in changing line spacing from the following:
    (a) To open the Format Menu
    (b) To select the paragraphs you want to change
    (c) To open the Paragraph Menu
    (d) To click the Line Spacing button.

38. Joystick, Mouse and Trackball are what kind of devices?
    (a) Pen input devices   (b) Data collection devices
    (c) Pointing devices   (d) Multimedia devices

39. "Save As… Dialog Box" is used for what purpose?
    (a) Used for saving the file for the first time
    (b) To save file in a format other than Word document
    (c) To save the File by some other alternative name
    (d) All the above.

40. Contents on the Clipboard remains same until
    (a) you copy another text.   (b) you shut down your computer.
    (c) you cut another text.   (d) All of them.

41. In MS-Word, Borders are probably used where
    (a) you need to surround the paragraphs with different styles of boxes.
    (b) you need to draw lines above and below or to left and right of paragraphs.
    (c) you need to add emphasis to particular paragraphs.
    (d) All of them.

42. Where is the Formatting toolbar option applied?
    (a) To character selection only
    (b) To paragraph selection only

(c) To both character as well as paragraph selections
(d) None of them.

43. What is the use of page break in MS-Word?
    (a) Used to create a blank page at the top of the document
    (b) Used to create a new page that cannot be deleted
    (c) Used to create a new page at the bottom of the document
    (d) Used to create a new page at the insertion point.

44. Letter wizard command appears in which Word menu?
    (a) Format   (b) Table   (c) Tools   (d) Insert

45. Split cells command appears in which Word menu?
    (a) Table   (b) Tools   (c) Insert   (d) Format

46. What type of keys is displayed in the Status bar?
    (a) Scroll lock key   (b) Num lock key   (c) Caps lock key   (d) All of them.

47. In MS-Excel, the intersection of a row and column is known as _____.
    (a) Worksheet   (b) Cell   (c) Cubicle   (d) Square

48. In MS-Excel, once a range has been declared, you can go to a range _____.
    (a) by selecting ranges using the name box.
    (b) by selecting ranges using the [F5] key.
    (c) Both (a) and (b).
    (d) None of them.

49. Which of the following statement is not true?
    (a) In the default settings, the word processor does not hyphenate the text.
    (b) MS-Word hyphenates text in its default settings.
    (c) By hyphenating, the looks of the justified thin columns will look greatly improved.
    (d) Hyphenating helps when you are dealing with thin columnar text.

State True or False

1. Animation effects option appears in the Standard toolbar.
2. BIOS means Basic Integrated Operating System.
3. The LEN() function is used to calculate the length of the string.
4. The floating text or the text which is not associated with objects in the chart cannot be moved in the chart area.
5. You can preview a chart before printing in the same way as previewing a worksheet before printing.
6. You need to select Header and Footer option from the File menu, to insert header or footer to your worksheet.
7. In Windows, it is not possible to add items to the Start menu.
8. It is not possible to interchange the functionality between the left and right mouse buttons.
9. The AutoContent Wizard is used to create the structure and contents based on the customized choices.

10. MS-PowerPoint is loaded with more than 24 slide layouts options.
11. The option of Bullets and Numbering is not in the standard toolbar.
12. In MS-Excel, the cell names are not case sensitive.
13. In MS-PowerPoint you can add color scheme to the current slide or to all the slides in your presentation.
14. In MS-Excel 29 sales is a valid name for a cell.
15. MS-PowerPoint allows you to differentiate between your own animation effects.
16. Internet is classified as non-commercial information service.
17. Network NSFnet was renamed as Internet.
18. The IP address space is divided into five classes from A through E.
19. The Request for Comments (RFCs) core topics are not from Internet and the TCP/IP protocol suites.
20. The Back and Forward buttons are used to navigate between the pages from the same website.
21. POP1 is the protocol used for fetching the e-mail from the mailbox.
22. English is the language used for all the conversations on the IRC.
23. ISP means Internet Service Provider.
24. The smiley faces are the sequence of ordinary printable characters or small images, used to represent the human facial expressions to convey their emotions.
25. In MS-Word, you can stop the spelling checker option any time by clicking the close button.
26. In MS-Word, View menu is used to add header and footer.
27. Check-boxes are required to present options that need individual On/Off decisions in Message boxes.
28. Firmware means software that is embedded in the hardware device.
29. Secondary memory has smaller storage capacity than Primary memory.
30. F1 key can be used to get the Windows Help option.
31. In MS-Word you select an entire document by moving the pointer to the left of any document text until it changes to a right-pointing arrow, and then double-clicking it.
32. In MS-Word, [Ctrl] + [U] key allows you to underline the selected text.
33. A blank line is also considered as a paragraph and called an empty paragraph.
34. [Del] key deletes the character from the left side of the insertion point.
35. MS-Word has a number of AutoCorrect entries, which can only be used without any modification.
36. MS-Word allows you to create your own dictionaries.
37. The Insert function dialog box is used to enter your customized formula that contains a function in the worksheet functions.
38. In MS-Word, character spacing can be altered from the toolbar.
39. E-Commerce means distributing, buying, selling and marketing of products and services over Internet.
40. Word template includes the option of style formatting.

41. The Blank Web Page template of Word contains pre-formatted or pre-designed options.
42. In MS-Word, the Word organizer does not copy the AutoText entries.
43. In MS-Excel, different cells within the same row can have different heights.
44. In MS-Excel, the AutoFit to contents option enables the word to widen or narrow column dimensions based upon the inserted text.
45. Print Preview option does not allow you to do any kind of modification in the document.
46. Using the Mail Merge Helper dialog box, you can open an existing data source but cannot create a new one.
47. The name box is placed at the left end of the Formula bar.
48. In MS-Excel, delete and clear commands performs the same function.
49. Font style command cannot change the font style of the entire document by a single command.
50. Spelling and grammar check option can only be used once the text is selected.

ANSWER KEYS

Multiple Choice Questions

1. (a)   2. (c)   3. (b)   4. (d)   5. (c)   6. (a)   7. (b)   8. (c)
9. (d)   10. (b) 11. (b) 12. (d) 13. (d) 14. (a) 15. (c) 16. (a)
17. (d) 18. (a) 19. (b) 20. (c) 21. (c) 22. (a) 23. (b) 24. (d)
25. (a) 26. (c) 27. (d) 28. (a) 29. (b) 30. (b) 31. (a) 32. (c)
33. (d) 34. (a) 35. (c) 36. (d) 37. (b) 38. (c) 39. (d) 40. (d)
41. (d) 42. (c) 43. (d) 44. (c) 45. (a) 46. (d) 47. (b) 48. (c)
49. (b)

State True or False

1. False   2. False   3. True   4. False   5. True   6. False   7. False   8. False
9. True   10. True   11. True   12. True   13. True   14. False 15. True   16. True
17. False 18. True   19. False 20. False 21. True   22. False 23. True   24. True
25. True   26. True   27. True   28. True   29. False 30. True   31. False 32. True
33. True   34. False 35. False 36. True   37. True   38. False 39. True   40. True
41. False 42. False 43. False 44. True   45. False 46. False 47. True   48. False
49. False 50. False

SOLVED PAPER – 2

Multiple Choice Questions

1. The news readers present newsgroup articles in the _____.
   (a) Mail (b) Threads (c) Column (d) None of them.

2. What is the advantage of using Fiber optical cable?
   (a) It is free from any kind of interference. (b) It is easy to install than twisted wire.
   (c) It uses direct line-of-sight. (d) It is cheaper to install.

3. You can set up the margin for which of the following?
   (a) Footers (b) Headers (c) Both (a) and (b). (d) None of them.

4. Windows distinguishes between different drives through their naming convention; select the symbol designating the drive.
   (a) An asterisk (b) A semicolon
   (c) A colon (d) An exclamation point

5. Which of the following is a valid character while naming a file or folder in Windows?
   (a) ? (b) : (c) > (d) _

6. Select the presentation graphics software from the following.
   (a) MS-Excel (b) MS-PowerPoint (c) MS-Windows (d) MS-Word

7. To ensure that your presentation runs smoothly on different computers, you can bring _____.
   (a) your fonts (b) a copy of Microsoft PowerPoint Viewer
   (c) a copy of PowerPoint to install (d) None of them.

8. What should you do to update the slide each time you make original data changes, to the data you import?
   (a) Embed the data (b) Break the link
   (c) Link the data (d) Insert the data as an object.

9. In a PP slide, footer area appears at the _____.
   (a) bottom of the page (b) left of the page (c) top of the page (d) center of the page

10. Which of the following is a type of slide animation?
    (a) Flash once (b) Fly from top (c) Typewriter (d) All of them.

11. Which of the following is a slide transition effect?
    (a) Bit by bit (b) Dissolve (c) Wipe all over (d) None of them.

12. What is the purpose of built-in default copying in MS-Excel?
    (a) To use mixed position when copying formulas
    (b) To use absolute position when copying formulas
    (c) To use relative position when copying formulas
    (d) None of them.

13. Which of the following is responsible for governing the Internet?
    (a) IETF (Internet Engineering Task Force)
    (b) W3C (World Wide Web Consortium)
    (c) InterNIC (Internet Network Information Center)
    (d) None of them.

14. Which of the following is not the feature of MS-Excel?
    (a) Database functions such as filtering, sorting, etc.
    (b) Desktop publishing capabilities
    (c) Automatic calculation of numbers and formulas
    (d) Charging capabilities.

15. What is the e-mail component of Internet Explorer known as?
    (a) Message box
    (b) Outlook Express
    (c) Messenger Mailbox
    (d) None of them.

16. What is the 'USENET'?
    (a) A bulletin board system that helps in posting and responding to the messages on the Internet
    (b) Abbreviation of United States Electronic Network
    (c) A precursor to the Internet that has now become obsolete
    (d) A set of tools reserved exclusively for Internet administrators.

17. The CPU (Central Processing Unit) comprises of the following:
    (a) Input, Processing and Storage
    (b) Input, Output and Processing
    (c) Control unit, Arithmetic-logic and Primary storage
    (d) Control unit, Primary storage and Secondary storage.

18. What is the Control unit's function in CPU?
    (a) To perform logical operations
    (b) To transfer data top primary storage
    (c) To store program instructions
    (d) To decode program instructions.

19. Select the ascending order of a data hierarchy from the following.
    (a) Bit–byte–field–record–file–database
    (b) Byte–bit–record–file–field–database
    (c) Byte–bit–field–record–file–database
    (d) Bit–byte–record–field–file–database

20. Select the input device from the following.
    (a) Central Processing Unit
    (b) Motherboard
    (c) Keyboard
    (d) System Unit

21. Which kind of the following storage device is portable?
    (a) Main memory   (b) System cabinet   (c) Diskette   (d) Hard disk

22. When your computer is on but does not respond to the system reset, then the computer is said to be _____.
    (a) Insensitive   (b) Hung   (c) Off   (d) Dead

23. GIGO means _____.
    (a) "Gigabytes In, Gigabytes Out"
    (b) "Garbage Input, Garbage Output"
    (c) "Garbage In, Garbage Out"
    (d) None of them.

24. The memory stores the data _____ while the storage device stores the data _____.
    (a) Temporary, Permanent
    (b) Permanent, Temporary
    (c) Slow, Fast
    (d) None of them.

25. Which key should you use to go to slide number?
    (a) Slide Number + [Enter]
    (b) [PgUp] or [PgDown]
    (c) Both (a) and (b).
    (d) None of them.

26. Which of the following keys will help you to delete the selected sentence?
    (a) [Backspace]   (b) [Del]   (c) Both (a) and (b)   (d) None of them.

27. Computer understands _____ to execute its commands.
    (a) machine language
    (b) system program
    (c) application software
    (d) None of them.

28. What is the use of arithmetic and logical operators?
    (a) To perform both calculations and logical comparisons
    (b) To perform logical comparisons, such as equal to, greater than or less than
    (c) To perform calculations such as addition, subtraction, multiplication, and division
    (d) It is used to confirm data accuracy.

29. Why do we use MOVE command?
    (a) To rename directories
    (b) To move one or more files to the desired location
    (c) Both (a) and (b).
    (d) None of them.

30. GUI is an interface between
    (a) Hardware and Software
    (b) Software and User
    (c) User and Computer
    (d) None of them.

31. What do you understand by the word 'E-Mail'?
    (a) Exchange of messages over the computer
    (b) Mail concerning electronic device.
    (c) Exchange of letters, messages and memos over a communications network
    (d) None of them.

32. E-mail
    (a) is not capable of providing security to first class mail.
    (b) cannot address too many users.
    (c) Requires bridge to send messages between different networks.
    (d) None of them.

33. Which of the following is a capability of most of the workstations?
    (a) Numeric processing
    (b) Graphics
    (c) Text manipulation
    (d) None of them.

34. You can use the selection feature for which of the following?
    (a) A paragraph
    (b) Complete document
    (c) Single word or a line
    (d) All of them.

35. What do you mean by the term 'Word Wrap'?
    (a) To move text automatically to the next line
    (b) To insert spaces between words
    (c) To align text with the right margin
    (d) None of them.

36. What is the first step you follow in MS-Word to change line spacing?
    (a) To open the Paragraph menu.
    (b) To select the paragraphs you want to change.
    (c) To click the Line Spacing button.
    (d) To open the Format menu.

37. What do you mean by the Cell address B$6 in a formula?
    (a) It is an Absolute cell reference.
    (b) It is a Relative cell reference.
    (c) It is a Mixed cell reference.
    (d) All of them.

38. Why do we use Undo button?
    (a) To add the new text and delete the original text
    (b) To delete the new text and add the original text back
    (c) To delete the old text and add the new text back
    (d) None of them.

39. Which device is used to provide the power backup to the computer, when the power supply is disturbed?
    (a) Universal Power Protection and Supply (UPPS)
    (b) Uninterruptible Power Supply (UPS)
    (c) Universal Surge Protector (USP)
    (d) Power Supply Unit (PSU)

40. You've formatted some text, how can you quickly apply that formatting on other texts of the document?
    (a) By using the Format Painter button.
    (b) By using Formatting toolbar.
    (c) By using the Reveal Formatting option.
    (d) None of them.

41. How can you change the margin settings in MS-Word?
    (a) By using the Page setup
    (b) By using the ruler
    (c) Both (a) and (b).
    (d) None of them.

42. Template in MS-Word can be created _____.
    (a) based on an existing template
    (b) from the scratch
    (c) based on an existing document
    (d) All of them.

43. Letter wizard command is viewed in the _____ menu of the MS-Word.
    (a) Table   (b) Insert   (c) Format   (d) Tools

44. The use of sheet tab in the Letter wizard of MS-Word is for _____.
    (a) Recipient Info   (b) Letter Format   (c) Both (a) and (b).   (d) None of them.

45. Which of the following statements is not correct?
    (a) =SUM(above) formula is used to sum the values of all above cells of the current cell.
    (b) MS-Word is not capable of performing simple calculations.

(c) In MS-Word, you can perform simple calculations in a table using formula command.
(d) Simple calculations in a table means addition, subtraction, multiplication, division, etc.

46. What happens when you select Active Window option while using the Mail Merge Helper?
    (a) It opens a new document window.
    (b) It activates the document and automatically attaches it to the data source.
    (c) It creates a master document in the currently active document window.
    (d) None of them.

47. Which of the following are tear-off palettes?
    (a) FillColour   (b) FontColour   (c) LineColour   (d) All of them.

48. You can open a worksheet using the following option:
    (a) Open button   (b) Start button   (c) Both (a) and (b). (d) None of them.

49. Which of the following is the easiest step to select a column?
    (a) By pressing [Ctrl + A]
    (b) By dragging the top cell of the column to the last cell of the column
    (c) By double-clicking on any cell of the column
    (d) By clicking the heading of the column.

50. Which of the following options helps you to navigate in a Word document?
    (a) By moving to a specific page   (b) By scrolling
    (c) Both (a) and (b).   (d) None of them.

State True or False

1. It is possible to install Windows OS using your product key with different Windows OS software CD.
2. Hybrid computer is a combination of analog as well as digital computers.
3. It is not possible to alter the default decimal settings by using the increase and decrease decimal buttons.
4. In MS-Excel you can set the default currency symbol by setting it through the Regional Settings in Control Panel before opening the MS-Excel window.
5. In MS-Excel, the cell/range name should be the same as the cell/range reference.
6. In MS-Excel, the command '=SUM(Sheet1:Sheet12!B6)' adds all the values in cell B6 of all the worksheets ranging between Sheet 1 to Sheet 12.
7. In MS-Excel, omitting parenthesis while declaring a formula and pressing the [Enter] key, will not produce an error message.
8. The TIME() function is used to show the current time.
9. 3-D charts requires a category (x) axis a value (y) axis and a third (z) axis.
10. The purpose of using a Pie chart is to represent multiple series of data.
11. The Bubble chart can represent three variables on a two-dimensional chart.
12. After deleting a word sheet, you can click Undo button to bring back the sheet.
13. It is not possible to add different header and footer to each sheet of the workbook.
14. You can add a sheet at the end of the workbook.

15. In MS-PowerPoint, the Slide Sorter View automatically sorts the slides alphabetically.
16. In MS-PowerPoint, the font size and line spacing of the text adjust themselves to fit in the placeholder.
17. In MS-PowerPoint, you can split more than one cell of a table in a slide at a time.
18. In MS-PowerPoint, use F5 key to go to Slide Show View.
19. The different elements of a chart do not have different transitions.
20. 'Lycos' is not an example of Web portal or an Internet search engine.
21. Surfing is the process of browsing Web sites over Internet.
22. MSN Messenger is an e-mail component of Internet Explorer.
23. Netscape Communicator 4.0 includes the Netscape Messenger as the e-mail client.
24. There is no difference between the Usenet and the Internet.
25. You cannot select the data to be drawn as a chart in between the Chart wizard.
26. The Word Templates are saved with .dot extension.
27. Microcomputer consists of micro-processors.
28. BIOS means Basic Integrated Operating System.
29. A smart terminal does not have built-in processing feature.
30. The control unit is responsible for fetching the commands for its execution.
31. You can open as many Word documents at the same time as your Taskbar can display on the screen.
32. Before formatting a paragraph you need to select the paragraph to be formatted.
33. In MS-Word, the default Normal view displays 100% document screen.
34. MS-Word allows you to create your own dictionaries.
35. In MS-Word, you can apply spelling and grammar check only after selecting the text.
36. In MS-Word, you cannot apply different page-numbering styles to different sections of a document.
37. In MS-Excel, you use hash sign (#) to indicate absolute references.
38. In MS-Word, the View menu is used to add header and footer to your document.
39. You can converse on the IRC in different languages.
40. The word document can also be saved in html format by saving the document with .html extension.
41. In MS-Word, the new column added to the table retains the same format of the column next to which it is added.
42. You can shrink a document to a single page.
43. In MS-Word, Styles can be used to create table of contents quickly.
44. In MS-Word, the simplest way to resize a picture is by dragging its edges to adjust the size and shape to your requirement.
45. MS-Word does not allow you to add Graphics in the headers and footers of the document.
46. The Mail Merge Helper dialog box can be used to open an existing data source but cannot be used to create a new one.

47. In MS-Word, blank fields will be skipped by default; therefore, the merge will not be affected if the blank entries are in the data form.
48. In MS-Excel, the standard width of a column is 8.43.
49. In MS-Excel, [Ctrl] + [Spacebar] keys are used to select the entire row.
50. In MS-Word, we use [Ctrl] + [U] keys to underline the selected text.

ANSWER KEYS

Multiple Choice Questions

1. (b)	2. (a)	3. (c)	4. (c)	5. (d)	6. (b)	7. (b)	8. (d)		
9. (a)	10. (d)	11. (b)	12. (c)	13. (d)	14. (c)	15. (b)	16. (a)		
17. (b)	18. (d)	19. (a)	20. (c)	21. (c)	22. (b)	23. (c)	24. (a)		
25. (b)	26. (c)	27. (a)	28. (a)	29. (b)	30. (c)	31. (c)	32. (d)		
33. (d)	34. (d)	35. (a)	36. (b)	37. (c)	38. (d)	39. (b)	40. (a)		
41. (c)	42. (c)	43. (d)	44. (d)	45. (b)	46. (c)	47. (a)	48. (d)		
49. (d)	50. (c)								

State True or False

1. False	2. True	3. False	4. True	5. False	6. True	7. False	8. False
9. True	10. False	11. True	12. False	13. False	14. True	15. False	16. True
17. True	18. True	19. False	20. False	21. True	22. False	23. True	24. False
25. False	26. True	27. True	28. False	29. False	30. True	31. False	32. True
33. True	34. True	35. False	36. True	37. False	38. True	39. True	40. True
41. True	42. True	43. True	44. True	45. False	46. False	47. False	48. True
49. False	50. True						

SOLVED PAPER – 3

Multiple Choice Questions

1. Spelling command is displayed under _____ menu.
   (a) Edit   (b) Windows   (c) Tools   (d) View

2. What will happen, when we click the right mouse button on the Windows desktop?
   (a) The context-sensitive menu will be displayed.
   (b) The Display Properties dialog box will appear on the screen.
   (c) Control Panel will be displayed on the screen.
   (d) It will minimize all the opened applications.

3. What is the default alignment while typing numbers in a cell?
   (a) Center-aligned   (b) Justified   (c) Left-aligned   (d) Right-aligned

4. What do you mean by the Cell address $C$6 in a formula?
   (a) It is an Absolute cell reference.   (b) It is a Relative cell reference.
   (c) It is a Mixed cell reference.   (d) All of them.

5. In MS-Excel, whenever you create a chart on a separate sheet of the same workbook it is known as _____.
   (a) View chart   (b) View sheet   (c) Embedded chart   (d) Chart sheet

6. In MS-Excel, the page break command in the Insert menu will insert page break _____.
   (a) in the middle of the selected row   (b) above the selected row
   (c) below the selected row   (d) None of them.

7. What should you do in MS-Excel to print a specific area of the worksheet?
   (a) Use Page Setup dialog box to set the print area
   (b) Use File menu to set the print area
   (c) Both (a) and (b).
   (d) None of them.

8. You can use which of the following keys to quickly move between the open program windows?
   (a) Shift + Alt   (b) Shift + Tab   (c) Ctrl + Tab   (d) Alt + Tab

9. Why do we use AutoContent Wizard?
   (a) To create a new template for future use
   (b) To create new looks for an existing presentation
   (c) To create a new presentation with sample slides and suggestions about the information to be added
   (d) To create a new blank presentation with an attractive background and fonts.

10. In MS-PowerPoint, slide sorter command is displayed under _____ menu.
    (a) Edit   (b) View   (c) Tools   (d) File

11. While designing the slide presentation, your primary motive should be _____.
    (a) to make the information easy to read and understand
    (b) to make the slides interesting and exciting
    (c) to attract your audience
    (d) to coordinate with your company logo and color scheme.

12. In MS-Excel, the shortcut fill menu comprises of the _____.
    (a) Fill series   (b) Fill weekdays   (c) Both (a) and (b).   (d) None of them.

13. Alignment button is available in which toolbar?
    (a) Status bar
    (b) Standard toolbar
    (c) Formatting toolbar
    (d) None of them.

14. In MS-Excel, the Paste Special dialog box contains which options?
    (a) Formats and Formulas
    (b) Values
    (c) Transpose
    (d) All of them.

15. In MS-PowerPoint, you can add action buttons to the slide, by the Action button command in
    (a) Insert menu
    (b) Slide Show menu
    (c) View menu
    (d) None of them.

16. What should you do to update the Word document each time you make original data changes, to the data you import?
    (a) Embed the data
    (b) Break the link
    (c) Link the data
    (d) Insert the data as an object

17. Which of the following is an example of Slide Show option?
    (a) Browsed at a kiosk
    (b) Browsed by an individual
    (c) Presented by a speaker
    (d) All of them.

18. Which of the following is the first network that laid the foundation stone for the Internet?
    (a) Inet   (b) Vnet   (c) NSFnet   (d) ARPANET

19. If you want to create a small website, you need to buy web space from which of the following?
    (a) Telephone Exchange
    (b) Network Administrator
    (c) ISP
    (d) None of them.

20. What is the name of first graphical web browser?
    (a) Netscape   (b) Mosaic   (c) Veronica   (d) Lynx

21. Which of the following switching technology is used by the Internet?
    (a) Hybrid switching
    (b) Packet switching
    (c) Circuit switching
    (d) None of them.

22. IPO means _____.
    (a) Input Process Output
    (b) Internet Process Output
    (c) Interface Program Output
    (d) None of them.

23. The output of a computer displayed on the monitor screen is known as the _____.
    (a) COM   (b) Hardcopy   (c) Softcopy   (d) None of them.

24. How does the CPU read the information from secondary memory?
    (a) First, information is transferred to the main memory, from where the CPU reads it.
    (b) Through cache
    (c) Through DMA
    (d) None of them.

25. Which of the following options is not available in the edit menu of MS-PowerPoint?
    (a) Copy   (b) Delete slide   (c) Cut   (d) Page setup

26. In MS-Word, the templates are in ____ format.
    (a) .dot   (b) .dop   (c) .tmp   (d) .doc

27. The laser printer requires _____ for printing.
    (a) heat-sensitive paper   (b) raster scan
    (c) camera lens   (d) None of them.

28. What is the primary purpose of using the Tape storage?
    (a) Rarely used software   (b) Backups
    (c) Installing new programs   (d) None of them.

29. GUI means _____.
    (a) Geographical User Interface   (b) Great User Interface
    (c) Graphical User Interface   (d) None of them.

30. Define Word Processor.
    (a) It is the CPU of a microcomputer.
    (b) It is a program used to create, view, edit and manipulate the text before printing.
    (c) It is a program used for processing the word, such as giving frequency of words, sorting of words, etc.
    (d) None of them.

31. Which of the following protocol is responsible for governing the fetching of e-mail?
    (a) POP   (b) SMTP   (c) PPP   (d) SLIP

32. In MS-Word, we use Find and Replace option to _____.
    (a) replace both text and formatting   (b) replace document's name with a new name
    (c) replace text of a document only   (d) replace formatting only

33. Why do we use the Spelling and Grammar check option in MS-Word?
    (a) To highlight the misspelled words in the document
    (b) To allow you to correct the misspelled word manually
    (c) To display the misspelled words in a dialog box
    (d) All of them.

34. In MS-Word, the purpose of using Borders is
    (a) to draw lines above and below or to left and right of paragraphs.
    (b) to surround the paragraphs with different styles of boxes.
    (c) to add emphasis to particular paragraphs.
    (d) All of them.

35. In MS-Word, Drop caps is applied to which of the following?
    (a) Characters   (b) Words   (c) Sentences   (d) None of them.

36. Which of the following terms is used to describe "The appearance of your final document would be exactly the same as you might expect when the document is printed on the paper"?
    (a) Search & Replace   (b) Softcopy   (c) Pagination   (d) WYSIWYG

37. In MS-Excel, you can use Borders to
    (a) add a single line or multiple lines, along one side of the cell or around it.
    (b) add lines above, below or to either side of the cell.
    (c) Both (a) and (b).
    (d) None of them.

38. A Word file can be saved as a Web Page, which is a document that consists of one or more parts
    (a) that are readable by a Web browser.
    (b) saved in HTML.
    (c) that helps distribute information over the Internet.
    (d) All of the above.

39. What is the limit of a file's name length in Windows95/98/XP?
    (a) It can contain only one space.
    (b) It is limited to 11 characters.
    (c) It is limited to 255 characters.
    (d) It is not limited in length.

40. In MS-Excel, which of the following actions cannot be performed once the table is created?
    (a) Insertion of a row in a table
    (b) Splitting a single table into two tables
    (c) Deletion and Insertion of columns
    (d) None of them.

41. The Magnifier option is available in which of the following toolbar?
    (a) Print Preview toolbar
    (b) Formatting toolbar
    (c) Standard toolbar
    (d) None of them.

42. In MS-Word, you can use print dialog box to select which of the following options?
    (a) All pages in a range
    (b) Even pages
    (c) Odd pages
    (d) Any of them.

43. In MS-Word, the print preview command is displayed under _____ menu.
    (a) View   (b) File   (c) Edit   (d) Tools

44. The existing data sources can be used with master documents only when_____.
    (a) data source has some fields that may or may not be in the master document
    (b) data source has the same fields as present in the master document
    (c) data source has the same fields as those present in the master document
    (d) None of them.

45. Which of the following keys are displayed in the Status bar?
    (a) Scroll lock key   (b) Num lock key   (c) Caps lock key   (d) All of them.

46. In the default settings, the number of sheets in the workbook can be extended to:
    (a) 3,255
    (b) 16,225
    (c) the limit of available memory
    (d) 3,225

47. In MS-Excel, once the range is defined, you can go to the range
    (a) by selecting ranges using the name box.
    (b) by selecting ranges using the [F5] key.
    (c) Both (a) and (b).
    (d) None of them.

48. In MS-Excel, we use AutoSum to
    (a) add grand totals to a range containing other totals.
    (b) total any selected range.
    (c) locate and total the rows or columns in a range nearest to the current cell.
    (d) All of them.

49. Which one of the following is an invalid number in a cell?
    (a) "1,500.00"   (b) 1.1e+2   (c) (2000.00)   (d) All of them.

50. Why do we use page break?
    (a) To create a blank page at the top of the document
    (b) To create a new page that cannot be deleted
    (c) To create a new page at the bottom of the document
    (d) To create a new page at the insertion point.

State True or False

1. You get the option of Grayscale color as Grayscale submenu.
2. Analog computers are not capable to process variable type of data.
3. A function or a formula can also begin with a "$" sign.
4. While printing you can enlarge the size of the sheet up to 400%.
5. Print area option allows you to select a limited area for printing.
6. You cannot search for a file in Windows without knowing the full file name.
7. In MS-PowerPoint, you can reuse the deleted slide as it is not deleted from the file.
8. The structure and contents created by the Auto Text is based upon your customized choices.
9. MS-PowerPoint is not an example of word processor developed by Microsoft.
10. Change of capitalization for a sentence can be done using the Change Case command.
11. In MS-PowerPoint, it is possible to print slides for overhead projector transparencies.
12. Unit price is not a valid name for a cell/range.
13. In MS-Word, we can use <Ctrl + B> keys to give the selected text a Bold effect.
14. In MS-Excel, "£" is the only valid currency symbol.
15. In MS-PowerPoint, you can continue working while background printing is turned on to get the print.
16. E-mail address has the options of To, CC, BCC and Subject fields for sending mails.
17. Protocols are the set of rules to be followed for communicating over the network.
18. Internet connection can be obtained from ISP.
19. Hypertext allows users to read, navigate and visualize the information in a nonlinear manner depending on what he wants to know next.
20. The symbol '@' is used to divide an e-mail address in two parts.
21. In SMTP, the length of the message is not a concern.

22. HTML files are the simple text files saved with .html extension.
23. While designing a website, the title of the website should be very attractive, descriptive and accurate.
24. A person's feelings and moods can be expressed using emoticons, which are a pictorial representation of a facial expression made using punctuation marks, numbers and letters.
25. In MS-PowerPoint, you can use Design toolbar to draw objects in your presentation.
26. A new worksheet can be created by selecting the worksheet option from the file menu.
27. Soft Page Break is a dotted line that extends on a page in a multi-page document.
28. Numerals have equal widths but are specified in a spaced font.
29. It is not possible to use different page-numbering styles in different sections of the document.
30. In MS-Word, the ruler is not displayed by default.
31. In MS-Word, Even pages and Odd pages cannot have different footers.
32. In MS-Word, Headers and Footers are not displayed in the normal view.
33. The AutoFit to contents helps Word to widen or narrow columns based on the text inserted.
34. AutoFormat command enables you to analyze the formatting requirement and automatically create styles in the document.
35. The Page preview option shows the image of the page in WYSIWYG mode.
36. In MS-Word, Print Preview option does not allow you to perform any editing to the document.
37. In MS-Excel, to copy a formula into a range, select the cell that contains the formula and drag the Fill handle downward, upward, and right or left till it reaches the desired location.
38. In MS-Word, the simplest way to resize a picture is by dragging its edges to adjust the size and shape to your requirement.
39. The Website where entries are made in the style of journal and displayed in reverse chronological order is known as blog.
40. In MS-Excel, it is not possible to select multiple non-adjacent ranges.
41. In MS-Excel, we use [Home] key to move the active cell to column A of the current row.
42. The combination of [Shift] + [Spacebar] helps to select the entire column.
43. It is always possible to copy or move sheets from one workbook to another.
44. In MS-Excel, [Ctrl] + [End] key takes you to the last cell having contents of the worksheet.
45. In MS-Excel, whenever you copy a formula, the relative cell references do not change.
46. In MS-Excel, the delete and clear commands do not perform the same function.
47. In MS-Excel, you cannot add multiple rows in a sheet.
48. In MS-Excel, the Insert menu has the Worksheet option, which is used to insert a new sheet to the workbook in front of the current sheet.
49. In MS-Excel, manual page breaks are ignored when you select the Fit To option of the Page Setup.
50. In MS-Word, we use Styles to create the table of contents quickly.

ANSWER KEYS

Multiple Choice Questions

1. (c) 2. (a) 3. (d) 4. (a) 5. (d) 6. (b) 7. (b) 8. (d)
9. (c) 10. (b) 11. (a) 12. (a) 13. (c) 14. (d) 15. (b) 16. (c)
17. (d) 18. (d) 19. (d) 20. (b) 21. (b) 22. (a) 23. (c) 24. (a)
25. (d) 26. (a) 27. (d) 28. (b) 29. (c) 30. (b) 31. (a) 32. (a)
33. (d) 34. (a) 35. (a) 36. (d) 37. (c) 38. (d) 39. (d) 40. (b)
41. (a) 42. (d) 43. (b) 44. (a) 45. (d) 46. (c) 47. (b) 48. (d)
49. (a) 50. (d)

State True or False

1. True 2. False 3. False 4. True 5. True 6. False 7. False 8. False
9. True 10. True 11. True 12. True 13. True 14. False 15. True 16. True
17. True 18. True 19. True 20. True 21. False 22. True 23. True 24. True
25. False 26. False 27. True 28. False 29. True 30. True 31. False 32. True
33. True 34. True 35. True 36. False 37. True 38. True 39. True 40. False
41. True 42. False 43. True 44. True 45. False 46. True 47. False 48. True
49. True 50. True

SOLVED PAPER – 4

Multiple Choice Questions

1. Web sites should be registered with various _____ so that the viewers can locate it easily.
   (a) search engines
   (b) mail servers
   (c) backbone providers
   (d) online services

2. Which technique is used to analyze the network communication, and confirm that the packets are the part of on-going communication between sender and receiver?
   (a) Stateful inspection
   (b) Packet filtering
   (c) Application proxy filtering
   (d) Intrusion detection system

3. In MS-Word, minimum Zoom is supported up to which of the following options?
   (a) 0.15
   (b) 0.25
   (c) 0.04
   (d) 0.1

4. Select the valid conditional formatting operator in the New Formatting Rule dialog box from the following options.
   (a) Outside
   (b) In between
   (c) More
   (d) Greater than

5. How can you add Comments to the cells?
   (a) Insert → Comment
   (b) View → Comments
   (c) File → Comments
   (d) Edit → Comments

6. In MS-Excel, what happens when you copy a formula?
   (a) MS-Excel changes the cell references in the newly copied formula.
   (b) MS-Excel does not adjust the relative cell references.
   (c) MS-Excel adjusts the absolute cell references.
   (d) MS-Excel erases the original copy of the formula.

7. In MS-Excel, when you create a vertical page break, _____.
   (a) the active cell must be in column A.
   (b) the active cell must be in row 1.
   (c) the active cell can be anywhere in the worksheet.
   (d) the active cell must be A1.

8. The broadband bus topology follows which type of transmission?
   (a) Unidirectional transmission
   (b) Switching transmission
   (c) Bidirectional transmission
   (d) None of them.

9. Which of the following geographic domain extension is invalid?
   (a) cd – Canada
   (b) ind – India
   (c) jp – Japan
   (d) All of them.

10. Select the valid e-mail id from the following.
    (a) Enquires?Center.company.co.@.uk
    (b) finance@information.marketing.co.in
    (c) @sales.information@company.co.uk
    (d) sales.enquiry.company.co.com

11. Select the domain name suffixes from the following.
    (a) .com
    (b) .nat
    (c) Both (a) and (b).
    (d) None of them.

12. Which of the following is a shortcut to Undo an action?
    (a) Ctrl + X   (b) Ctrl + Z   (c) Ctrl + U   (d) Ctrl + Y

13. How can you protect your computer from viruses?
    (a) Do not use your computer.
    (b) Do not turn your computer off at night.
    (c) Do not use Microsoft Office Programs.
    (d) Do not download unknown documents or programs.

14. Select the word processing software from the following.
    (a) MS-Word   (b) WordPerfect   (c) Easy Word   (d) All of them.

15. The first e-mail sent was mailed in _____.
    (a) 1982   (b) 1977   (c) 1992   (d) 1971

16. Challenge–Response is an authentication verification technique that needs users to reply to an e-mail challenge message
    (a) after the original e-mail that triggered the challenge is delivered at the receiver's end.
    (b) before the original e-mail that triggered the challenge is delivered at the receiver's end.
    (c) Both (a) and (b).
    (d) None of them.

17. _____ is a process of selecting appropriate recipients for a specific e-mail campaign, using the demographics and related information about the customers from the customer's database.
    (a) Demo graphing   (b) Targeting   (c) Both (a) and (b)   (d) None of them.

18. The list developed by anyone receiving or processing e-mail on its way to the recipient containing domains or IP addresses of any e-mailers suspected of sending spam is called _____.
    (a) Wrong list   (b) Blacklist   (c) Both the above.   (d) None of the above.

19. Which of the following options helps you to play a photo album slide show continuously?
    (a) Launch an online broadcast
    (b) Use random slide transition
    (c) Loop continuously
    (d) All of them.

20. In MS-PowerPoint, how can you preview a presentation?
    (a) File → Print Preview
    (b) Click Print Preview button on the standard toolbar
    (c) Both (a) and (b).
    (d) None of them.

21. In MS-PowerPoint, which key helps you to move back to the previous slide during presentation?
    (a) Left Arrow key   (b) Right Arrow key   (c) Space bar   (d) Shift key

22. Which of the following devices can hold two IP addresses?
    (a) Router   (b) Computer   (c) Gateway   (d) All of them.

23. _____ in Web sites help you to switch between the different web pages.
    (a) Bars   (b) Strings   (c) Links   (d) Threads

24. Which of the following hardware device is considered as the brain of computer?
    (a) Secondary storage   (b) Data input   (c) RAM chip   (d) CPU

25. Which of the following entries should be made while logging into the network?
    (a) Job Profile   (b) Full name   (c) Username and password   (d) Money

26. DVD means _____.
    (a) Digital Video Disc
    (b) Double Volume Density
    (c) Disk Virtual Drive
    (d) Digital and Video Drive

27. What does the term 'Binary' indicate?
    (a) The same as a byte, 8 bits.
    (b) That computers needs more than two options.
    (c) There are three options: 0, 1 and 2.
    (d) There are two possibilities, ON and OFF.

28. How many characters can be created in ASCII?
    (a) 256   (b) 128   (c) 255   (d) 1024

29. Why do we use Algorithms and Flowcharts?
    (a) To direct the output to a printer.
    (b) To understand the problem completely and clearly.
    (c) To know about the Memory capacity.
    (d) To identify the base of a number system.

30. What does analog computer do?
    (a) It never converts input to digital form.
    (b) First it converts the input to digital form.
    (c) It displays the output in digital form.
    (d) All of them.

31. Select the largest 16-bit positive number from the following.
    (a) 34567   (b) 32767   (c) 32768   (d) 36789

32. What is the name of the process for converting data from one medium to another?
    (a) Transformation   (b) Manipulation   (c) Collection   (d) Conversion

33. _____ is a model that supports online non-commercial interaction between local and central government and the commercial business sector, rather than private individuals
    (a) Government-to-Citizen or Government-to-Consumer (G2C)
    (b) Government-to-Business (G2B)
    (c) Government-to-Government (G2G)
    (d) Government-to-Employees (G2E)

34. In MS-PowerPoint, Slide _____ is responsible to control the text characteristics, background color and special effects, such as bullet style and shadowing.
    (a) Presentation   (b) Sort   (c) Master   (d) Show

35. Which of the following is two-dimensional representation of an image?
    (a) Image reasoning   (b) Image resolution   (c) Image routing   (d) None of them.

36. Which of the following is responsible for exchanging the word processing files that include formatting styles such as text alignment, font sizes, and font styles?
    (a) Rich Text Format (RTF)
    (b) BCD
    (c) ASCII
    (d) None of them.

37. In MS-Word, what is the color of the wavy underline that appears below the misspelled word?
    (a) Black   (b) Green   (c) Blue   (d) Red

38. In MS-Word, Ctrl + U key combination performs the following action?
    (a) Move file from /U directory
    (b) Move file to /U directory
    (c) Move a file
    (d) None of them.

39. IIS means _____.
    (a) Internal IP Scheme.
    (b) International Institute For Standards.
    (c) Internet Information System.
    (d) Internet Information Server.

40. Is it possible to change the mouse scroll property?
    (a) Yes
    (b) No
    (c) Yes, during installation
    (d) Yes, at any time.

41. In MS-Word, how many options are available in menu bar?
    (a) Nine   (b) Twelve   (c) Three   (d) Six

42. Which of the following options helps you to add a link to your Web site?
    (a) Format Painter
    (b) Insert Hyperlink
    (c) Insert Word Table
    (d) None of them.

43. How can you open the Print preview window?
    (a) File → Print Preview option from the File menu.
    (b) By selecting the Print Preview option from the standard toolbar.
    (c) Both (a) and (b).
    (d) None of them.

44. How can you create a new document?
    (a) By selecting the New option from the standard toolbar.
    (b) File → New option from the file menu.
    (c) By using Ctrl + N combination of keys.
    (d) All of them.

45. Which of the following keys is used to remove one character to the left of the cursor?
    (a) Shift   (b) Enter   (c) Delete   (d) Backspace

46. You place the mouse pointer in the selection bar and double-click on it, to select a _____.
    (a) Paragraph   (b) Sentence   (c) Word   (d) Letter

47. In MS-Word, the alignment refers to the position of the text in relation to the _____.
    (a) Paragraphs   (b) Margins   (c) Header   (d) Footer

48. In MS-Word, how can you end the current paragraph and begin the new paragraph?
    (a) By pressing the Enter key twice.
    (b) By pressing Escape key and Enter key once.
    (c) By pressing the Enter key once.
    (d) By pressing the Enter key and Spacebar key once.

49. In MS-Word, whenever you insert an object in a document, the object is said to be present in which document?
    (a) Original   (b) Source   (c) Destination   (d) Primary

50. The speed of a Mouse is _____.
    (a) Adjustable.
    (b) Nonadjustable.
    (c) Adjustable through the control panel.
    (d) Adjustable by double clicking the middle button of mouse.

State True or False

1. When an e-mail is not delivered to the recipient due to temporary error, such as when mailbox full, it is known as Soft bounce.
2. In the binary system, the digit 1 represents OFF, that is, electronic state is off indicating absence of an electronic charge.
3. In MS-Excel, the meaning of file extension .XLA is MS-Excel add-in.
4. The search engines use software programs called as 'SPIDERS' for roaming around the WWW.
5. The software program Acrobat reads and converts the documents into PDF format.
6. Cracking is not the name of a process for overcoming hacking.
7. Phone lines or fiber-optics are the requirements for Wireless Local Area Network.
8. Carrying on discussions does not require the bulletin board service.
9. In networking, Client machines do not require any assistance from the Server machines.
10. 'abc' is a domain name in the e-mail address 'abc@books.edu'.
11. The meaning of B2C is Business-to-Consumer.
12. In MS-Excel, whenever you press Enter key, the cell accepts your entry as its contents.
13. Operating System is a program that manages all other programs installed in the computer.
14. You can remove multiple worksheets from a workbook by going to File → Save As → Save As Type → Excel 4.0 Work Sheet.
15. Delivered e-mail is the number of e-mails sent less the number of bounces and filtered messages.
16. Newsletter is a broadcast where comments by members or subscribers go only to the message sender and is a one-to-many technique of sharing information.
17. In MS-PowerPoint, Page Orientation can be used to set the page layout as Portrait or Landscape.
18. In MS-PowerPoint, you can print either nine or fifteen hand-outs in a presentation.
19. Templates are the readymade styles that are readily available to be used in your presentations.
20. You can perform editing in design template by selecting View → Master → Slide Master from the menu bar.
21. In MS-PowerPoint, you cannot re-record the narration for your Show.
22. It is not possible to export PowerPoint presentation outline or speaker notes directly from PowerPoint to an MSWord document.
23. In networking, SMTP, FTP, Telnet and HTTP do not require Ethernet protocol.
24. Band Pass Filters are required to apply multi-access in GSM.
25. Converter acts as a translator between two dissimilar protocols.
26. In MS-Word, you can add an image from a file.
27. Computer is capable of solving most types of problems.
28. Meaning of Procedures and Software is the same.
29. Communication among the computers is described by the term called as connectivity.

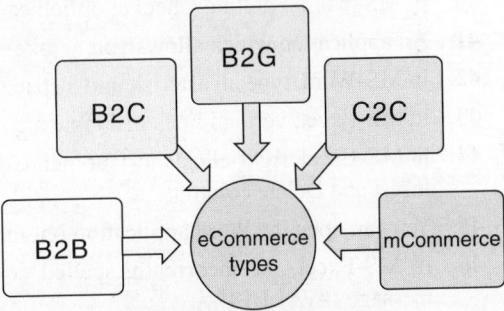

Types of eCommerce

30. An encyclopedia with its structured data is a database, even if the users cannot modify its contents.
31. In binary system, the bits in a byte are in the range from zero to eight.
32. MS Windows and Linux operating system can be installed in a single computer.
33. Accessories menu holds an option of 'Add/Remove Tools'.
34. Linux has hierarchical file structure.
35. Hot key combination is used to enlarge the window to its maximum size.
36. Whenever your computer is idle, the Screen Saver will be displayed on the screen.
37. Shift + Enter key moves your location to the first cell in the row.
38. Computer will not print the Background color or picture added through Format → Background.
39. PC network makes the Internet access faster.
40. In MS-Word, Spelling Checker option can be activated using F8 key.
41. An application which allows you to take notes and save them in a file is called as Assistance.
42. In MS-Word, type an asterisk and a space or a tab, to automatically begin bullet list.
43. In MS-Excel, vertical lines in a table are not defined as Rows.
44. In MS-Excel, right-click shortcut menu, opened while the column is selected, contains option to Insert and Delete columns.
45. You can open the Word application only through office shortcut bar.
46. In MS-Excel, the incorrectly spelled cell or function in a formula is indicated by the error message '#VALUE!'.
47. You cannot format a comment.
48. C4:H12 is a cell reference for a range of cells that begins from cell C4 and goes over to column H and down to row 12.
49. You can change the cell content using the F4 key.
50. The use of symbol '?' and '#' in a primary filename is valid.

ANSWER KEYS

Multiple Choice Questions

1. (d)   2. (a)   3. (d)   4. (d)   5. (a)   6. (a)   7. (c)   8. (a)
9. (b)   10. (b) 11. (a) 12. (b) 13. (d) 14. (a) 15. (d) 16. (a)
17. (b) 18. (b) 19. (c) 20. (b) 21. (a) 22. (b) 23. (c) 24. (d)
25. (c) 26. (a) 27. (d) 28. (a) 29. (b) 30. (a) 31. (b) 32. (d)
33. (b) 34. (c) 35. (b) 36. (a) 37. (d) 38. (d) 39. (d) 40. (c)
41. (a) 42. (b) 43. (c) 44. (d) 45. (d) 46. (a) 47. (b) 48. (c)
49. (b) 50. (c)

State True or False

1. True   2. False   3. True   4. True   5. True   6. True   7. False   8. False
9. False   10. False 11. True   12. True   13. True   14. True   15. True   16. False
17. True   18. False 19. True   20. False 21. False 22. False 23. True   24. True
25. True   26. True   27. True   28. False 29. True   30. True   31. False 32. True
33. False 34. True   35. True   36. True   37. False 38. False 39. False 40. False
41. False 42. True   43. True   44. True   45. False 46. False 47. False 48. True
49. False 50. False

SOLVED PAPER – 5

Multiple Choice Questions

1. The term Base station and MSC are related to which of the following options?
   (a) ISO-OSI model
   (b) Cellular radio
   (c) ARPANET structure
   (d) None of them.

2. World Wide Web is defined as _____.
   (a) a software application
   (b) a computer game
   (c) a synonym of Internet
   (d) the part of the Internet that enables information-sharing via interconnected pages.

3. Which of the following allows you to compose, send, receive, delete and print messages?
   (a) E-mail   (b) FTP   (c) Both (b) and (d).   (d) Telnet

4. You can access all the files on WWW via _____.
   (a) Internet   (b) Intranet   (c) Both (a) and (b).   (d) None of them.

5. In MS-PowerPoint, which of the following types of sound files can be added to the presentation?
   (a) .wav file and .jpg file
   (b) .jpg file and .gif file
   (c) .wav file and .gif file
   (d) .wav file and .mid file

6. What kind of file is saved with .wav and .mid as extension?
   (a) Picture file   (b) Image file   (c) Sound file   (d) None of them.

7. In MS-PowerPoint, _____ helps you to take notes printout with a miniature slide.
   (a) Audience Handouts
   (b) Slides with animation
   (c) Outline View
   (d) Notes Page

8. Which of the following keys bring back the bullet to its previous level?
   (a) Shift + Tab key   (b) Tab key   (c) Shift key   (d) Enter key

9. In MS-PowerPoint, _____ view options helps you to add, delete, copy and move the slides.
   (a) Normal   (b) Slide Sorter   (c) Notes   (d) Outline

10. Which of the following fonts has the finishing stokes?
    (a) Sans serif   (b) Courier
    (c) Times New Roman   (d) Tahoma

11. In MS-PowerPoint, the collection slides is defined as a _____.
    (a) File   (b) Presentation   (c) Document   (d) Workbook

12. Google Chrome is an example of _____.
    (a) Internet browser
    (b) E-mail program
    (c) Both (a) and (b).
    (d) None of them.

13. Select an IP address of B class from the following:
    (a) 192.128.32.56 (b) 191.023.21.54 (c) 10.14.12.34 (d) 125.123.123.2

14. Netscape Communicator suite programs help you to perform which of the following operations?
    (a) E-mail
    (b) Create Web pages
    (c) Group discussions
    (d) All of them.

15. In networking, the advantage of bridging and switching is _____ transparency.
    (a) Encryption
    (b) Lower layer protocol
    (c) Upper layer protocol
    (d) None of them.

16. Computer modem does not
    (a) demodulate analog signals into digital signals.
    (b) line modulates electrical digital signals into analog signals.
    (c) produce sounds like you hear on the touch tone telephone.
    (d) collect signals from low speed terminals and transmit them over a single.

17. What is an ideal range for a Bluetooth device to carry radio wave information?
    (a) 300 Km (b) 30 yards (c) 30 Km (d) 30 feet

18. Which is an ideal network to connect a computer and other network devices in a limited geographical area, such as for home, school, office building or computer laboratory?
    (a) Local area network (LAN)
    (b) Metropolitan area network (MAN)
    (c) Wide area network (WAN)
    (d) All of them.

19. What do you mean by the term 'Gopher'?
    (a) Search Tool
    (b) Internet Duet Tape
    (c) Protocol
    (d) Both (a) and (b).

20. Web pages are also called as multimedia pages because they may contain _____.
    (a) video clips, sound, text and pictures
    (b) text, pictures and sound
    (c) text and pictures only
    (d) None of them.

21. Which of the following actions can be performed with the files attached with an e-mail?
    (a) Saved (b) Examined (c) Detached (d) All of them.

22. Which of the following options is used by the browser to contact the Web Server to check whether the Web page has been changed since it was stored in the catcher folder?
    (a) Reload (b) Refresh (c) Cache (d) Either (a) or (b).

23. Which of the following is responsible for Internet standards approval resource allocation?
    (a) IETF (b) IAB (c) InterNIC (d) None of them.

24. Which of the following unit is used to measure the computer's clock speed?
    (a) Bits (b) Gigabytes (c) Gigahertz (d) Megabits

25. In MS-PowerPoint, what is the name of a slide that can be used as an agenda slide and contains the list of the titles from selected slides in your presentation?
    (a) Title Slide
    (b) Index Slide
    (c) Summary Slide
    (d) Slide Master

26. Which combination of keys from the keyboard can be used to display the start menu?
    (a) Ctrl + Alt + Del (b) Alt + S (c) Ctrl + Space + Del (d) Ctrl + Esc

27. Which of the following command is used to list the contents of the current directory of a disk?
    (a) Copy   (b) Dir   (c) CD   (d) Tree

28. Select the valid statement from the following.
    (a) 1 MB = 1000 kilobytes   (b) 1 MB = 2048 bytes
    (c) 1 KB = 1024 bytes   (d) 1 KB = 1000 bytes

29. What do you name to a directory within a directory?
    (a) Sub Directory   (b) Directory   (c) Junior Part   (d) Mini Directory

30. CRT means _____.
    (a) Cathode Ray Tube   (b) Cathodic Ray Tub
    (c) Cathode Ray Tub   (d) Cathodic Ray Tube

The Internet Client–Server model

31. What do you call the records in a file when they have the same number of bytes?
    (a) Fixed length record   (b) Record
    (c) Variable length record   (d) None of them.

32. What are the three color combinations comprising the Pixel?
    (a) Red, Yellow, Blue   (b) Red, Green, Blue
    (c) Red, White, Black   (d) None of them.

33. Which of the following device is not an output device?
    (a) Speaker   (b) Plotter   (c) Mouse   (d) Printer

34. _____ is responsible to load the software component in a Server.
    (a) User   (b) Administrator   (c) Either (a) or (b).   (d) None of them.

35. Folders automatically created in /Documents and Settings can be accessed by _____.
    (a) Default Users   (b) All Users
    (c) Folders are not created automatically   (d) Both (a) and (b).

36. What is Title?
    (a) A valid command   (b) Used to set title of command prompt window
    (c) An MS-Window command   (d) All of them.

37. The URLs and links of the Web pages recently visited through the Web browser are maintained in the _____.
    (a) Page List   (b) History List   (c) Link List   (d) All of them.

38. Which of the following actions can be performed with the icons on the desktop?
    (a) Delete icon   (b) Resize icon   (c) Hide icon   (d) All of them.

39. Which of the following program saves the information from Web server onto the client's computer?
    (a) Virus   (b) Cache   (c) Cookie   (d) None of them.

40. In MS-Word, how can you keep the track of the number of words typed in the document?
    (a) MS-Word is not capable to count the number of words typed.
    (b) You can use word count to calculate the number of words typed.
    (c) MS-Word automatically keeps the record of number of words typed.
    (d) You can use the text count feature to calculate the number of words typed.

41. To create a table, use
    (a) the Insert Table button present on the Standard Toolbar.
    (b) the Draw Table command on the Tools menu.
    (c) the Draw Table button on the Tables and Formatting toolbar.
    (d) All of these.

42. In MS-Word, Alignment feature can be used to _____ the document.
    (a) filter   (b) condition   (c) merge   (d) enhance

43. Select the word processing application from the following.
    (a) WordPerfect   (b) MS-Word   (c) Easy Word   (d) All of them.

44. In portrait prints, the document has
    (a) lesser characters per line than the same document in landscape.
    (b) more characters per line than the same document in landscape.
    (c) the same characters per line as the same document in landscape.
    (d) similar fonts to fit in the same amount of characters per line as landscape.

45. MS-Word allows users to work with _____
    (a) Mouse only   (b) Keyboard only
    (c) Mouse and Keyboard   (d) None of these.

46. In MS-Excel, which function is used to print the current date?
    (a) Now()   (b) Date()   (c) Today()   (d) None of these.

47. Under which menu will you find the option of Auto Format to change the appearance of your document?
    (a) Format   (b) Tools   (c) Edit   (d) View

48. For printing a portion of the sheet, you need to select that portion and _____.
    (a) use the Print button.
    (b) use the PRINT SCREEN key.
    (c) select Print selection in the Print dialog and then print.
    (d) select Print selection on Page Setup → Sheet and then print.

49. Which of the following is a valid IF function?
    (a) "IF(A3>=C2,B4,""Too small"")"
    (b) "IF(A3>=C2,B4,Too small)"
    (c) =IF(A3>=C2,B4,"Too small")
    (d) "IF(A3>=C2,B4;""Too small"")"

50. Which of the actions can be performed by a multifunction printer?
    (a) Printing   (b) Scanning   (c) Copying   (d) All of them.

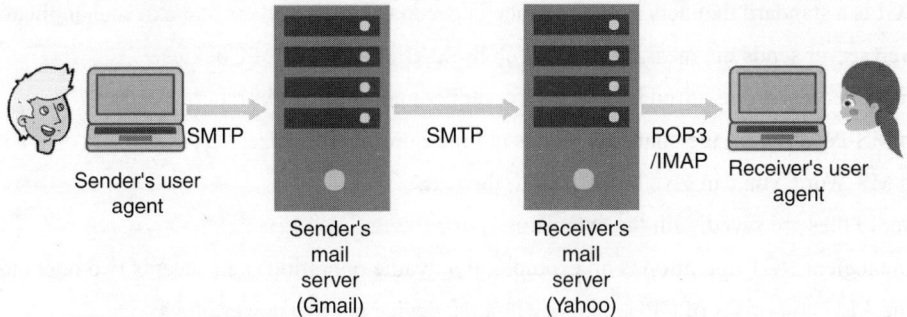

SMTP and POP3/IMAP servers for dispatch and delivery of e-mail

State True or False

1. In MS-PowerPoint, you cannot show hidden slide during the slide show.
2. 100 KB is approximately 100,000 bytes.
3. Spam mails are the unwanted, unsolicited junk e-mail sent to a large number of recipients.
4. Bounced e-mails do not reverse the messages back to the sender.
5. Broadcast is the process of not sending the same e-mail to multiple recipients.
6. In MS-PowerPoint, you can print the presentation in Landscape mode only.
7. In MS-PowerPoint, you can add XY type of chart to the slide.
8. In MS-PowerPoint, you can rename a file when it is open.
9. In MS-PowerPoint, you can use Ctrl + H key to get help on related topics.
10. In MS-PowerPoint, you can import data to the presentation from photo album data source.
11. In MS-PowerPoint, Placeholders are the objects of the slide to hold text.
12. The IMAP and POP protocol are not used by the e-mail clients.
13. MS-PowerPoint is a sub-part of Windows Operating System.
14. Firewall is a software program used to prevent unauthorized access to the network.
15. In MS-PowerPoint, Slide Master can maintain only one standard design.
16. FSK is a frequency modulated binary PCM technique.
17. Spam mails are the unsolicited commercial e-mails.
18. The computer can be added to the network using the device called Repeater (circuit board or card).
19. 191.23.21.54 is an example of an IP address from B class.
20. TCP/IP model avoids collision by following flow control and congestion management.
21. E-mails are exchanged using SMTP protocol.

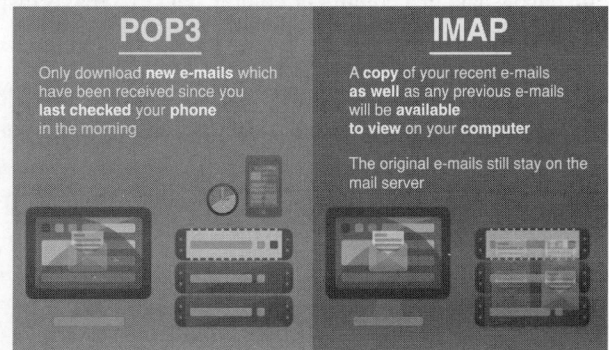

22. CGI is a standard that acts as an interface between the Web Servers and external applications.
23. Web server sends the message to the Web browser in the form of Cookies.
24. Proxy servers are required by every computer connected to an intranet or extranet.
25. In MS-PowerPoint, the character size is not measured in font size.
26. In MS-Word, you can give bold effect to the text.
27. Audio files are saved with the extension '.jpg'.
28. The logical NOT operation is an example of a dyadic operation (i.e., accepts two operands).
29. The ALU comprises of CPU, memory boards, device boards, power plugs.
30. Icons of the desktop are symbolic links to the system softwares.
31. Folder can also be defined as a directory.
32. Print Scheduler is responsible to manage more than one printer connected to a computer.
33. NTFS is an example of Windows File Storage.
34. An Operating System is not responsible to manage all the devices connected to the computer.
35. A computer can install more than one web browser.
36. In MS-Word, Tools menu can be used to access utilities such as spell check, mail merge and macros.
37. In-house list is the list of e-mail addresses that a company has acquired from previous customer contacts, Web sign-ups or through other valid means.
38. The spreadsheet and word processing applications have in-built subprograms that transform data into graphs or charts.
39. Chatting is an on-line text-based communication between two or more users on the network.
40. In MS-Word, you cannot make changes to the Font size of the text.
41. Excel automatically saves your work in a temporary file because AutoRecover is turned on as a default in Excel 97 and higher, and is set to save every 10 minutes.
42. You can change everything in an existing chart.
43. Tools menu has a Sort command that can be used arrange the data in ascending or descending order.
44. In MS-Excel, Status bar shows the current status of certain keys of the keyboard.
45. Create names dialog box can be used to name a constant.
46. Row data in a column or column data in a row is displayed by Transpose function.
47. To move to one cell down or to the next cell in sequence you can use Shift + Tab key as shortcut.
48. In MS-Excel, you can move to the first cell in the row using directional keys.
49. In MS-Excel, use decrease decimal option in the Formatting toolbar to move decimal point one place to the left.
50. The Quick Access Toolbar has maximum limit of 20 buttons.

ANSWER KEYS

Multiple Choice Questions

1. (b) 2. (d) 3. (a) 4. (a) 5. (d) 6. (c) 7. (d) 8. (a)
9. (b) 10. (c) 11. (b) 12. (a) 13. (b) 14. (d) 15. (b) 16. (c)
17. (d) 18. (a) 19. (d) 20. (a) 21. (d) 22. (d) 23. (a) 24. (c)
25. (a) 26. (d) 27. (b) 28. (c) 29. (a) 30. (a) 31. (a) 32. (b)
33. (c) 34. (b) 35. (d) 36. (a) 37. (a) 38. (d) 39. (c) 40. (b)
41. (c) 42. (d) 43. (d) 44. (d) 45. (c) 46. (c) 47. (a) 48. (c)
49. (c) 50. (d)

State True or False

1. True 2. True 3. True 4. False 5. False 6. False 7. True 8. False
9. False 10. True 11. True 12. False 13. False 14. True 15. True 16. True
17. True 18. False 19. True 20. True 21. True 22. True 23. True 24. True
25. False 26. True 27. False 28. False 29. False 30. True 31. True 32. False
33. True 34. False 35. True 36. True 37. True 38. True 39. True 40. False
41. True 42. True 43. False 44. True 45. True 46. True 47. False 48. False
49. True 50. True

SOLVED PAPER – 6

Multiple Choice Questions

1. What would you enter to change the cell reference D3:D8 to an absolute row and column reference?
   (a) None (b) $D$3:$D$8 (c) D$3:D$8 (d) D3:D8

2. Which of these is not a financial function?
   (a) NPV() (b) SUM() (c) PMT() (d) FV()

3. Which of these is not a text function?
   (a) ABS() (b) LEN() (c) CHAR() (d) VAR()

4. How many of rows are there in a worksheet?
   (a) 256 (b) 64536 (c) 36500 (d) 1,048,576

5. Which of the following is displayed each time the formatted number does not fit within the cell?
   (a) None (b) #DIV/0 (c) #DIV@ (d) #####

6. Which symbol is used to enter a number as a text?
   (a) + (b) = (c) " (d) '

7. Which of the following is defined as the concatenating operator?
   (a) Hash (#) (b) Exclamation (!) (c) Ampersand (&) (d) Apostrophe (')

8. Which key is used to select multiple non-adjacent cells in a worksheet?
   (a) Ctrl (b) Shift (c) ALT (d) Ctrl + Shift

9. Now() function returns _____.
   (a) None
   (b) serial number of the current date and time
   (c) serial number of the current date
   (d) serial number of the current time

10. What should be the output of the formatted cell having 5439.1 as '#,##0.00'?
    (a) 7.8 (b) 5,439.00 (c) 5,439.10 (d) 5,439.1

11. Which symbol is used to specify the fixed column or rows in a formula?
    (a) * (b) $ (c) % (d) @

12. _____ tool button is used in Excel 2010, to sum a large range of data.
    (a) Auto Format (b) AutoCorrect (c) Auto Sum (d) AutoFill

13. What should you do to keep the specific row and column from scrolling off the screen?
    (a) Keep the cursor on the row you want to retain on the screen
    (b) Keep the cursor to right of the column you want to retain on the screen
    (c) Keep the cursor below the row you want to retain on the screen
    (d) Keep the cursor both below and right of the row and column you want to retain on the screen.

14. What command will you use to convert a column of data into row?
    (a) Paste Special of Clipboard Group
    (b) Paste Special in the Front Group
    (c) Cut and Paste in the Clipboard Group
    (d) None.

15. The two printers and five workstations of Printek India are known as _____.
    (a) None   (b) LAN   (c) MAN   (d) WAN

16. In Internet terminology, the ISP stands for _____.
    (a) Internet Service Provider
    (b) Internal Service Provider
    (c) International Service Provider
    (d) Intranet Service Provider

17. Which combination of keys you would use to open a new tab in the foreground, from the address bar?
    (a) None   (b) Ctrl + G   (c) Ctrl + W   (d) Alt + Enter

18. Which of the following is not an Internet search engine?
    (a) Excite   (b) Google   (c) Scientia   (d) Web crawler

19. The most convenient place to save the contact information for quick retrieval is_____.
    (a) None   (b) Address box   (c) Message box   (d) Address book

20. Which of the following sentence is incorrect for Digital Signature?
    (a) It cannot be duplicated.
    (b) It is a mechanism for authentication.
    (c) It is created by encrypting information.
    (d) It is the scanned image of one's signature.

21. Which tab is used to insert a video from PowerPoint 2010 file?
    (a) Insert tab of media group
    (b) Home tab of editing group
    (c) Insert tab of Images group
    (d) Insert tab of symbols group

22. Select the menus that have Background.
    (a) Slide Show   (b) Format   (c) Insert   (d) View

23. Which of the PowerPoint view displays only text (bullets and title)?
    (a) Notes Page View   (b) Slide Sorter View   (c) Outline View   (d) Slide Show

24. Select the default page setup orientation of a slide in PowerPoint.
    (a) Portrait   (b) Vertical   (c) Landscape   (d) None

25. What is the meaning of Handout master?
    (a) Handout content formatting for Word export
    (b) Layout of audience handout notes
    (c) Slide formatting
    (d) All of the above.

26. Mathematic operations such as addition, subtraction, division, multiplication and logical are performed by _____.
    (a) ALU   (b) Registers   (c) Control Unit   (d) None

27. Select that which can be used as a primary memory.
    (a) None   (b) Cartridge tape   (c) Optical Disk   (d) Hard Disk

28. Which of the following is not an output device?
    (a) Keyboard (b) Plotter (c) Printer (d) Monitor
29. Select the odd one out.
    (a) eScan (b) Norton (c) None (d) McAfee
30. Printer resolution is measured in _____.
    (a) Hz
    (b) Dots per Inch (DPI)
    (c) Megabits
    (d) Inches (Diagonal)
31. _____ is a utility used to increase the speed of the computer programs.
    (a) None (b) Disk Cleanup (c) Disk Formatter (d) Disk Fragmenter
32. Which of the following charts is not part of the analysis of presentation graphics package?
    (a) Line (b) Pie (c) Bar (d) Temperature
33. A printer that gives the output by pressing print element and an inked ribbon against the paper form is known as _____.
    (a) None
    (b) Scanning printers
    (c) Non-Impact printer
    (d) Impact printer
34. What is Virtual Memory?
    (a) None
    (b) Part of secondary storage used in program execution
    (c) Part of main memory only used for swapping
    (d) A technique to allow a program, of size more than size of the main memory to run.
35. What is Baud rate?
    (a) None
    (b) Transmission speed of channel
    (c) Transmission capacity
    (d) The difference between the lowest and the highest frequency transmitted.
36. Select the file extension used to save the graphic file?
    (a) BMP and GIF (b) TXT and STK (c) JPEG and TXT (d) BMP and DOC
37. ENIAC, the first electronic computer, was designed by _____.
    (a) All of them.
    (b) Joseph M Jacquard
    (c) Van-Neumann
    (d) J Presper Eckert and John W Maunchly
38. _____ converts an entire program into machine language.
    (a) Simulator (b) Compiler (c) Commander (d) Interpreter
39. _____ translates one program instruction at a time into a machine language.
    (a) Interpreter (b) CPU (c) Compiler (d) None
40. All the instructions executed to start the computer are saved in _____.
    (a) CD-ROM
    (b) RAM (Random Access Memory)
    (c) ROM (Read only Memory)
    (d) All the above.
41. Shortcut key for copyright symbol?
    (a) Ctrl + Shift + C (b) Alt + Ctrl + C (c) Ctrl + C (d) Alt + C
42. What is the smallest and largest font size available in Font size tool?
    (a) None (b) 8 and 64 (c) 8 and 72 (d) 12 and 72

43. Which of the following sound effect file can be added to the MS PowerPoint presentation?
    (a) .wav and .jpg   (b) .jgp and .gif   (c) .wav and .gif   (d) .wav and .mid
44. Which of these is an invalid data type in spreadsheet?
    (a) Character   (b) Number   (c) Date/Time   (d) Label
45. Which option helps you to select more than one slide in the presentation?
    (a) Ctrl + Click each slide   (b) Alt + Click each slide
    (c) Shift + Drag each slide   (d) Shift + Click each slide
46. The image quality of a printer is measured in _____.
    (a) Pixels   (b) Dots per inch
    (c) Pages per minute   (d) Characters per second
47. The statement in spreadsheet used to perform calculation is known as _____.
    (a) Formula   (b) Parameter   (c) Reference   (d) Argument
48. _____ is the number system that forms the basis for computer operations.
    (a) ASCII   (b) Octal System
    (c) Hexadecimal System   (d) Binary System
49. Select the Diagnostic Software from the following.
    (a) Unix   (b) Windows XP   (c) Norton Antivirus   (d) Office XP
50. What does CAD stand for?
    (a) All of them.   (b) Computer application in design
    (c) Computer algorithm design   (d) Computer aided design

State True or False

1. Plotter gives the best quality graphics reproduction.
2. RAM allows you to perform read and write operations simultaneously.
3. SRAM, DRAM and VRAM are all different types of ROM.
4. Page Layout tab of the spreadsheet is used for entering formulas and values.
5. VisiCalc is the oldest spreadsheet package.
6. You can select the Draw Table tool command from Page Layout of Page Setup group.
7. 1.1e+2 is a valid number entry for the cell in spreadsheet.
8. In Windows, each different drive name is designated by a letter followed by a colon.
9. Wipe all over is a slide transition effect.
10. All the web pages of Amaozon.com form its website.
11. The value for '=ROUND(3.32,2)', when entered in the spreadsheet cell, is 3.32.
12. Whenever your computer does not respond to system reset, then the computer is said to be Dead.
13. The Internet uses circuit switching technique for data delivery.
14. The cell address A$8 used in a formula is an absolute cell reference.
15. When copying formulas, relative cell addressing is used.
16. The value for '=MOD(-53,5)', when entered in the spreadsheet cell, is 2
17. Domain name is used to locate the specific web page and its computer on the web.
18. Firefox is a system software.

19. A group of 8 binary digits is called a word.
20. Code written in binary language can be directly executed by the computer.
21. RAM is used to backup large amount of data.
22. Dot matrix printer can print only using the standard font.
23. Barcode reader is used to convert a printout into its digital image.
24. Joystick is an input device used for CAD/CAM applications.
25. Information is a collection of raw facts or figures.
26. The operating system acts as an intermediary between a user and computer hardware.
27. Multi-processing operating system uses more than one CPU.
28. Time sharing operating system has rigid time requirement on data processing.
29. The latest version of Windows is Windows 8.1.
30. Linux is an Apple-based operating system.
31. Jump List makes recent item lists of each application.
32. Internet Explorer can be used to manage files and folders stored in the computer system.
33. To select multiple non-consecutive files, you will use the Shift key.
34. You cannot insert charts in MS Word.
35. Title bar contains buttons for frequently used commands.
36. You cannot see header and footers in Draft Layout.
37. Status bar displays information about the document like the total number of pages and words.
38. Redo button is used to reverse the effect of Undo.
39. To select a paragraph, double click on it.
40. To get capital letter, press the letter along with Ctrl key.
41. Fiber optic cables use radio waves to transmit data.
42. Cable modem connection uses coaxial cable to provide Internet access.
43. Ping command is used to check if the server is running.
44. Client provides information or services to other programs.
45. SMTP is a protocol that defines a set of rules to exchange documents on the World Wide Web.
46. Gopher is a program that organizes information on the Internet using a system of menus.
47. Wireless LANs use light waves.
48. Hotmail is now known as Outlook.com.
49. Normal Layout displays the time of each slide in your presentation.
50. WordArt feature is present in the Insert tab.

ANSWER KEYS

Multiple Choice Questions

1. (c) 2. (b) 3. (a) 4. (d) 5. (d) 6. (d) 7. (b) 8. (a)
9. (b) 10. (c) 11. (b) 12. (c) 13. (d) 14. (a) 15. (b) 16. (a)
17. (d) 18. (d) 19. (d) 20. (d) 21. (a) 22. (b) 23. (c) 24. (b)
25. (b) 26. (a) 27. (a) 28. (a) 29. (c) 30. (b) 31. (d) 32. (a)
33. (d) 34. (c) 35. (b) 36. (a) 37. (d) 38. (b) 39. (a) 40. (c)
41. (b) 42. (c) 43. (d) 44. (a) 45. (d) 46. (b) 47. (a) 48. (d)
49. (c) 50. (d)

State True or False

1. True 2. True 3. False 4. False 5. True 6. False 7. False 8. True
9. False 10. True 11. True 12. False 13. False 14. True 15. True 16. False
17. True 18. False 19. False 20. True 21. True 22. True 23. False 24. True
25. False 26. True 27. True 28. False 29. False 30. False 31. True 32. False
33. False 34. False 35. False 36. True 37. True 38. True 39. False 40. False
41. False 42. True 43. True 44. False 45. False 46. True 47. False 48. True
49. False 50. True

SOLVED PAPER – 7

Multiple Choice Questions

1. What is the short key for CUT?
   (a) Ctrl + X (b) Ctrl + C (c) Ctrl + M (d) None of the above.

2. What is the short key for GO-TO menu in MS-Word?
   (a) Ctrl + F (b) Ctrl + X (c) Ctrl + G (d) None of the above.

3. A Plotter is an _____.
   (a) Input Device (b) Output Device (c) Both (d) None of the above.

4. To name a file or folder, _____ key is used.
   (a) F1 (b) F2 (c) F3 (d) None of the above.

5. Undo is done by _____.
   (a) Ctrl + A (b) Ctrl + Y (c) Ctrl + Z (d) None of the above.

6. The extension of a video file is _____.
   (a) .3gp (b) .rhtml (c) .jpg (d) None of the above.

7. The extension of graphic file is _____.
   (a) .hhtm (b) .gif (c) .blog (d) None of the above.

8. The extension of MS-Access is _____
   (a) .accdb (b) .http (c) .html (d) None of the above.

9. The default page orientation in Excel is _____.
   (a) Landscape (b) Horizontal (c) Portrait (d) None of the above.

10. Which one of the following can be entered as a number in a cell?
    (a) 1,300.00 (b) 5000.00 (c) 1.1e+2 (d) All of the above.

11. Which of the following is sent out by a search engine continuously, starting on a homepage of a server and pursuing all links stepwise?
    (a) Spiders (b) Packets (c) Cookies (d) None of the above.

12. What would you use for immediate, real-time communication with a friend?
    (a) Instant Messaging (b) E-mail (c) Usenet (d) Blog

13. The Internet uses _____.
    (a) Circuit switching
    (c) Hybrid switching
    (b) Packet switching
    (d) None of the above.

14. Software instructions intended to satisfy a user's specific processing needs are called _____.
    (a) System software
    (c) Documentation
    (b) Microcomputer
    (d) Application software

15. In computer terminology, information means _____.
    (a) raw
    (b) data
    (c) data in more useful or intelligible form
    (d) alpha numeric data program

16. The first page that you normally view at a Web site is its _____.
    (a) Home page   (b) Master page   (c) First page   (d) Banner page

17. What is the function of the justification buttons on the toolbar?
    (a) To display a drop-down list of justification options
    (b) To display the four options for aligning text
    (c) To open the justification dialog box
    (d) To center the current line.

18. The binary number system has a base _____.
    (a) 2   (b) 4   (c) 8   (d) 16

19. The arithmetic/logic unit performs the following actions:
    (a) Checks data for accuracy
    (b) Does calculations using addition, subtraction, multiplication, and division
    (c) Does logical comparisons, such as equal to, greater than, less than
    (d) Both calculations and logical comparisons.

20. CPU reads the information from secondary memory _____.
    (a) Directly
    (b) First, information is transferred to main memory and from there, the CPU reads
    (c) Through registers
    (d) None of these.

21. A plotter is _____.
    (a) an input device to produce good quality graphics
    (b) an output device to produce drawings and graphics
    (c) a fast output device using camera lenses
    (d) None of these.

22. A _____ is a collection of buttons which represent various operations that can be carried out within an application.
    (a) Buttons   (b) Menu   (c) Toolbar   (d) None of the above.

23. The topmost bar in any application window is the_____.
    (a) Title bar   (b) Menu bar   (c) Toolbar   (d) Status bar

24. Supercomputers are primarily useful for _____.
    (a) input–output intensive processing
    (b) mathematical intensive scientific applications
    (c) data retrieval operations
    (d) None of these.

25. E-mail is _____.
    (a) mail concerning electronic devices
    (b) network transaction of messages within a computer
    (c) transaction of letters, messages and memos over a communication.
    (d) None of these.

26. To be sure that your presentation will run on a different computer, you could bring _____.
    (a) your fonts
    (b) a copy of PowerPoint to install
    (c) a copy of Microsoft PowerPoint Viewer
    (d) None of the above.
27. If you import data and want to update the slide when the original data changes, you must _____.
    (a) embed the data
    (b) link the data
    (c) insert the data as an object
    (d) break the link
28. Excel has a number of features that make it a very powerful spreadsheet program. What feature below is NOT a major advantage to using Excel?
    (a) Database functions such as filtering, sorting, etc.
    (b) Automatic calculation of numbers and formulas
    (c) Charting capabilities
    (d) Desktop publishing capabilities.
29. The arithmetic/logic unit performs the following actions:
    (a) Checks data for accuracy
    (b) Does calculations using addition, subtraction, multiplication, and division
    (c) Does logical comparisons such as equal to, greater than, less than
    (d) Both calculations and logical comparisons.
30. A client program used to access the Internet services and resources available through the World Wide Web.
    (a) ISP
    (b) Web Browsers
    (c) Web Servers
    (d) None of the above.
31. When a computer prints a report, this output is called _____.
    (a) hard copy
    (b) soft copy
    (c) Both (a) and (b).
    (d) None of the above.
32. Which hardware connects RAM, ROM, CPU and expansion card together?
    (a) None
    (b) Motherboard
    (c) Hard disk
    (d) Floppy disk
33. Which storage device has the fastest information retrieval?
    (a) Hard disk
    (b) Pen drive
    (c) CD
    (d) All of them.
34. RAM stands for _____.
    (a) Read Access Memory
    (b) Read Also Memory
    (c) Random Also Memory
    (d) Random Access Memory
35. Choose the output device from the following:
    (a) Web Camera
    (b) Printer
    (c) Keyboard
    (d) Mouse
36. Define the control unit function of the CPU.
    (a) To perform logic functions
    (b) To store program instructions
    (c) To decode program instruction
    (d) To transfer data to primary storage.
37. CD stands for _____.
    (a) Change Data
    (b) Copy Density
    (c) Compact Disk
    (d) Command Description
38. What does 'Hibernate' mean in Windows XP/Windows7?
    (a) To restart the computer in Hibernate Mode
    (b) To shut down the computer without closing the already-running applications

(c) To restart the computer in the Safe Mode
   (d) To shut down the computer while terminating all the running applications.

39. _____ displays the function of a button each time you point to a button.
   (a) Screen List
   (b) Screen Bar
   (c) Screen Alert
   (d) Screen Tip

40. _____ contains the list of commonly used programs on the computer, most of which are accompanied by the Windows Operating System.
   (a) Accessories
   (b) Necessities
   (c) Helper Programs
   (d) Utilities

41. _____ is used to manage the files and folders in the Windows Operating System.
   (a) Control Panel
   (b) Office
   (c) Accessories
   (d) Windows Explorer

42. _____ gives access to all the active applications by showing title box of all the open applications.
   (a) Start Menu
   (b) Title Bar
   (c) Task Bar
   (d) None

43. What is the shortcut used to make the Word text Italic?
   (a) Ctrl + B
   (b) Ctrl + I
   (c) Ctrl + U
   (d) None

44. The default left aligned tab that Word automatically places is at every_____.
   (a) 0.5"
   (b) 0.3"
   (c) 0. 2"
   (d) 0.4"

45. How many scroll bars are visible in the text area of your document when it is above 200%?
   (a) One
   (b) Two
   (c) Three
   (d) Four

46. Which Ribbon you will use to add a chart in your document?
   (a) Page Layout
   (b) Reference
   (c) View
   (d) Insert

47. Which Ribbon you will use to modify the margins of the document?
   (a) View
   (b) Reference
   (c) Page Layout
   (d) Insert

48. What are the items displayed in the status bar of a document?
   (a) Number of pages in the document, spelling/grammar check, word count
   (b) Number of spellings errors, document name, page number
   (c) Spell check, name of document, insert button
   (d) Word count, web layout, size of margins.

49. What does NOT the Insert Ribbon include?
   (a) Page Numbers
   (b) Clip Art
   (c) Thesaurus
   (d) Shapes

50. _____ is the first electronic worksheet.
   (a) VisiCalc
   (b) Lotus 1-2-3
   (c) MS Excel
   (d) None

State True or False

1. Computers are not useful in decision making process.
2. You can access the data saved on the magnetic tape randomly.
3. You require an Operating System to work on the computer.
4. You are not allowed to undo the actions like saving, opening, printing and creating the documents in Word.

5. You can use the Insert menu to insert objects like headers and footers, page numbers, pictures, etc.
6. Formula bar is a part of MS Word 2010.
7. A0 is the address of first cell in Excel 2010.
8. You can locate the domain name of an e-mail address from where the e-mail address is hosted.
9. Inbox stores all the received e-mails.
10. Transferring the information from client PC to server is known as Uploading.
11. Web browsers are the documents used by HTTP.
12. The dial-up connection does not require modem to connect the computer to an ISP server.
13. Web browser is also called as the Web client.
14. You can save the URLs of the frequently visited web pages using the favorite feature of the Internet Explorer.
15. To revisit the Web pages or to complete the website browsing, you can add them to the list of favorite sites.
16. Internet Explorer saves the Web Pages the user visited in the Internet list folder on the computer hard disk.
17. To view a presentation in PowerPoint, you have ten view options available to choose from.
18. You can insert a table in your PowerPoint presentation only when Word is installed on your computer.
19. You can add animation effects from the Design tab.
20. Rotate option is used to change the direction of the clip art image.
21. The best view for setting transition effect for all slides in a presentation is the Slide sorter view.
22. The first successful GUI was launched by Macintosh computers in 1984.
23. Motherboard is the main circuit board that connects CPU, memory and other components together.
24. MS Windows does not work without mouse.
25. In the Spreadsheet, #REF! is an error that appears when the formula refers to an invalid cell.
26. Whenever the text size in a Spreadsheet exceeds its character limit, it displays #####.
27. 1 and 2 digits are used as the binary representation.
28. High-end laser printers are capable to offer printing resolution as high as 300 dpi.
29. A presentation normally holds a single slide.
30. Inkjet printer is an impact printer.
31. In Word, Header is not displayed in the Web Layout view.
32. You can insert text anywhere in the presentation slide.
33. The character size is measured in points.
34. Linux is an example of proprietary software.
35. 18.43 is the standard width of the column in a Spreadsheet.
36. In Linux, you can search a line with specified pattern in a specified file using Grep command.
37. Railway Ticket Reservation System cannot be considered as an example for on-line processing system.

38. Speech synthesizer is used to transform text information into spoken sentences.
39. Video camera is an input device used for capturing video data.
40. A0 is the first cell of the worksheet in MS Excel.
41. The red wavy line is used to mark the incorrect spellings in the document.
42. The workbook has 3 sheets as the default settings and this number can be increased to 255 sheets.
43. Word holds the track of last seven files used.
44. Wipro developed the Portable Document Format.
45. Additional items can be added to the Start menu of Windows.
46. Word allows you to create your own dictionaries.
47. F1 button can be used to invoke help in Windows.
48. BIOS means Basic Integrated Operating System.
49. Internet is the renamed form of the network NSFnet.
50. POP3 is the protocol used to fetch e-mail from mailbox.

ANSWER KEYS

Multiple Choice Questions

1. (a)	2. (c)	3. (b)	4. (b)	5. (c)	6. (a)	7. (b)	8. (a)
9. (c)	10. (a)	11. (a)	12. (a)	13. (b)	14. (d)	15. (c)	16. (a)
17. (b)	18. (a)	19. (d)	20. (b)	21. (b)	22. (c)	23. (a)	24. (b)
25. (c)	26. (c)	27. (b)	28. (d)	29. (d)	30. (b)	31. (a)	32. (b)
33. (a)	34. (d)	35. (b)	36. (a)	37. (c)	38. (b)	39. (d)	40. (a)
41. (d)	42. (c)	43. (b)	44. (a)	45. (b)	46. (d)	47. (c)	48. (a)
49. (c)	50. (a)						

State True or False

1. False	2. False	3. True	4. True	5. True	6. False	7. False	8. True
9. True	10. True	11. False	12. True	13. True	14. True	15. True	16. False
17. True	18. True	19. False	20. True	21. True	22. True	23. True	24. False
25. True	26. True	27. True	28. True	29. False	30. False	31. True	32. True
33. True	34. False	35. False	36. True	37. True	38. False	39. True	40. False
41. True	42. False	43. True	44. False	45. True	46. True	47. True	48. False
49. False	50. True						

SOLVED PAPER – 8

Multiple Choice Questions

1. Who is the father of WWW?
   (a) Tim Berners-Lee (b) Charles Babbage (c) Shwet Tripathi (d) None of the above.

2. Redo is done by _____.
   (a) Ctrl + Z (b) Ctrl + Y (c) Y (d) None of the above.

3. PROM, EP-ROM, and EEPROM are the examples of _____.
   (a) ROM (b) Hard disk (c) RAM (d) None of the above.

4. Removing a video properly requires _____ it.
   (a) Uninstalling (b) Removing (c) Deleting (d) None of the above.

5. What is the short key for insertion of a new slide in MS-PowerPoint?
   (a) Ctrl + Insert (b) Ctrl + O (c) Ctrl + N (d) None of the above.

6. ALU stands for _____.
   (a) Artur Log Unit
   (b) Armetur Leg Unit
   (c) Arithmetic Logic Unit
   (d) None of the above.

7. What is the short key for HYPERLINK?
   (a) Ctrl + K (b) G (c) K (d) None of these.

8. What is the short key for BOLD?
   (a) Ctrl + C (b) Ctrl + B (c) Ctrl + A (d) None of these.

9. What is the full form of BIOS?
   (a) Basic Input Output System
   (b) BIOSSS
   (c) BIO Settlement
   (d) None of these.

10. What is the short key for COPY?
    (a) Ctrl + B (b) Ctrl + C (c) Ctrl + A (d) None of these

11. The format of correct e-mail is _____.
    (a) username@domainname
    (b) username
    (c) Name + domain
    (d) None of the these.

12. The extension of MS-Word is _____.
    (a) .docx (b) .xls (c) .ppt (d) None of these.

13. The extension of web page is _____.
    (a) .html (b) .mp4 (c) .hhtm (d) None of these.

14. The extension of image file is _____.
    (a) .mp3 (b) .jpg (c) .amr (d) None of these.

15. Which of the following is a graphics software used for making presentations?
    (a) MS-Windows   (b) MS-Excel   (c) MS-PowerPoint   (d) MS-Word
16. Following is a type of Slide animation:
    (a) Fly from top   (b) Flash once   (c) Typewriter   (d) All of them.
17. Internet is governed by _____.
    (a) W3C (World Wide Web Consortium)
    (b) Interknit (Internet Network Information Center
    (c) IETF (Internet Engineering Task Force)
    (d) None of these.
18. USENET is:
    (a) a set of tools reserved exclusively for Internet administrators.
    (b) short for United States Electronic Network.
    (c) a bulletin board system that allows for posting and responding to messages on the Internet.
    (d) a precursor to the Internet that is now obsolete.
19. The ascending order of a data hierarchy is:
    (a) Bit-byte-record-field-file-database
    (b) Byte-bit-field-record-file-database
    (c) Byte-bit-record-file-field-database
    (d) Bit-byte-field-record-file-database.
20. To change the size of the chart without changing its proportion, you have to press _____ as you drag a corner handle.
    (a) [Shift]   (b) [Alt]   (c) [Ctrl]   (d) [F11]
21. The first computer is _____.
    (a) Anatur   (b) Calculator   (c) Abacus   (d) None of the above.
22. ALU is a part of _____.
    (a) CPU   (b) CU   (c) Memory   (d) None of the above.
23. To open a file in MS-Word, we use _____.
    (a) Ctrl + O   (b) Ctrl + N   (c) O   (d) None of the above.
24. The extension of MS-Excel is _____.
    (a) .xls   (b) .gif   (c) .doc   (d) None of these.
25. The extension of WordPad is _____.
    (a) .rtf   (b) .ttf   (c) .txt   (d) None of these.
26. Windows distinguishes between the different drives by means of a naming convention. Each drive is designated by a letter followed by _____.
    (a) a colon
    (b) an exclamation point
    (c) a semicolon
    (d) an asterisk.
27. The following is a slide transition effect.
    (a) Wipe all-over   (b) Bit by bit   (c) Dissolve   (d) None of these.
28. What is the control unit's function in the CPU?
    (a) To decode program instructions
    (b) To transfer data to primary storage
    (c) To perform logical operations
    (d) To store program instructions.

29. The purpose of the MOVE command is to _____.
    (a) move one or more files to the location you specify
    (b) rename directories
    (c) Both (a) and (b).
    (d) None of the above.

30. GUI is used as an interface between _____.
    (a) hardware and software
    (b) man and machine
    (c) software and user
    (d) None of these.

31. To create a new blank presentation you could _____.
    (a) click on the New button
    (b) use the File New command
    (c) Both of the above.
    (d) None of the above.

32. How do you make an inserted sound file play continuously over several slides?
    (a) In the Custom Animation task pane, open Effects Options and set the sound to play for the desired number of slides.
    (b) Using the Record Sound feature, press the Record button and play your music as you click through the whole slide show.
    (c) Using the Play CD Audio Track feature, set the CD to play for the desired number of tracks.
    (d) All of the above.

33. The area on a slide that holds text that will appear in the presentation outline is a _____.
    (a) Textbox   (b) Title box   (c) Placeholder   (d) Bullet point

34. The purpose of Auto Format command in Excel is to
    (a) create a professional and consistent look for your data.
    (b) choose between standard table formats that include borders, shading, font colors and other formatting options.
    (c) easily apply a consistent format throughout a workbook.
    (d) All of the above.

35. The ascending order of a data hierarchy is:
    (a) Bit-byte-record-field-file-database
    (b) Byte-bit-field-record-file-database
    (c) Byte-bit-record-file-field-database
    (d) Bit-byte-field-record-file-database

36. What is meant by computer literacy?
    (a) Ability to write computer programs
    (b) Knowing what a computer can and cannot do
    (c) Knowing computer related vocabulary
    (d) Ability to assemble computers.

37. The software application that is used most often is _____.
    (a) Word processing
    (b) Database
    (c) graphical presentation
    (d) Spreadsheet

38. What is the first step in MS-Word to change line spacing?
    (a) To open the Format menu
    (b) To click the Line Spacing button
    (c) To select the paragraphs you want to change
    (d) To open the Paragraph menu.

39. A mouse, trackball, and joystick are examples of_____.
    (a) pointing devices
    (b) pen input devices
    (c) data collection devices
    (d) multimedia devices

40. The Save As dialog box can be used
    (a) for saving the file for the first time.
    (b) to save a file by some alternative name.
    (c) to save a file in a format other than Word.
    (d) All of the above.

41. The contents of the Clipboard remain the same until
    (a) you cut another text.
    (b) you shut down your computer.
    (c) you copy another text.
    (d) All of the above.

42. You will probably use Borders in Word where
    (a) you wish to add emphasis to particular paragraphs.
    (b) you wish to draw lines above and below or to the left and right of paragraphs.
    (c) you wish to surround the paragraphs with different styles of boxes.
    (d) All of the above.

43. The Formatting Toolbar option is applied
    (a) to paragraph selection only.
    (b) to character selection only.
    (c) to both character as well as paragraph selections.
    (d) None of the above.

44. A page break is used to do what?
    (a) Create a new page at the insertion point
    (b) Create a new page at the bottom of the document
    (c) Create a new page that cannot be deleted
    (d) Create a blank page at the top of the document.

45. The most common input device used today is the _____.
    (a) Motherboard
    (b) Central processing unit
    (c) System unit
    (d) Keyboard

46. Which kind of storage device can be carried around?
    (a) Hard disk   (b) Diskette   (c) Main memory   (d) System cabinet

47. If a computer is on but does not respond to a system reset, what is it said to be?
    (a) Dead   (b) Insensitive   (c) Off   (d) Hung

48. GIGO stands for _____.
    (a) Garbage Input, Garbage Output
    (b) Gigabytes in, Gigabytes out.
    (c) Garbage In, Garbage out
    (d) None of the above.

49. The difference between memory and storage is that memory is _____ and storage is _____.
    (a) temporary, permanent
    (b) permanent, temporary
    (c) slow, fast
    (d) None of the above.

50. To go to slide number press.
    (a) Slide number + [Enter]
    (b) [Pug]
    (c) Both (a) and (b).
    (d) All of these.

State True or False

1. ROM is a Permanent memory.
2. RAM is a Temporary memory.
3. Docx is the extension of MS-Excel.
4. Tim Berners-Lee is the father of WWW.
5. Charles Babbage is the father of computer.
6. 56. KB stands for kilobit.
7. USB stands for Union Serial Bus.
8. Internet is the example of connectivity.
9. 1TB = 1024 MB
10. Debugging is the process of finding errors in the software code.
11. The Windows key will launch the START button.
12. Computers cannot understand the binary language.
13. TB stands for Tango byte.
14. To move the beginning of a line of next, press END key.
15. CPU is the brain of a computer.
16. Mother-board is also known as System Board.
17. 1 MB equals to 1024 KB.
18. 0 and 1 are used in binary language.
19. CPU transforms input data into output.
20. LAN is small, single-site network.
21. Keyboard is an output device.
22. Personal computers can be connected together to form a network.
23. Mouse is a pointing device.
24. LAN, MAN and WAN are the types of network.
25. You can stop using the spelling checker at any time by clicking the close button.
26. The View menu in Word is used to create header and footer.
27. Check boxes are used to present options requiring individual on/off decisions in Message boxes.
28. A blank line is also called as a paragraph. It is called as an empty paragraph.
29. [Del] key deletes the text to the left of the insertion point.
30. Word includes a number of AutoCorrect entries. We can use these entries but cannot modify them.
31. You can create your own dictionaries in Word.
32. When you create a formula that contains a function, the Insert Function dialog box helps you enter worksheet functions.
33. In Word, you can change the character spacing from the toolbar.
34. E-commerce consists primarily of the distributing, buying, selling, marketing and servicing of products or services over electronic systems such as the Internet.

35. Word template does not include style formatting.
36. The Blank Web page template of Word contains pre-formatted or pre-designed options.
37. The Word organizer does not copy the AutoText entries.
38. Different cells within a row can have different heights.
39. The AutoFit to contents enables Word to widen or narrow columns based on the contents you insert in Insert Table.
40. Print Preview of Word does not allow you to do any editing.
41. From the Mail Merge Helper dialog box, you can only open an existing data source but cannot create a new one.
42. The name box is at the left end of the formula bar.
43. In Excel, the delete and clear commands perform the same function.
44. You cannot change the Font style of the entire workbook by a single command. It can be changed only worksheet by worksheet.
45. The spelling and grammar check can only be done once the text is selected.
46. Firmware is software that is embedded in a hardware device.
47. Primary memory has higher storage capacity than secondary memory.
48. Pressing F1 is a common way to invoke help in Windows.
49. To select an entire document in Word, move the pointer to the left of any document text until it changes to a right-pointing arrow, and then double-click.
50. [Ctrl] + [U] selects the italics style for the selected text.

ANSWER KEYS

Multiple Choice Questions

1. (a)	2. (b)	3. (a)	4. (c)	5. (c)	6. (c)	7. (a)	8. (b)
9. (a)	10. (b)	11. (a)	12. (a)	13. (a)	14. (b)	15. (c)	16. (b)
17. (d)	18. (c)	19. (d)	20. (a)	21. (c)	22. (a)	23. (a)	24. (a)
25. (a)	26. (a)	27. (c)	28. (a)	29. (a)	30. (c)	31. (c)	32. (d)
33. (c)	34. (d)	35. (d)	36. (c)	37. (a)	38. (c)	39. (a)	40. (d)
41. (d)	42. (d)	43. (c)	44. (a)	45. (d)	46. (b)	47. (d)	48. (c)
49. (a)	50. (a)						

State True or False

1. True	2. True	3. False	4. True	5. True	6. False	7. False	8. True
9. False	10. True	11. True	12. False	13. False	14. False	15. True	16. True
17. True	18. True	19. True	20. True	21. False	22. True	23. True	24. True
25. False	26. False	27. True	28. True	29. False	30. True	31. True	32. True
33. True	34. True	35. False	36. True	37. False	38. False	39. True	40. True
41. False	42. True	43. False	44. True	45. False	46. True	47. False	48. True
49. True	50. False						

SOLVED PAPER – 9

Multiple Choice Questions

1. CD stands for _____.
   (a) Compact Disk (b) Computer disk (c) Connector DJ (d) None of these.
2. OMR stands for _____.
   (a) Optical Mark Reader (b) Optical Mark Reading
   (c) Optical Mark Radar (d) None of these.
3. AMD stands for _____.
   (a) Advantage Micro Distance (b) And Mad Dam
   (c) Advanced Micro Devices (d) None of the above.
4. CD-R stands for _____.
   (a) Compact Disk – Recordable (b) Collect Data – Radium
   (c) Color Data – Ring (d) None of these.
5. LAN stands for _____.
   (a) Local Area Network (b) Limited Area Network
   (c) Limit and Notice (d) None of the above.
6. WWW stands for _____.
   (a) World Wide Web (b) World Wide Websites
   (c) World Wider Webs (d) None of the above.
7. TB stands for _____.
   (a) Tetra Byte (b) Tera Byte (c) Team Byte (d) None of these.
8. What is the short key for PASTE?
   (a) Ctrl + V (b) Ctrl + A (c) Ctrl + B (d) None of these.
9. What is the short key for Help?
   (a) F1 (b) F2 (c) F4 (d) None of these.
10. What is the short key for search?
    (a) F2 (b) F3 (c) F4 (d) None of these.
11. What is the short key for REBOOT?
    (a) Del (b) Alt + Del (c) Ctrl + Alt + Del (d) None of these.
12. ASCII stands for _____.
    (a) Australia Standard Code for Inter Interchange
    (b) American Standard Code for Inter Interchange
    (c) American Standard Code for Information Interchange
    (d) None of the above.
13. A tape drive offers _____ access to data.
    (a) timely (b) sequential (c) random (d) None of these.

14. CU is the part of _____.
    (a) ALU (b) CPU (c) CU (d) None of these.

15. www.testonnet.blogspot.com is an example of a _____.
    (a) Website (b) BLOG (c) Facebook Page (d) None of these.

16. SRAM stands for _____.
    (a) Shri RAM (b) Satyam RAM (c) Static RAM (d) Storage RAM

17. IMAC is the name of a _____.
    (a) Machine (b) Processor (c) Modem (d) None of these.

18. FLASH is a _____.
    (a) ROM (b) Hardware (c) Software (d) None of these.

19. Ctrl + B is used for _____.
    (a) Underline (b) Bold (c) Italic (d) None of these

20. Who is father of computer?
    (a) Lady Ada Lovelace
    (b) Charles Babbage
    (c) Tim Berner Lee
    (d) George Boole

21. Find a right e-mail.
    (a) shwet@india.com (b) ShwetIndia.com (c) satyam.com (d) None of the above.

22. The extension of MS-Powerpoint is _____.
    (a) .html (b) .xls (c) .ppt (d) None of these.

23. The extension of NotePad is _____.
    (a) .txt (b) .doc (c) .ttf (d) None of these.

24. Most news readers present newsgroup articles in:
    (a) Threads (b) Mail (c) Column (d) None of these.

25. Fiber optics has the advantage of _____.
    (a) being cheaper to install
    (b) being easier to install than twisted wire
    (c) having no interference
    (d) using direct line-of-sight

26. We can set up the margin for _____.
    (a) Headers (b) Footers (c) Both (a) and (b). (d) None of these.

27. Which of the following characters is allowed in a Windows file name or folder?
    (a) : (b) ? (c) _ (d) >

28. In slide master, the footer area appears at _____.
    (a) left of the page
    (b) center of the page
    (c) top of the page
    (d) bottom of the page

29. The built-in default copying in Excel is programmed to _____.
    (a) use relative position when copying formulas
    (b) use absolute position when copying formulas
    (c) use mixed position when copying formulas
    (d) None of the above.

30. The e-mail component of Internet Explorer is called _____.
    (a) Messenger Mailbox
    (b) Message Box
    (c) Outlook Express
    (d) None of these.

31. The CPU (central processing unit) consists of:
    (a) Input, Output and Processing
    (b) Control unit, Primary storage and Secondary storage
    (c) Control unit, Arithmetic-logic unit and Primary storage
    (d) Input, Processing and Storage.

32. To delete the selected sentence, we can press the following key:
    (a) [Del]   (b) [Backspace]   (c) Both (a) and (b).   (d) None of these.

33. The language that the computer can understand and execute is called:
    (a) System program
    (b) Application software
    (c) Machine language
    (d) None of these.

34. In Excel, if you click on the Gridlines and Draft Quality check box on the sheet tab property sheet of page setup dialog box then _____.
    (a) gridlines will be printed
    (b) gridlines will not be printed
    (c) sometimes print
    (d) None of these.

35. Which of the following statements about search engines and directories are true?
    (a) A search engine does not discriminate between good and bad sites.
    (b) A search engine displays all Web pages that contain your keywords and may list thousands of unordered results.
    (c) We can manipulate the results of a search engine by using SEO techniques.
    (d) All of the above.

36. When a computer prints a report, this output is called_____.
    (a) soft copy   (b) hard copy   (c) COM   (d) None of these.

37. ROUND(2.15,1) entered in a cell displays _____.
    (a) 2   (b) 2.1   (c) 2.2   (d) None of these.

38. MOD(-3,2) entered in a cell displays _____.
    (a) −1.5   (b) 1   (c) 0   (d) −1

39. The default page orientation in Excel is _____.
    (a) Landscape   (b) Horizontal   (c) Portrait   (d) None of these.

40. Which of the following is a part of the Central Processing Unit?
    (a) Keyboard
    (b) Printer
    (c) Tape
    (d) Arithmetic Logic Unit

41. A floppy disk contains _____.
    (a) circular tracks only
    (b) sectors only
    (c) both circular tracks and sectors
    (d) None of these.

42. Which of the following is a graphical package?
    (a) Corel DRAW   (b) MS-Excel   (c) MS-Word   (d) None of these.

43. The gigantic work of simulating the airflow around an entire aircraft can only be done by using fast _____.
    (a) Microcomputers (b) Minicomputers (c) Supercomputers (d) None of these.

44. Which of the rule mentioned below for range names is incorrect?
    (a) Names cannot be the same as a cell reference.
    (b) In a range name you are allowed to use spaces or commas.
    (c) The only separators allowed are under score characters and/or periods between words.
    (d) Range names can be directly used in formulas.

45. In which Word menu, Letter wizard command appears?
    (a) Format (b) Tools (c) Insert (d) Table

46. In Word, split cells command appears in _____ menu.
    (a) Table (b) Format (c) Insert (d) Tools

47. Status bar shows different types of keys:
    (a) Num lock key (b) Scroll lock key (c) Caps lock key (d) All of these.

48. In Excel the intersection of a row and column is called a _____.
    (a) square (b) cubicle (c) cell (d) worksheet

49. In Excel, once a range has been named, you can go to the range _____.
    (a) by selecting ranges using the name box
    (b) by selecting ranges using the [F5] key
    (c) Both (a) and (b).
    (d) None of these.

50. One of the statements is not true:
    (a) In its default settings, a word processor does not hyphenate the text.
    (b) Hyphenating helps when you are dealing with thin columnar text.
    (c) By hyphenating, the looks of the justified thin columns will look greatly improved
    (d) Microsoft Word hyphenates text in its default settings.

State True or False

1. Bold, Italic and Bold-Italic are available for all fonts.
2. ALU and CU consist of CPU.
3. A1 is an example of absolute cell reference.
4. A serial port transmits data, one bit at a time.
5. The title bar displays the name of current active word document.
6. Courier is a font.
7. In Unix, commands are case-sensitive.
8. Main memory is a software component.
9. WWW is another name of Internet.
10. SMTP is associated with e-mail.
11. FTP moves files between devices.

12. All web address starts with :http//.
13. Internet Explorer is a web browser.
14. TCP provides packet level reliability.
15. In star topology, any node can communicate with another node directly.
16. ASP stands for Active Server Pages.
17. HTTP uses TCP and DNS uses UDP.
18. Read Only Memory is the full form of RAM.
19. The Request for Comments (RFCs) core topics are Internet and the TCP/IP protocol suites.
20. The Back and Forward buttons can be used to visit only pages from the same website.
21. A protocol used for fetching e-mail from a mailbox is POP1.
22. All conversations on the IRC are in English.
23. The full form of ISP is Information Source Provider.
24. A smiley is a sequence of ordinary printable characters, or a small image, intended to represent a human facial expression and convey an emotion.
25. LENGTH() function is used to find the length of the string.
26. The floating text (text not associated with objects in the chart) cannot be moved in the chart area.
27. You can add items to the Start menu of Windows.
28. You can swap over the functionality of the left and right mouse buttons.
29. The AutoContent Wizard creates the structure and contents based on the choices you make.
30. To insert a header or footer in a worksheet, select Header and Footer option in the File menu.
31. PowerPoint has more than twenty-four slide layouts.
32. Bullets and numbering appears in the standard toolbar.
33. The Cell/Range names are case sensitive.
34. Animation effects appear in the Standard toolbar.
35. BIOS stands for Basic Integrated Operating System.
36. Just as you can preview a worksheet before printing, it is not possible to preview a chart.
37. You can apply a color scheme to the current slide or to all slides in your presentation.
38. 99 sales is a valid name for a cell or a range.
39. PowerPoint allows you to differentiate your own animation effects.
40. Internet is not a commercial information service.
41. The network NSF net was later renamed as Internet.
42. The IP address space is divided into five classes five, which are given letters A through E.
43. LAN stands for Local Area Network.
44. Linux is an open-source operating system.
45. Nibble is equal to 4 bits.
46. Audio Output device can output only music.
47. In a spreadsheet, ordinary text is called a 'label'.

48. Function keys are programmable keys.
49. TCP allows several concurrent logins to the same host.
50. MEM and CLS are internal DOS commands.

ANSWER KEYS

Multiple Choice Questions

1. (a)	2. (a)	3. (c)	4. (a)	5. (a)	6. (a)	7. (b)	8. (a)
9. (a)	10. (b)	11. (c)	12. (c)	13. (b)	14. (b)	15. (a)	16. (c)
17. (a)	18. (a)	19. (b)	20. (b)	21. (a)	22. (c)	23. (a)	24. (b)
25. (d)	26. (c)	27. (c)	28. (d)	29. (a)	30. (c)	31. (c)	32. (c)
33. (c)	34. (a)	35. (d)	36. (b)	37. (c)	38. (b)	39. (c)	40. (d)
41. (c)	42. (a)	43. (c)	44. (b)	45. (b)	46. (a)	47. (d)	48. (c)
49. (a)	50. (d)						

State True or False

1. True	2. False	3. True	4. True	5. True	6. True	7. True	8. False
9. False	10. True	11. True	12. True	13. True	14. True	15. False	16. True
17. True	18. False	19. True	20. False	21. False	22. False	23. False	24. True
25. True	26. False	27. True	28. True	29. True	30. False	31. True	32. True
33. False	34. True	35. False	36. False	37. True	38. True	39. True	40. True
41. False	42. True	43. True	44. True	45. True	46. False	47. True	48. True
49. True	50. True						

MCQ SETS FROM VARIOUS PAPERS

MCQ Set 1

1. Which light-sensitive device converts printed text, drawings or images into digital form?
   - (a) Scanner
   - (b) Plotter
   - (c) OMR
   - (d) Keyboard
   - (e) None of them.

2. Which protocol is used to transfer e-mails between different hosts?
   - (a) FTP
   - (b) SMTP
   - (c) HTTP
   - (d) TELNET
   - (e) None of them.

3. _____ developed the basic computer architecture.
   - (a) John Von Neumann
   - (b) Garden Moore
   - (c) Charles Babbage
   - (d) John Napier

4. In MS-Excel, which operator is used to enter a formula in a cell?
   - (a) @
   - (b) #
   - (c) +
   - (d) =
   - (e) $

5. Into how many generations has the evolution of computers been classified till now?
   - (a) 3
   - (b) 4
   - (c) 5
   - (d) 6
   - (e) None of them.

6. The Fifth-generation computers are designed on _____.
   - (a) Artificial Intelligence
   - (b) Programming Intelligence
   - (c) VVLSI
   - (d) System Knowledge

7. The First-generation computers was designed on which of the following technology?
   - (a) Transistor
   - (b) Registers
   - (c) Vacuum Tube
   - (d) VLSI
   - (e) LSI

8. In which computer generation, Microprocessor were introduced?
   - (a) First Generation
   - (b) Second Generation
   - (c) Third Generation
   - (d) Fourth Generation

9. The Second-generation computers were made of _____.
   - (a) Transistors
   - (b) Registers
   - (c) LSI
   - (d) VLSI
   - (e) Vacuum Tubes

10. Select the non-volatile memory from the following options.
    - (a) RAM
    - (b) DRAM
    - (c) SRAM
    - (d) ROM

11. GUI means _____.
    - (a) Graph Use Interface
    - (b) Graphical User Interface
    - (c) Graphical Unique Interface
    - (d) Graphical Users Interchange

12. The instructions or data of any kind given to the computer is defined as the _____.
    (a) Information (b) Input (c) Output
    (d) Storage (e) Process

13. The processing time required by the computer to complete a job is known as the _____.
    (a) Real Time (b) Waiting Time (c) Execution Time (d) Delay Time

14. Select the circuit that is used as a 'Memory Device' in computers.
    (a) Attenuator (b) Rectifier (c) Comparator (d) Flip Flop

15. The memory size of mainframe and advanced microcomputers is expressed in _____.
    (a) Bits (b) Bytes (c) Kilobytes
    (d) Megabytes (e) Gbytes

16. _____ is not an application software.
    (a) Microsoft Office (b) Redhat Linux
    (c) Adobe Pagemaker (d) Photoshop

17. Which of the following is an invalid statement?
    (a) Photoshop is a graphical design tool by Adobe.
    (b) Windows XP is an operating system by Microsoft.
    (c) Linux is an open-source and freely available software.
    (d) Microsoft owns and sells the Linux Operating System.

18. In computer terminology, an error is also called as _____.
    (a) Bug (b) Debug (c) Cursor (d) Icon

19. MS-Word is an_____.
    (a) Operating System (b) Application Software
    (c) Input Device (d) Processing Device

20. The graphical images used to represent the files and folders is known as _____.
    (a) Task Bar (b) Icons (c) Windows (d) Desktop

21. Which of the following statements is not an advantage of magnetic disk storage?
    (a) Disk storage is less expensive than tape storage.
    (b) Disk storage is longer lasting than magnetic tape.
    (c) The access time of magnetic disk is much less than that of magnetic tape.
    (d) None of them.

22. 0 and 1 in the binary system, known as Binary Digits, are also described as _____.
    (a) Bits (b) Bytes (c) Decimal Bytes (d) Kilo bytes

23. What is the size of the commonly used floppy diskette?
    (a) 3.25" (b) 3.5" (c) 4.5"
    (d) 5.5" (e) None of them.

24. Which of the following is used to make the IC chip used in computers?
    (a) Iron Oxide (b) Chromium (c) Silicon (d) Silica

25. IBM developed which of the following operating systems?
    (a) Android (b) Windows (c) OS-2 (d) DOS

26. Which of the following processors performs arithmetical and logical operations?
    (a) ALU   (b) Register   (c) Control   (d) Cache Memory
27. Choose an early mainframe computer from the following options.
    (a) BRAINIA   (b) FUNTRIA   (c) UNIVAC   (d) ENIAC
28. Select the first processor introduced by Intel.
    (a) 3080   (b) 4004   (c) 8080   (d) 8086
29. Which protocol is used to transfer e-mail in the network?
    (a) IP   (b) FTP   (c) POP3   (d) SMTP
30. In which year was the first e-mail sent?
    (a) 1963   (b) 1969   (c) 1971   (d) 1972
31. Operating System is an example of what type of software?
    (a) Application (b) System   (c) Communication (d) Word Processing
32. Arithmetic logic unit (ALU) is used to _____.
    I. Store data
    II. Perform arithmetic operations
    III. Perform comparison
    IV. Communicate with the input devices
    (a) I only   (b) II only   (c) I and II only
    (d) II and III only   (e) None of the above.
33. The RAM _____.
    (a) allows the computer to save data electronically
    (b) stores the data unless you delete it
    (c) is a secondary memory
    (d) All of the above.
34. The advantage of supercomputers is that they can perform _____.
    (a) data retrieval operations
    (b) input–output intensive processing
    (b) mathematically intensive scientific programs
    (d) All of the above.
35. The operating system is responsible to manage _____.
    (a) memory   (b) processor   (c) disk and I/O devices   (d) All of the above.
36. Select the non-volatile memory that may be written only once.
    (a) RAM   (b) PROM   (c) EPROM   (d) EEPROM
37. Which of the following memory is programmed at the time of manufacturing?
    (a) RAM   (b) ROM   (c) PROM   (d) EPROM
38. Select the volatile memory from the following options.
    (a) RAM   (b) ROM   (c) EPROM   (d) PROM
39. Which of the following is the fastest?
    (a) CPU   (b) Magnetic Tapes and Disks
    (c) Video Terminal   (d) Sensors, Mechanical Controllers

40. The kilobyte (KB) is equivalent to how many bytes?
    (a) 512 bytes   (b) 814 bytes   (c) 1000 bytes   (d) 1024 bytes
41. Which of the following devices helps to transmit the computer's output over the telephone line?
    (a) Teleport   (b) Multiplexer   (c) Modem   (d) Cable
42. Which of the following devices is not required in a LAN?
    (a) Computers   (b) Modem   (c) Printer   (d) Cable
43. Which of the following initial program is saved in ROM?
    (a) Kernel   (b) OS Version
    (c) Bootstrap Loader   (d) Computer Start-up Loader
44. Computer virus is type of a _____.
    (a) memory   (b) bacteria   (c) hardware   (d) software
45. EEPROM means _____.
    (a) Electrically Enabled Programmable Read Only Memory
    (b) Electrically Erasable Programmable Read-Only Memory
    (c) Electronically Enabled Programmable Read Only Memory
    (d) Electronically Erasable Programmable Read-Only Memory
46. _____ is the most advanced version of ROM.
    (a) PROM   (b) RAM   (c) Cache Memory   (d) EEPROM
47. The Main Memory of the computer is also known as the _____.
    (a) RAM   (b) ROM   (c) Floppy Disk   (d) Hard Disk
48. The MS-Word document in Office 2007 is saved with which of the following extensions?
    (a) .docx   (b) .doc   (c) .pdf   (d) .txt
49. The computer port is required to accomplish which of the following tasks?
    (a) To Surf Internet.   (b) To Download Files.
    (c) To Communicate with Hard Disks.   (d) To Connect other Computer Devices.
50. One Megabyte (MB) is equivalent to_____.
    (a) 1024 Byte   (b) 1000 KB   (c) 1024 KB   (d) 1024 GB
51. Laser, Deskjet, Inkjet and Dot-matrix are all examples of which computer devices?
    (a) Printers   (b) Software   (c) Keyboards   (d) Monitors
52. Internet Explorer is an example of _____.
    (a) IP Address   (b) Browser   (c) Compiler   (d) Operating System
53. Which of the following developed the Audio Video Interleave (AVI) format?
    (a) Apple   (b) Adobe   (c) Macromedia   (d) Microsoft
54. Choose the high-speed memory used in computer from the following options.
    (a) RAM   (b) BIOS   (c) Cache   (d) Hard Disk
55. In a client–server model, what is the client's program usage?
    (a) To request for information   (b) To provide information and files
    (c) To serve software files to other computers   (d) To distribute data files to other computers.

56. Select an example of Operating System from the following options.
    (a) MS-Access   (b) MS-Excel   (c) MS-Windows   (d) MS-Word

57. Which of the following is not used as secondary storage?
    (a) Semiconductor Memory
    (b) Magnetic Disks
    (c) Magnetic Drums
    (d) Magnetic Tapes

58. General-purpose computers are those that can be adapted to countless uses simply by changing its _____.
    (a) Output Devices   (b) Input Device   (c) Program
    (d) Processor   (e) None of these.

59. Eight bits are equivalent to a _____.
    (a) Nibble   (b) Byte   (c) Word   (d) Record

60. Usually a modern computer comprises of _____.
    (a) LSI Chips
    (b) more than 10,000 vacuum tubes
    (c) magnetic tape for primary memory
    (d) magnetic cores for secondary storage

61. The term 'memory' is used in which of the following context?
    (a) Input device   (b) Output device   (c) Logic   (d) Storage

62. Which of the following devices is used to get the hardcopy of a document?
    (a) Printer   (b) CRT   (c) Card Reader   (d) Computer Console

63. Select the most powerful computer from the following options.
    (a) Mainframe   (b) Superconductor   (c) Supercomputer   (d) Microcomputer

64. Select the valid statement in the context of primary storage from the following options.
    (a) It is a part of the CPU.
    (b) It is relatively more expensive.
    (c) It gives very fast access to data.
    (d) All of them.

65. What do you call the list of instructions used by a computer to perform an operation?
    (a) Output   (b) Program   (c) CPU   (d) Text

66. What do you call the process of copying data from a memory location?
    (a) Writing   (b) Reading   (c) Controlling   (d) Booting

67. What do you call the process of saving data into a storage location?
    (a) Writing   (b) Reading   (c) Controlling   (d) Booting

MCQ Set 2

1. Select the outcome of data processing from the following options.
   (a) Information   (b) System
   (c) Software Program   (d) Data

2. Which of the following is not an example of an input device?
   (a) Keyboard   (b) Speaker   (c) Mouse   (d) Scanner

3. In Internet terminology, DNS means _____.
   - (a) Data Name System
   - (b) Domain Name System
   - (c) Dynamic Name System
   - (d) Distributed Name System

4. The term 'portable program' means it can run _____.
   - (a) independently from its authors
   - (b) independently on any platform
   - (c) program with wheels
   - (d) None of them.

5. Which of the following memories can only be read?
   - (a) RAM
   - (b) DRAM
   - (c) ROM
   - (d) Virtual Memory
   - (e) Secondary Memory

6. The CPU manages_____.
   - (a) Controls Memory
   - (b) the Input Data
   - (c) all Input, Output and Processing
   - (d) None of the above.

7. USB means _____.
   - (a) Unique Serial Bus
   - (b) Universal Serial Bus
   - (c) Unique Sequential Bus
   - (e) Universal Sequential Bus

8. ALU means _____.
   - (a) Arithmetic Long Unit
   - (b) Arithmetic Logic Unit
   - (c) Arithmetic Local Unit
   - (d) Arithmetic Logic Utility

9. CPU means _____.
   - (a) Central Processing Unit
   - (b) Control Processing Unit
   - (c) Common Processing Unit
   - (d) Central Performance Unit

10. Which of the following computer part installs the ROM, RAM and CPU together?
    - (a) ALU
    - (b) Hard Disk
    - (c) Mother Board
    - (d) None of them.

11. Which of the following technique converts an analog signal into a digital bit stream?
    - (a) Pulse Code Modulation
    - (b) Digital Signal Generator
    - (c) Pulse Signal Modulation
    - (d) None of them.

12. Which optical input device interprets pencil marks on paper media?
    - (a) OMR
    - (b) Magnetic Tape
    - (c) Optical Scanners
    - (d) Punch Card Reader

13. Which of the following computer program converts the data into a code system?
    - (a) Trigger
    - (b) Emulator
    - (c) Encoder
    - (d) Decoder

14. DRAM means _____.
    - (a) Data Random Active Memory
    - (b) Data Random Access Memory
    - (c) Double Random Access Memory
    - (d) Dynamic Random Access Memory

15. What is the use of Cache RAM?
    - (a) It is similar to the hard disk.
    - (b) Memory to save secret data like passwords
    - (c) Faster memory used for data accessed often
    - (d) Extended memory used to control hard disk overload.

16. Cache RAM represents which of the following options?
    (a) PROM   (b) SRAM   (c) Flash   (d) DRAM
17. Which of the following is responsible for holding the computer's BIOS?
    (a) SRAM   (b) Flash   (c) EEPROM   (d) DRAM
18. Which of the following memory holds the clients programs when the computer is shut down?
    (a) RAM   (b) ROM   (c) Cache   (d) Hard Disk Drive
19. What is Peripheral Component Interconnect (PCI)?
    (a) Computer Monitor   (b) A kind of graphics
    (c) A modem standard   (d) Type of system bus.
20. Which of the following companies does not manufacture microprocessors?
    (a) AMD(Advanced Micro Devices)   (b) IBM
    (c) Intel   (d) Microsoft
21. Why do we need system bus?
    (a) To carry instructions
    (b) To stores data and instructions
    (c) To connect with other computers
    (d) To connect the different components of the computer.
22. Which of the following company does not manufacture PC?
    (a) Gateway   (b) Intel   (c) Compaq   (d) Dell
23. LAN means _____.
    (a) Local Area Network   (b) Leased Area Network
    (c) Latency Around Network   (d) Largest Affordable Network
24. Internet Browser understands which of the following programming languages to display information from the World Wide Web?
    (a) Assembly Language   (b) HTML
    (c) C++   (d) Machine Code
25. Which wireless technology is used by electronic gadgets for exchanging data over short distances?
    (a) Wi-Fi   (b) Bluetooth   (c) Modem   (d) USB
26. Name the process of buying and selling of products over the Internet?
    (a) Net Banking   (b) Online Shopping (c) E-Commerce (d) Digital Marketing
27. Select the two categories of computer monitors.
    (a) CRT and DVD   (b) LCD and DVD   (c) CRT and LCD   (d) DVD and VCD
28. What is the basic building block for digital circuit?
    (a) Logic Gate   (b) BIOS   (c) CMOS   (d) DMOS
29. Which of the following keys are present at the top row of the keyboard?
    (a) Numeric   (b) Type Writer   (c) Function   (d) Navigation
30. Which of the following computers are used in Banking, Railways, and Airlines department?
    (a) Super Computer   (b) Micro Computer
    (c) Mini Computer   (d) Mainframe Computer

31. Who invented the computer mouse?
    (a) Chester Carlson (b) John Mauchly
    (c) J Presper Eckert (d) Douglas Engelbart

32. Which of the following is used to start the computer?
    (a) ROM (b) RAM (c) USB (d) All of these.

33. Which of the following memory saves the data temporarily while you are working on the computer?
    (a) ROM (b) RAM (c) CPU (d) Flash Memory

34. _____ are responsible for carrying data between the components on the motherboard.
    (a) Peripherals (b) Bays (c) CMOS (d) Buses

35. Data in the spreadsheet is organized in which of the following manner?
    (a) Height and Width (b) Layers and Planes
    (c) Rows and Columns (d) Lines and Spaces

36. Which of the following is a valid statement?
    (a) Bit represents grouping of digital numbers.
    (b) Eight-digit binary number is equivalent to a bit.
    (c) Eight-digit binary number is equivalent to a byte.
    (d) Byte is a single digit in a binary number system.

37. Which of the following converts input to output?
    (a) Storage (b) Memory
    (c) CPU (d) Input–Output Unit

38. In binary system, how many options are given?
    (a) Zero (b) One (c) Two (d) Three

39. The collection of web pages is called _____ whereas the very first page of a website is known as the _____.
    (a) Web-page, Web-site (b) Web-site, Home-page
    (c) Web-page, Home-page (d) Home-page, Web-page

40. The pointer changes its shape to hand each time it is positioned over the _____.
    (a) Grammar Error (b) Spelling Error (c) Screen Tip (d) Hyperlink

41. What is the program or instructions to perform a task?
    (a) Icon (b) Information (c) Software (d) Hardware

42. 'www' means _____.
    (a) World Work Web (b) World Wide Web
    (c) World Whole Web (d) World Word Web

43. Which of the following menu has the cut, copy, and paste options?
    (a) File (b) Edit (c) Tools (d) Home

44. Tab key is used to _____.
    (a) move the cursor across the screen (b) indent a paragraph
    (c) move the cursor down the screen (d) Both (a) and (b).

45. Which of the following computers is considered to be the most important and powerful computer in any network?
    (a) Network Station (b) Network Server (c) Network Client (d) Desktop

46. Which of the following defines the connectivity of a computer system?
    (a) Internet (b) Data (c) Power Cord (d) Hard Disk

47. The software converts data into _____.
    (a) Web sites (b) Programs (c) Information (d) Objects

48. Which of the following saves data in a temporary area to paste it later at another location?
    (a) ROM (b) Hard Disk (c) CD-ROM (d) Clipboard

49. Which of the following science deals with the knowledge similar to that of human beings?
    (a) Artificial Intelligence (AI) (b) Nanotechnology
    (c) Computer science (d) Simulation

50. What is the name of the process of making changes to an existing document?
    (a) Adjusting (b) Editing (c) Creating (d) Modifying

51. Which of the following systems is used by the computer to store data and make calculations?
    (a) Octal (b) Binary (c) Hexadecimal (d) Decimal

52. Select the largest storage unit from the following options.
    (a) Kilobyte (KB) (b) Megabyte (MB) (c) Gigabyte (GB) (d) Terabyte (TB)

53. Which of the following keys will activate the Start button?
    (a) Esc (b) Shift (c) Windows (d) Shortcut

54. Name the process of searching for errors in software coding.
    (a) Running (b) Testing (c) Compiling (d) Debugging

55. Which of the following keys helps to move the cursor to the beginning of a line of text?
    (a) Shift (b) Home (c) Enter (d) Page Up

56. Which of the following words describes the contents of the message while sending an e-mail?
    (a) Subject (b) To (c) CC (d) Contents

57. Which of the following holds various system applications and tells the computer how to use its various components?
    (a) Application Program (b) Network
    (c) Folder (d) Operating System

58. In computer terminology, what does the term 'backup' means?
    (a) Accessing data on tape
    (b) Filtering old data from the new data
    (c) Adding more components to the network
    (d) Preventing data loss by making a copy of the original data.

59. Which of the following statement is an advantage of using a dial-up-internet?
    (a) It uses broadband technology.
    (b) Router secures the network.
    (c) The speed of Modem is very fast.
    (d) It uses an existing telephone line.

60. In Internet terminology, the unsolicited e-mails are described as _____.
    (a) Spam (b) Starred (c) Unread (d) Drafts

61. What is created when two or more computers are connected to each other for sharing information?
    (a) Pipeline (b) Tunnel (c) Network (d) Router

62. Which of the following computers are portable and can be carried along while travelling?
    (a) Servers (b) Supercomputers
    (c) Laptops (d) Mini Computers

63. Which network technology can be used to connect two LANs that are spread geographically apart on a large area?
    (a) LAN (b) MAN (c) WAN (d) SAN

64. Web page coding is done in which of the following languages?
    (a) JAVA Script (b) Hyper Text Markup Language
    (c) C Language (d) Fifth-generation language

65. _____ saves the frequently given instructions to the computer application for further use.
    (a) The Hard Disk (b) Cache Memory (c) RAM (d) Registers

66. In Internet terminology, what are the personal logs or journal entries displayed on the Web page?
    (a) Listservs (b) Blogs (c) Mails (d) Webcasts

67. Which of the following is not a broadband internet connection?
    (a) DSL (b) Satellite (c) Cable (d) Dial-up

68. Which of the following suits to the term 'Linux' operating system?
    (a) Mac (b) Microsoft (c) Windows (d) Open-source

69. Choose the correct data elements from smallest to the largest?
    (a) Character, record, field, database, file
    (b) Character, file, record, field, database
    (c) Character, field, record, file, database
    (d) Bit, byte, character, record, field, file, database

70. With respect to a file, which of the following statements is invalid?
    (a) File extension is a different name of the file type.
    (b) Each file in same folder must have a unique name.
    (c) Files may either share the same name or the same extension but not both.
    (d) The file extension comes before the dot (.) followed by the file name.

71. Which of the following problems may not be an indicator of a computer virus?
    (a) CD-ROM stops functioning.
    (b) Existing program files and icons disappears.
    (c) Web browser opens an unusual home page.
    (d) Unexpected messages or images are displayed on the screen.

72. Select the correct relationship between hardware and its function.
    (a) Mouse → Input (b) Monitor → Input
    (c) CPU → Storage (d) Hard Disk → Processing

73. Which of the following keys helps to move the cursor to the bottom of the document?
    (a) Shift Key (b) Ctrl + End key (c) Ctrl + Home key (d) End key

74. The document is printed in which of the following print mode by default?
    (a) Landscape
    (b) Portrait
    (c) Page setup
    (d) Print Preview

75. SMTP means _____.
    (a) Server Message Transfer Process
    (b) Simple Messaging Text Process
    (c) Simple Mail Transfer Protocol
    (d) Slow Messaging Transfer Protocol

76. Which of the following is considered to be the 'backbone' of World Wide Web?
    (a) File Transfer Protocol (FTP)
    (b) Uniform Resource Locator (URL)
    (c) Hyper Text Transfer Protocol (HTTP)
    (d) Hyper Text Mark-Up Language (HTML)

77. Which of the following applications helps to access the 'World Wide Web'?
    (a) Search Engine
    (b) Browser
    (c) High Bandwidth
    (d) Instant Messaging

78. What type of waves is used by the wireless network to transmit signals?
    (a) Sound
    (b) Radio
    (c) Magnetic
    (d) Mechanical

79. What device includes an adapter that decodes data sent in radio signals?
    (a) Modem
    (b) Digital Translator
    (c) Router
    (d) Switch

80. Which of the following is generally not a feature of a computer?
    (a) Accuracy
    (b) Speed
    (c) Versatility
    (d) Intelligence

81. Which of the following is generally not a feature of an e-mail?
    (a) Low cost
    (b) Speed
    (c) Paper waste reduction
    (d) Record maintenance in database

82. Which of the following input devices is not required while working with MS Office?
    (a) Scanner
    (b) Light Pen
    (c) Joystick
    (d) Mouse

83. Name the process of loading Operating System onto the RAM.
    (a) Saving
    (b) Booting
    (c) Compiling
    (d) Scanning

84. Which of the following device cannot perform calculations?
    (a) Notebook Computer
    (b) Tablet Computer
    (c) Mobile Phones
    (d) Scanners

85. Name the bar at the top of a window that displays the name of the window.
    (a) Menu bar
    (b) Taskbar
    (c) Title bar
    (d) Status bar

86. URL means _____.
    (a) Universal Research List
    (b) Universal Recourse List
    (c) Uniform Resource Locator
    (d) Uniform Research Locator

87. Which of the following key combinations is used to "Undo" the last action done in a document?
    (a) Ctrl + U
    (b) Ctrl + X
    (c) Ctrl + Y
    (d) Ctrl + Z

88. Which of the following is also described as 'Chip'?
    (a) Register
    (b) Transistor
    (c) Semiconductor
    (d) Integrated Circuit

89. Which of the following applications helps to navigate and surf the World Wide Web?
    (a) Internet
    (b) Networks
    (c) Hypertext
    (d) Web Browsers

90. Usually what is the normal storage capacity of a CD-ROM?
    (a) 680 Bytes   (b) 680 KB   (c) 680 MB   (d) 680 GB
91. Which of the following storage devices allows you save the data but you cannot erase or edit it?
    (a) Tape Drive   (b) Hard Disk   (c) CD-ROM   (d) Floppy Disk
92. Choose the largest manufacturer of Hard Disk Drives from the following options.
    (a) 3M   (b) IBM   (c) Samsung   (d) Seagate
93. Which of the following programs are permanent as hardware and saved in ROM?
    (a) Modules   (b) Firmware   (c) Software   (d) Hardware
94. Which of the following options is used to save an existing document in a different location?
    (a) Save   (b) Share   (c) Save As   (d) Save as Web Page
95. Which of the following does not manufactur Computer Hard Disk drives?
    (a) Intel   (b) Samsung   (c) Seagate   (d) Western Digital
96. Choose the drawback of the laser printer from the following options?
    (a) It is very slow.   (b) The output is of a lower quality.
    (c) It is quieter than an impact printer.   (d) None of them.
97. Different components on the motherboard of a PC processor unit are linked together by sets or parallel electrical conducting lines. What are these lines called?
    (a) Conductors   (b) Busses   (c) Connectors
    (d) Connectivity   (e) None of these.
98. What does the term 'dedicated computer' imply?
    (a) Computer that uses one kind of software.
    (b) Computer that is used by only one person.
    (c) Computer that is meant for application software.
    (d) Computer that is assigned for one task.
99. Which of the following code represents the instructions and memory addresses?
    (a) Binary word   (b) Binary codes   (c) Character code   (d) Parity bit
100. Hard Disks are _____ as compared to diskettes.
    (a) less rigid   (b) more portable   (c) more expensive   (d) slowly accessed
101. The secondary storage devices can only store data but they cannot perform _____.
    (a) Arithmetic Operations   (b) Logic Operations
    (c) Fetch Operations   (d) Any of the above.
102. Which of the following companies is the largest manufacturer of microprocessors?
    (a) AMD   (b) IBM   (c) Intel   (d) Motorola
103. Which of the following computer memory stores data and programs being processed by the CPU currently?
    (a) PROM   (b) Mass memory
    (c) Internal memory   (d) Non-volatile memory
104. Which of the following DOS command is used to set a name to a disk?
    (a) VOL   (b) VOLUME   (c) LABEL   (d) DISKLABEL

105. Which of the following file begins MS-Word application?
    (a) Word.exe   (b) Word2019.exe   (c) MSword.exe   (d) Winword.exe

106. In MS-WORD 2007, which menu shows the 'Symbol' dialog box?
    (a) View   (b) Insert   (c) Mailings   (d) Page Layout

107. What do the terms Superscript, Subscript, Outline, Emboss, and Engrave represent?
    (a) Font styles   (b) Font effects   (c) Text effects   (d) Word art

108. What do the term Shimmer, Sparkle text, Blinking Background etc. represent?
    (a) Font Styles   (b) Font Effects   (c) Text Effects   (d) Word Art

109. In MS-Word, which of the following is not a Font Spacing option?
    (a) Normal   (b) Loosely   (c) Condensed   (d) Expanded

110. What do the term Bold, Italic, Regular represent?
    (a) Font styles   (b) Font effects   (c) Text effects   (d) Word art

111. In MS-Excel, after entering data into a cell, if you don't want your entry placed into that cell, then:
    (a) Press Esc
    (b) Press the erase key
    (c) Press the Enter button
    (d) Press the Edit Formula button.

112. Which of the actions will not cut the data?
    (a) Pressing Ctrl + C
    (b) Pressing Ctrl + X
    (c) Selecting Edit → Cut
    (d) Clicking on the standard cut button.

113. Computers connected to a LAN (Local Area Network) can _____.
    (a) run faster
    (b) go online
    (c) share information and/or share peripheral equipment
    (d) E-mail

114. Choose the self-replicating application similar to virus that was used from a 1970s science fiction novel by John Bruner entitled "The Shockwave Rider".
    (a) Vice   (b) Bug   (c) Lice   (d) Worm

115. VDU represents _____.
    (a) Screen   (b) Monitor   (c) Both (a) and (b)   (d) Joystick

116. Which of the following applications would help you the most in billing account system?
    (a) Spreadsheet
    (b) Web Authoring
    (c) Word Processing
    (d) Electronic Publishing

117. Which of the following is not a computer programming language?
    (a) C   (b) BASIC   (c) Java   (d) Microsoft

118. Why is it advisable to keep electronic devices such as computers in the Sleep mode?
    (a) To have backup
    (b) To improve download speed
    (c) To reduce power consumption
    (d) To write contents of RAM to hard disk.

119. The computer virus cannot _____.
    (a) erase the files
    (b) crash motherboard
    (c) corrupt the program
    (d) crash disk

120. How does the Firewall work?
    (a) Prevents fire attacks
    (b) Prevents virus attacks
    (c) Prevents data-driven attacks
    (d) Prevents unauthorized access

121. Which of the following is the backup file extension?
    (a) .bak
    (b) .bas
    (c) .com
    (d) .txt

122. What are the special-purpose software that perform specific tasks called?
    (a) Applications
    (b) Hardware
    (c) Shareware
    (d) Network software

123. Define computer output.
    (a) Data the user enters in processor
    (b) Data the processor receives from user
    (c) Data that user provides to the processor
    (d) Result the user receives from the processor

124. In MS-Word, what is the most efficient way to shift a paragraph from one place to another?
    (a) Cut and Copy
    (b) Cut and Paste
    (c) Copy and Paste
    (d) Copy, Cut and Paste

125. Define Hardware.
    (a) All devices that provide input to the computer
    (b) Code of instructions that the computer runs or executes
    (c) All devices connected to computer that provide input and output data
    (d) All devices engaged in processing data including the CPU, memory and storage.

126. Which of the following is used to locate a particular word or phrase in a word document?
    (a) Search
    (b) Lookup
    (c) Find
    (d) Replace

127. What does the term 'User Interface' mean?
    (a) The VDU of the computer
    (b) Means through which the user and computer interact
    (c) Manner in which the operating system reacts to user commands
    (d) Means through which the user interacts with the hardware of the computer.

128. Which of the following options helps to create a new word document?
    (a) Open
    (b) New
    (c) Close
    (d) Save

129. In MS-Word, the background of the document _____.
    (a) always has white color
    (b) has same color for the entire document
    (c) can have any color of your choice
    (d) has color you set using the Options menu

130. Which of the following options can expose your computer to virus attack?
    (a) Using antivirus
    (b) Using pirated software
    (c) Opening any system application
    (d) Browsing a website without any additional transactions.

131. Name the application used for surfing the Web?
    (a) Internet
    (b) Network
    (c) Hypertext
    (d) Web Browser

132. Select the main difference between a supercomputer and mainframe from the following statements.
    (a) Supercomputer is much larger in size than the mainframe computers.
    (b) Supercomputers are much smaller in size than the mainframe computers.
    (c) Supercomputers are used to run limited programs at much faster speed while mainframes are used to run different programs concurrently.
    (d) Supercomputers are used to run different programs concurrently while mainframes are used to run limited programs at much faster speed.

133. Why does the Windows require 'Recycle Bin'?
    (a) To store word files   (b) To store deleted files
    (c) To store corrupted files   (d) To store temporary files

134. Select the latest version of MS Office from the following options?
    (a) Office XP   (b) Windows 10   (c) Office 2016   (d) Office 2019

135. Which of the following hardware cannot be shared in the network?
    (a) Projector   (b) Printer   (c) Keyboard   (d) Scanner

136. Which of the following scanning devices is used to read the bar coding made on products?
    (a) OCR   (b) MICR   (c) Wand   (d) Laser Scanner

137. What is the main difference between the desktop operating system and the Personal Digital Assistant (PDA) Operating system?
    (a) Desktop computer has an OS whereas the PDA does not.
    (b) Desktop OS has a graphical user interface whereas the PDA OS does not.
    (c) Desktop OS manages hardware resources whereas the PDA OS does not.
    (d) Desktop OS executes several programs simultaneously whereas PDA OS cannot.

138. Name the set of information that states the status of allotted resources to the process.
    (a) ALU   (b) Register Unit
    (c) Process Control (d) Process Description

139. Name the family of polynomial block codes designed to rectify the burst errors.
    (a) Gray Codes   (b) Bar Codes
    (c) Fire Codes   (d) Mnemonics Code

MCQ Set 3

1. What is MS-DOS operating system?
    (a) Command-driven interface, single-tasking operating system
    (b) Graphical user interface, multi-tasking operating system
    (c) Graphical user interface, single-tasking operating system
    (d) Command-driven interface, multi-tasking operating system.

2. Which of the following was an early desktop operating system with an integrated graphic user interface with point-and-click structure?
    (a) Unix   (b) Mac OS   (c) MS-DOS   (d) Gnome

3. The latest Mac OS version is built on which operating system platform?
    (a) Unix   (b) Linux   (c) CMOS   (d) Windows

4. Which of the following operating systems was developed in the early 1970s at AT&T's Bell Labs?
   (a) GNU   (b) Unix   (c) Linux   (d) DOS

5. What is the difference between Linux and Windows operating system?
   (a) Linux is proprietary OS, whereas Windows is not.
   (b) Linux OS cannot run with an Intel processor, whereas Widows OS can.
   (c) Linux OS has multiple versions, whereas Windows has only one version.
   (d) Programmer can revise Linux code, whereas Windows OS does not allow it.

6. Which of the following is a disadvantage of using an open-source operating system over proprietary versions OS?
   (a) Availability of source code   (b) Usage and distribution freedom
   (c) Technical Support availability   (d) Facility to change code.

7. Which of the following interfaces allows users to use icons and windows?
   (a) Menu-driven   (b) Graphical-user
   (c) Command-driven   (d) Windows-oriented

8. What is an advantage of using an offline device over an online device?
   (a) It minimizes operating errors while data recording.
   (b) It saves computer time.
   (c) It minimizes the space area at the computer lab.
   (d) All of the above.

9. Which property of an operating system controls multiple programs at the same time?
   (a) Multi-paging   (b) Multi-processing   (c) Multi-operating   (d) Multitasking

10. Name the computer-aided system that helps in recording and analyzing an existing hypothetical system.
    (a) Data flow   (b) Data link
    (c) Data Transmission (d) Distributed Processing

11. In Network terminology, which computer stores the files and performs data processing?
    (a) Node   (b) Terminal   (c) Server   (d) Modem

12. The behavior of a virus is that _____.
    (a) they are viruses   (b) they copy themselves to spread
    (c) Both (a) and (b).   (d) None of them.

13. Which of the following is not a virus source?
    (a) A plain-text mail   (b) Downloaded videos
    (c) Downloaded files over the text (d) An e-mail with attachment.

14. MIPS means _____.
    (a) Million Inputs per second   (b) Million Instructions per session
    (c) Million Instructions per second   (d) Many Instructions per second

15. Which of following supercomputers is developed in India?
    (a) Mira   (b) PARAM   (c) CRAY   (d) Titan

16. Which of the following units is used to measure the speed of a LAN?
    (a) BPS (Bits per second)   (b) KBPS (Kilo Bits per second)
    (c) MBPS (Mega Bits per second) (d) MIPS (Million Instructions per second)

17. The banking system follows which of the following techniques while processing cheques for payment?
    (a) Barcode technique
    (b) VRT (Volume Rendering Technique)
    (c) OCR (Optical Character Recognition)
    (d) MICR (Magnetic Ink Character Recognition)

18. What is the benefit of using UPS?
    (a) Provides power backup
    (b) Provides power on self-test
    (c) Increases computer speed
    (d) Enhances data storage capacity

19. QWERTY represents which of the following hardware?
    (a) Monitor
    (b) Mouse
    (c) Keyboard
    (d) Printer

20. What does the term "Zipping" a file indicate?
    (a) Transfer the data
    (b) Encrypting the data
    (c) Compressing the data
    (d) Downloading the data

21. Which of the following materials is used in computers' Integrated Circuits (IC) chips?
    (a) Silver
    (b) Silicon
    (c) Copper
    (d) Gold

22. Which of the following is not an operating system?
    (a) UNIX
    (b) LINUX
    (c) Internet
    (d) Windows

23. Which of the following coding technique is used to transform computer information between the terminals?
    (a) ASCII
    (b) BCDIC
    (c) BCD
    (d) OOPS

24. Which of the following terms describes the physical components of the computer?
    (a) Applications
    (b) Input
    (c) Software
    (d) Hardware

25. Data in a spreadsheet is organized in which of the following manner?
    (a) Tables
    (b) Boxes
    (c) Rows and Columns
    (d) Input and Output

26. VIRUS means _____.
    (a) Vital Information Reports Under Siege
    (b) Vital Information Recourse Under Siege
    (c) Vital Information Recourse Under System
    (d) Vast Information Recourse Under Siege

27. Which of the following means an unauthorized access to others' system?
    (a) Hacking
    (b) Commands
    (c) Encryption
    (d) Decryption

28. Select the first Web browser from the following browsers?
    (a) Mozilla Firefox
    (b) Netscape Navigator
    (c) World Wide Web
    (b) Internet Explorer

29. Which small piece of text is stored on the client's terminal by the Web browser to maintain its status?
    (a) Application
    (b) Session
    (c) Cookie
    (d) QueryString

30. Select the valid format of an e-mail address from the following options?
    (a) contactwebsite.info
    (b) contact.website.info
    (c) contact@website.info
    (d) contact@website@info

31. HTTP means _____.
    (a) Head Tail Transfer Print
    (b) Hypertext Transfer Program
    (c) Handle Timed Transfer Protocol
    (d) Hypertext Transfer Protocol

32. Which of the following is the smallest and basic information storage unit?
    (a) Bit
    (b) Byte
    (c) Newton
    (d) Mega Byte

33. Which of the following companies is also known as or nicknamed "Big Blue"?
    (a) Apple
    (b) TCS
    (c) IBM
    (d) Microsoft

34. Windows XP is an example of _____.
    (a) a Processor
    (b) an Operating System
    (c) a Storage Device
    (d) an Output Device

35. Which of the following manages and coordinates various computer resources and programs?
    (a) Application Software
    (b) Operating System
    (c) Motherboard
    (d) RAM

36. What kind of file is saved using the WAV file format?
    (a) Video
    (b) Image
    (c) Sound
    (d) Word Document

37. FTP means _____.
    (a) File Thread Protocol
    (b) File Transfer Protocol
    (c) File Transfer Program
    (d) File Thrashed Program

38. In e-mail, BCC means?
    (a) Blind Carbon Copy
    (b) Black Carbon Copy
    (c) Big Computerized Copy
    (d) Business Channel Copy

39. Select the shortcut key for printing a word document.
    (a) Alt + P
    (b) Shift + P
    (c) Ctrl + P
    (d) Ctrl + Alt + P

40. What kind of file is saved using the TMP file format?
    (a) Text File
    (b) Video File
    (c) Image File
    (d) Temporary File

41. BIOS means _____.
    (a) Basic Input Output System.
    (b) Basic Interrelated Operating Setup
    (c) Both Integrated Operating System.
    (d) Backup Input Output System

42. Select the non-storage device from the following devices.
    (a) Hard Disk
    (b) Mouse
    (c) Floppy Disk
    (d) DVD

43. Which of the following is the first e-mail service provider?
    (a) Yahoo Mail
    (b) Gmail
    (c) Hotmail
    (d) Rediff Mail

44. Which of the following is the first general-purpose electronic computer system?
    (a) IBM 405
    (b) Zuse Z3
    (c) CSIRAC
    (d) ENIAC

45. Which of the following devices is associated with the term 'Pentium'?
    (a) Memory
    (b) Hard Disk
    (c) Microprocessor
    (d) Multiplexer

46. The term 'BLOG' is made by combining two words_____.
    (a) Wave-log
    (b) Web-log
    (c) Worm-log
    (d) Word-log

47. E-mail means
    (a) Electric Mail   (b) Encrypted Mail   (c) Enlarged Mail   (d) Electronic Mail
48. Which of the following Web is not considered as a search engine?
    (a) Twitter   (b) Bing   (c) Yahoo   (d) Google
49. What is the function of ROM?
    (a) To shut down the computer
    (b) To boot the Operating System
    (c) To connect the hardware
    (d) To disconnect the computer.
50. What is 'URL'?
    (a) A System Application
    (b) A Web Server
    (c) An address of a web page
    (d) A Computer Hardware
51. Which of the following represents the term 'memory'?
    (a) Network Device   (b) Storage Device   (c) Input Device   (d) Output Device
52. What does the 'User Interface' represent?
    (a) What the user sees and interacts on the screen
    (b) Means by which OS gives its commands
    (c) Means through which the user and computers interact
    (d) All of them.
53. Which of the following storage devices has the maximum storage capacity?
    (a) Floppy Disk   (b) CD-RW   (c) VCD   (d) DVD
54. Which of the following relates to 'virtual memory'?
    (a) USB   (b) RAM   (c) ROM   (d) UPS
55. Which of the following companies controls and operates the 'Gmail' services?
    (a) Apple   (b) Google   (c) IBM   (d) Microsoft
56. In computer terminology, which of the following units is used to measure the length of a word?
    (a) Bits   (b) Byte   (c) Mbps   (d) Hertz
57. Which of the following personalities started e-mail service 'HOTMAIL' in 1996?
    (a) Vinod Dham   (b) Bill Gates   (c) Sabeer Bhatia   (d) V Rajaraman
58. Which of the following represents one billion memory locations approximately?
    (a) Kilobyte   (b) Megabyte   (c) Gigabyte   (d) Terabyte
59. In MS-Excel, name the process of making a single cell by combining two or more selected cells.
    (a) Merging   (b) Formatting   (c) Splitting   (d) Embedding
60. What kind of software is an operating system?
    (a) Application   (b) System   (c) Computing   (d) Network
61. Name the process of pressing and releasing the left mouse button twice?
    (a) Selecting   (b) Pointing   (c) Clicking   (d) Double-clicking
62. What are 'Protocols'?
    (a) Set of rules   (b) Set of devices   (c) Set of ports   (d) Set of Programs
63. Which of the following measuring unit is used to measure Hard Drive storage capacity?
    (a) Bits   (b) Mbps   (c) GB   (d) G Newton

64. Which of the following disk content is recorded during its manufacturing and cannot be edited later?
    (a) Read-only   (b) Write-only   (c) Run-only   (d) Memory-only

65. In computer terminology, alphanumeric data normally transforms to which of the following?
    (a) Garbage and irregular values   (b) Numbers and symbols
    (c) Encrypted data and shapes   (d) Numbers and alphabetical characters

66. Which of the following devices is used for displaying information in public domain?
    (a) Monitors   (b) Overheads
    (c) Monitors and overhead projections   (d) Youch Screen Kiosks

67. The real business and competitive value of information technology lies in:
    (a) The software applications that are used by many companies
    (b) The capabilities of software and the value of the information a business acquires and uses
    (c) The infrastructure of hardware, networks, and other IT facilities that are commonly used by many companies
    (d) The capabilities of the hardware and the speed at which it processes information.

MCQ Set 4

1. Which of the following is the first and the main page of any website?
   (a) Home Page   (b) Browser Page   (c) Search Page   (d) Bookmark Page

2. Which of the following must be copied in decompressed state from CDROM while installing to the hard disk?
   (a) Programming Software   (b) System Hardware
   (b) Application Hardware   (d) Application Software

3. How do you tag to the collection of interrelated file in the computer system?
   (a) Field   (b) Record   (c) Cell   (d) Database

4. Which of the following units represent a collection of 8 bits?
   (a) Nibble   (b) Byte   (c) Cell   (d) GB

5. The general-purpose computer can be adapted to various situations by making alterations to its _____.
   (a) Input Devices   (b) Output Devices   (c) Program   (d) Processor

6. Which of the following memories can be reached in a very short span of time by stating its address?
   (a) Mass Storage   (b) Secondary Memory
   (c) Random Access Memory   (d) Sequential Access Memory

7. Which of the following allows calculations on the data of rows and columns?
   (a) Flowcharts   (b) Graphics Presentation
   (c) Word Processing   (d) DBMS

8. What are the horizontal and vertical lines in a spreadsheet?
   (a) Sheets   (b) Grid-lines   (c) Cells   (d) Graphics

9. Which of the following options is used to delete a character to the right of the insertion point?
   (a) Enter key   (b) Backspace key   (c) Delete key   (d) Spacebar key

10. Which of the following is not the task of an operating system?
    (a) Manage computer memory and storage.
    (b) Control central processing unit (CPU).
    (c) Enable the users to edit the word document.
    (d) Means through which the computer and the user interacts.

11. Which of the following steps is not included in the system boot processes?
    (a) Loading Software programs
    (b) Executing power on self-test
    (c) Initiating basic input/output system (BIOS)
    (d) Loading of operating system into RAM

12. Which of the following in ROM loads an operating system from the hard drive into the RAM?
    (a) API   (b) BIOS   (c) Supervisor Program (d) Device Driver

13. Which of the following constitutes the basic input/output system (BIOS)?
    (a) RAM   (b) ROM   (c) CPU   (d) Hard Drive

14. Which of the following confirms that all the essential devices are connected and working properly?
    (a) ROM   (b) CMOS   (c) Configuration   (d) POST

15. Which of the following devices is associated with the term 'Hyper-threading'?
    (a) Processor   (b) RAM   (c) Hard disk   (d) Modem

16. Which of the following devices is manufactured by Intel and AMD?
    (a) Processor   (b) RAM   (c) Hard disk   (d) Router

17. Which of the following devices is connected using IDE (ATE) or SATA interface on the Mother Board?
    (a) Processor   (b) RAM   (c) LAN card   (d) Hard disk

18. USB is an example of _____.
    (a) Virus   (b) Processor   (c) Port   (d) Software

19. Which of the following techniques helps surgeons to perform complicated surgeries by using computer-aided devices?
    (a) Aseptic   (b) Robotics   (c) Forensics   (d) Forecasting

20. What is the name of the process of combining two or more strings?
    (a) Attaching   (b) Combining   (c) Fixing   (d) Concatenation

21. Which of the following programs intends to perform a task while simultaneously infecting the computer?
    (a) Virus   (b) Bug   (c) Trojan Horse   (d) Worm

22. Which of the following Melissa virus was broadcasted in 1999?
    (a) Time Bomb   (b) E-mail Virus   (c) Trojan Horse   (d) Macro Virus

23. Name the troubleshooting program that spreads from one program to another intentionally?
    (a) Virus   (b) Blog   (c) Time Bomb   (d) Trojan Horse

24. What is the name given to 'Malicious' software?
    (a) Corruptware   (b) Badware   (c) Maliciousware   (d) Malware
25. Which of the following represents the situation of collecting personal information and presenting as another individual for an illegal activity?
    (a) Hacking   (b) Spooling   (c) Spoofing   (d) Identity Theft
26. Which of the following represents the crime of cheating passwords?
    (a) Spooling   (b) Hacking   (c) Spoofing   (d) Identity Theft
27. Most of the time, the culprits of cyber-crimes are _____.
    (a) Insiders   (b) Hackers
    (c) Genius Tech Teenagers   (d) International Criminals
28. Limitation of which of the following sooner or later ends the worm virus?
    (a) Time   (b) CD-RW
    (c) CD Drive space   (d) Memory or Disk Space
29. Which of the following activates the logic bomb by a time-related event?
    (a) Virus   (b) Time bomb
    (c) Trojan Horse   (d) Time-related bomb sequence
30. Which logic bomb was produced to erupt on Michelangelo's birthday?
    (a) Virus   (b) Trojan Horse
    (c) Time bomb   (d) Time-related bomb sequence
31. Which of the following applications collects the user's information to redirect it to someone else on the Internet?
    (a) Spybot   (b) Virus   (c) TELNET   (d) Security Patch
32. Standardization of Microsoft programs and the Windows operating system has made the spread of viruses _____.
    (a) more complicated   (b) more difficult   (c) easier   (d) slower
33. Which of the following can be infected by the HTML viruses?
    (a) Computer   (b) Both the Web Page and the Client Computer
    (c) Web Page with HTML coding   (d) None of them.
34. Which of the following programs fixes the potential security breaches in an operating system?
    (a) Fragmentation   (b) Security Patches
    (c) Security Repairs   (d) Security Breach Fixes
35. In which situation is a client unable to access a Web site due to shelling of fake traffic?
    (a) Virus   (b) Trojan Horse
    (c) Hacking   (d) A Denial-of-Service attack.
36. Which of the following techniques allows one to take fingerprints and retinal scans for security access?
    (a) Laser   (b) Biometrics
    (c) Computer Security   (d) Routers
37. Which of the following is the most common tool used to control the computer system access?
    (a) User Log-in   (b) Passwords   (c) Computer keys   (d) Encryption

38. Which hardware or software safeguards against unauthorized access to the computer network?
    (a) Firewall
    (b) Hacker-resistant Server
    (c) Computer security
    (d) Encryption Safe Wall
39. Which of the following techniques helps in scrambling of code?
    (a) Firewall
    (b) Booting
    (c) Encryption
    (d) Scrambling
40. Which of the following will help you in securing your message?
    (a) Encryption Key
    (b) Cryptosystem
    (c) Cryptology Source
    (d) Encryption Software Package
41. In computer terminology, the instructions and memory addresses are represented in_____.
    (a) Bit
    (b) Binary Codes
    (c) Character Code
    (d) Binary Word
42. Which storage area stores the data to manage the speed difference at which various components handle the data?
    (a) Address
    (b) Buffer
    (c) Memory
    (d) Accumulator
43. Which of the following events will occur when the data is inserted into the memory location?
    (a) Deletion of the previous content
    (b) Addition to the content of the location
    (c) Conversion of address of the memory location
    (d) No meaningful result if there is already some data at the location.
44. From which of the following components does the ALU of a computer receive its commands?
    (a) Primary Memory
    (b) Cache Memory
    (c) Control Section
    (d) External Memory
45. Choose the synonym of the term 'Bug' that is an error in software or hardware of the computer?
    (a) Virus
    (b) Glitch
    (c) Slug
    (d) Worm
46. Which of the following represents the largest network of computers connected around the world?
    (a) MAN
    (b) LAN
    (c) Web
    (d) Internet
47. Which of the following terms represent the resolution of a laser printer?
    (a) PPI
    (b) Betamax
    (c) Pixels
    (d) DPI
48. How many bits make a byte?
    (a) 8 bits
    (b) 12 bits
    (c) 16 bits
    (d) 32 bits
49. Which main circuit board holds together the various components of the computer?
    (a) RAM
    (b) BIOS
    (c) Processor
    (d) Motherboard
50. What are 'dedicated computers'?
    (a) Computer allocated a single task only
    (b) Computer used by a single person only
    (c) Computer meant for application software
    (d) Computer working on single software.
51. Which of the following keyboard keys does not have its name printed on it?
    (a) Enter
    (b) Backspace
    (c) Space
    (d) Delete
52. QWERTY represents which of the following devices?
    (a) Monitor
    (b) Keyboard
    (c) Mouse
    (d) Memory
53. From where does the computer mouse get its name?
    (a) Its shape
    (b) Its functioning
    (c) Button like mouse teeth
    (d) Its wire cable looks like mouse tail.

54. What is the advantage of using a digitizing tablet?
    (a) Tracing Diagrams
    (b) Playing games
    (c) Sensing Bar-Codes
    (d) Document printing
55. Choose the pointing device from the following devices.
    (a) Scanner
    (b) Touch Screens
    (c) CD-ROM Drive
    (d) Flash Drive
56. Which of the following components is available in a light pen?
    (a) Lead
    (b) Ink capsule
    (c) Refillable ink
    (d) Light-sensitive elements
57. Which of the following would be the most suitable device used to navigate in a 3D environment?
    (a) Joystick
    (b) Keyboard
    (c) Tracker Ball
    (d) Space Mouse
58. Which of the following holds a magnetic strip on its body?
    (a) Sensors
    (b) Smart Card
    (c) Credit Card
    (d) Laser Light
59. Which of the following represents the hard copy?
    (a) Printed Copy
    (b) Data saved in ROM
    (c) Saving a copy in USB
    (d) Written with permanent ink
60. VAB means _____.
    (a) Video Audio Broadcast
    (b) Voice Answer Back
    (c) Visual Audio Buffer
    (d) Voice Audio Backup
61. Name the dots that create the picture on the monitor's screen.
    (a) Pixie set
    (b) Pixels
    (c) Bits
    (d) DPI
62. Which of the following devices describes a daisy wheel?
    (a) Storage Device
    (b) Pointing Device
    (c) Printing Device
    (d) Scanning Device
63. Which of the following devices can be used to automate the factory production lines?
    (a) VDUs
    (b) Plotters
    (c) Machine tools
    (d) None of them.
64. How does the impact printer print the characters on paper?
    (a) Using ink drums
    (b) Electrically charged ink
    (c) Using the color refills
    (d) Using inked ribbon and print head.
65. What would you not use with a flatbed plotter?
    (a) A pen
    (b) Eraser
    (c) Paper
    (d) None of these.
66. Which of the following is required in an ink jet printer?
    (a) Drum
    (b) Ribbon
    (c) Cartridge
    (d) Cassette
67. Which of the following is not required in laser printer?
    (a) Ribbon
    (b) Laser Beam
    (c) Print Head
    (d) Photo-conductive Drum
68. Which of the following represents disk data space or the amount of data it can store?
    (a) Speed
    (b) Dimension
    (c) Tracking Unit
    (d) Storage Capacity
69. Which of the following protects the access of the floppy disk?
    (a) Read
    (b) Write
    (c) Read and Write
    (d) All of them.
70. Which of the following is responsible for the backup of hard disk data?
    (a) Floppy Disk
    (b) Magnetic Tape
    (c) CD-ROM
    (d) Processor

71. In nonexistence of which of the following does the magnetic storage device represent binary 0?
    (a) Magnetic Tape
    (b) Static Power
    (c) Circuit
    (d) Magnetic Field
72. The magnetic tape represents _____.
    (a) Parallel Access Medium
    (b) Random Access Medium
    (c) Serial Access Medium
    (d) Universal Access Medium
73. Which of the following storage devices has the largest storage ability?
    (a) Floppy Disk
    (b) Flash Drive
    (c) CD-ROM
    (d) Magnetic Tape Storage
74. Which storage device stores data permanently?
    (a) CD-ROM
    (b) Flash Drive
    (c) Floppy Disk
    (d) Magnetic Tape Storage

ANSWER KEYS

MCQ Set 1

1. (a)   2. (b)   3. (a)   4. (d)   5. (c)   6. (a)   7. (c)   8. (d)
9. (a)   10. (d) 11. (b) 12. (b) 13. (c) 14. (d) 15. (d) 16. (b)
17. (d) 18. (a) 19. (b) 20. (b) 21. (d) 22. (a) 23. (b) 24. (c)
25. (c) 26. (a) 27. (d) 28. (b) 29. (d) 30. (c) 31. (b) 32. (d)
33. (a) 34. (c) 35. (d) 36. (b) 37. (b) 38. (a) 39. (a) 40. (d)
41. (c) 42. (b) 43. (c) 44. (d) 45. (b) 46. (d) 47. (a) 48. (a)
49. (d) 50. (c) 51. (a) 52. (b) 53. (d) 54. (c) 55. (a) 56. (c)
57. (a) 58. (c) 59. (b) 60. (a) 61. (d) 62. (a) 63. (c) 64. (d)
65. (b) 66. (a) 67. (a)

MCQ Set 2

1. (a)   2. (b)   3. (b)   4. (b)   5. (c)   6. (c)   7. (b)   8. (b)
9. (a)   10. (c) 11. (a) 12. (a) 13. (c) 14. (d) 15. (c) 16. (b)
17. (b) 18. (d) 19. (d) 20. (d) 21. (d) 22. (b) 23. (a) 24. (b)
25. (b) 26. (c) 27. (c) 28. (a) 29. (c) 30. (d) 31. (d) 32. (a)
33. (b) 34. (d) 35. (c) 36. (c) 37. (c) 38. (c) 39. (b) 40. (d)
41. (c) 42. (b) 43. (b) 44. (b) 45. (b) 46. (a) 47. (c) 48. (d)
49. (d) 50. (b) 51. (b) 52. (b) 53. (c) 54. (d) 55. (b) 56. (a)
57. (d) 58. (d) 59. (d) 60. (a) 61. (c) 62. (c) 63. (c) 64. (b)
65. (b) 66. (b) 67. (d) 68. (d) 69. (c) 70. (d) 71. (a) 72. (a)
73. (b) 74. (b) 75. (c) 76. (c) 77. (b) 78. (b) 79. (c) 80. (d)
81. (d) 82. (c) 83. (b) 84. (d) 85. (c) 86. (c) 87. (d) 88. (d)
89. (d) 90. (c) 91. (c) 92. (d) 93. (b) 94. (c) 95. (a) 96. (d)
97. (b) 98. (d) 99. (b) 100. (c) 101. (d) 102. (c) 103. (c) 104. (c)
105. (d) 106. (b) 107. (b) 108. (c) 109. (b) 110. (a) 111. (a) 112. (a)
113. (c) 114. (d) 115. (c) 116. (a) 117. (d) 118. (c) 119. (b) 120. (d)
121. (a) 122. (a) 123. (d) 124. (b) 125. (d) 126. (c) 127. (b) 128. (b)
129. (c) 130. (b) 131. (d) 132. (c) 133. (b) 134. (d) 135. (c) 136. (d)
137. (d) 138. (d) 139. (c)

MCQ Set 3

1. (a)	2. (b)	3. (a)	4. (b)	5. (d)	6. (c)	7. (b)	8. (b)	
9. (d)	10. (a)	11. (c)	12. (b)	13. (a)	14. (c)	15. (b)	16. (c)	
17. (d)	18. (a)	19. (c)	20. (c)	21. (b)	22. (c)	23. (a)	24. (d)	
25. (a)	26. (b)	27. (a)	28. (c)	29. (c)	30. (c)	31. (d)	32. (a)	
33. (c)	34. (b)	35. (b)	36. (c)	37. (b)	38. (a)	39. (c)	40. (d)	
41. (a)	42. (b)	43. (c)	44. (d)	45. (c)	46. (b)	47. (d)	48. (a)	
49. (b)	50. (c)	51. (b)	52. (a)	53. (d)	54. (b)	55. (b)	56. (a)	
57. (c)	58. (c)	59. (a)	60. (b)	61. (d)	62. (a)	63. (c)	64. (a)	
65. (d)	66. (d)	67. (b)						

MCQ Set 4

1. (a)	2. (a)	3. (d)	4. (b)	5. (c)	6. (c)	7. (d)	8. (b)	
9. (c)	10. (c)	11. (a)	12. (b)	13. (b)	14. (d)	15. (a)	16. (a)	
17. (d)	18. (c)	19. (b)	20. (d)	21. (c)	22. (b)	23. (a)	24. (d)	
25. (d)	26. (c)	27. (a)	28. (a)	29. (b)	30. (c)	31. (a)	32. (c)	
33. (c)	34. (b)	35. (d)	36. (b)	37. (b)	38. (a)	39. (d)	40. (b)	
41. (b)	42. (b)	43. (a)	44. (c)	45. (b)	46. (d)	47. (d)	48. (a)	
49. (d)	50. (a)	51. (c)	52. (b)	53. (d)	54. (a)	55. (b)	56. (d)	
57. (c)	58. (c)	59. (a)	60. (b)	61. (b)	62. (c)	63. (a)	64. (d)	
65. (c)	66. (c)	67. (d)	68. (d)	69. (b)	70. (c)	71. (a)	72. (c)	
73. (c)	74. (a)							